THOMAS AQUINAS, PREACHER AND FRIEND

Mary Ann Fatula, O.P.

A Michael Glazier Book
THE LITURGICAL PRESS
Collegeville, Minnesota

A Michael Glazier Book published by The Liturgical Press

Cover design by Don Bruno
Woodcut by Robert McGovern

1   2   3   4   5   6   7   8   9

Library of Congress Cataloging-in-Publication Data

Fatula, Mary Ann.
    Thomas Aquinas : preacher and friend / Mary Ann Fatula.
       p.   cm. — (Way of the Christian mystics; v. 15)
    "A Michael Glazier Book."
    Includes bibliographical references and index.
    ISBN 0-8146-5031-7
    1. Thomas, Aquinas, Saint, 1225?-1274. 2. Spirituality—Catholic Church—History. 3. Preaching—History—Middle Ages, 600-1500.
4. Friendship—Religious aspects—Christianity—History of doctrines—Middle Ages, 600-1500. 5. Catholic Church—Doctrines—History. 6. Thomas, Aquinas, Saint, 1225?-1274. I. Title.
II. Series.
BX4700.T6F38   1993
230'.2'092—dc20   92-27552
                                                 CIP

*To my teachers and friends, especially
William J. Hill, O.P.,
who have taught me to love Thomas.*

Contents

Abbreviations

Numbers in parentheses refer to an English translation or translations listed in the numbered bibliographic entries at the end of this book.

Ap Creed	*Sermons on the Apostles Creed* (3, 25, 36)
Char	*Charity* (Disputed Questions: *De Caritate*) (4)
Calo	Peter Calo, *Vita Sancti Thomae Aquinatis*
I Can	*First Canonization Enquiry* (44)
CG	*On the Truth of the Catholic Faith (Summa Contra Gentiles)* (19)
Com Div Nom	*Commentary on Dionysius' Divine Names*
Comp Theo	*Compendium of Theology* (11)
Contra Impugn	*An Apology for the Religious Orders (Contra impugnantes Dei cultum et religionem)* (1)
Contra Retrah	*Contra retrahentes*
Exiit	Sermon "Exiit qui seminat"
Exp in Job	*Exposition on the Book of Job*
Fr	Commentary on Books Eight and Nine of Aristotle's *Ethics, On Friendship* (6)
FVST	*Fontes Vitae Sancti Thomae*
Gui	Bernard Gui, *Vita Sancti Thomae Aquinatis* (44)
Hail Mary	*Sermons on the Hail Mary* (3, 36)
HE	*Historia Ecclesiastica* by William of Tocco (44)
Homo quidam	Sermon "Homo quidam fecit cenam magnam"
In 1 Cor	*Lectures on the First Epistle to the Corinthians*
In 2 Cor	*Lectures on the Second Epistle to the Corinthians*

9

In Eph	*Lectures on the Epistle to the Ephesians* (7)
In Gal	*Lectures on the Epistle to the Galatians* (8)
In Heb	*Lectures on the Epistle to the Hebrews*
In Jn	*Lectures on the Gospel of John* (9)
In Met	*Commentary on Aristotle's Metaphysics*
In Mt	*Lectures on the Gospel of Matthew*
In Phil	*Lectures on the Epistle to the Philippians* (9)
In Ps	*Lectures on the Psalms*
In Rom	*Lectures on the Epistle to the Romans*
In 1 Th	*Lectures on the First Epistle to the Thessalonians* (8)
Our Father	*Sermons on the Our Father* (3, 36)
Pot	*Disputed Questions: De Potentia* (18)
Quaest lib	*Quaestiones quod libetales* (21: qq. 1–2)
Rel St	*The Religious State, the Episcopate and the Priestly Office (De perfectione spiritualis vitae)* (23)
RSV	Revised Standard Version of the Bible
Rigans Montes	Thomas' Inaugural Address as Master of Theology
Sacraments	*Commentary on the Sacraments* (3)
Sent	*Commentary on Lombard's Four Books of Sentences (Scriptum super libros Sententiarum)*
ST	*Summa Theologiae* (29, 30)
ST Supp	*Summa Theologiae, Supplement* (29, 30)
Ten Com	*Sermons on the Ten Commandments* (3)
Tocco	William Tocco, *Vita Sancti Thomae Aquinatis*
Truth	*Disputed Questions: Truth (De Veritate)* (11)

Introduction

"No longer do I call you servants but *friends*" (John 15:15). In a world that suffers from so much loneliness, these beautiful words from the Gospel of John call out to an ache deep within each of us: the hunger for intimate friendship. Thomas Aquinas was no stranger to this longing at the core of who we are. In his writings he speaks with compelling power and depth of our need not for just any kind of love but for the love that is mutual, intimate friendship between equals. And in the above passage from John's Gospel Thomas found unveiled the answer to our longing: we who of ourselves are only creatures and servants have become, in Jesus, intimate friends of one another and of *God*.

Thomas was so moved by the depth and beauty of this truth that he let its power infuse his entire life and spirituality. Again and again he reflects on our own experience of friendship, which is so precious to us. In every important insight he develops, Thomas stresses the impossibility of our living a full human life, and therefore a true "spiritual" life, without our being bound together to God and to one another in the mutual, self-giving love that is friendship. Moreover, Thomas became convinced that we exist precisely in order to enjoy such close friendship—friendship with one another, and friendship with the triune God. But Thomas could not keep the glad tidings of this God pent up within himself. Thomas the friend *had* to become Thomas the preacher, and proclaiming the good news of God's friendship-love soon became Thomas' deepest act of friendship with others.[1]

Today Thomas invites us to experience for ourselves the beauty of this close friendship with God and one another, and to find the same joy of proclaiming God's goodness in the mutuality and interdependence of friendship with one another. It is this theme, so profound and so relevant to us today, which serves as the focus for this book. In the chapters that follow, we find Thomas himself speaking to us as a friend about the beautifully varied facets of our call to intimate friendship with the triune God and with one another, and our inseparable call to proclaim the joy of this God in the mutuality of friendship-love with each other.

In the first chapter we see Thomas reflecting on our hunger for friendship, and on the joys and struggles of friendship common to us all. The second and third chapters unfold Thomas' experience and understanding of *Jesus* as our beloved friend, and of the triune God whose merciful providence cares for us precisely as intimate friends. Chapter four reflects on the Spirit of love who makes us dear friends of God and one another, while chapter five considers Thomas' thought on prayer as an act of intimate, joyful friendship with God. In chapters six and seven we ponder Thomas' profound insights on charity as the friendship-love binding us to God and to one another, and on our own call to proclaim God's friendship-love with others. Chapter eight focuses on the peace that is meant to fill us as we share the good news of God's friendship, and chapter nine considers Thomas' insights on the Spirit's gifts as the source of our ability to share this good news with others. In chapter ten we reflect on Thomas' most intimate experience of friendship-love with Jesus in the Eucharist. Finally, in chapter eleven we consider the way Thomas increasingly spent himself in proclaiming the good news, until he yielded himself in death to the triune God whose intimate friend he had become.

In these chapters we meet Thomas, the mendicant friar and preacher, for this renowned philosopher, theologian, and doctor of the Church[2] lived for most of his brief life as a humble Dominican. He was not a particularly handsome man; though he was tall, "virile," and "robust,"[3] with a healthy complexion, "like ripe wheat,"[4] he was also "stout," with a "bald forehead."[5] But because he was always so "gentle and approachable," so "generous,"[6] and "wonderfully kind-hearted,"[7] he was loved and known by many people simply as "good Brother Thomas." In the chapters that follow, Thomas shows himself to be this same "good brother" to us, a singularly wonderful companion for us in our own faith-journey today.

Thomas' times were astonishingly like ours. His thirteenth-century world was bursting with new ideas, new movements toward equality and interdependence, new awareness of the world in its international character. Intellectual, social, and spiritual currents of great vitality were springing up everywhere. Many people were being grasped by a fierce secular urge to investigate the mysteries of the created world, as translations of Aristotle were making available to ordinary students his world-affirming philosophy. People, too, were throwing off the chains of feudalism with its rigid class system, and migrating to the cities where free trade and commerce were making equality and upward mobility an exciting, new possibility.[8] But many people, too, were rediscovering the Scriptures and the *vita apostolica,* a gospel way of life centered on preaching and voluntary poverty. Tommaso d'Aquino was one of these persons.

Thomas' Call to Preach the Good News of God's Friendship

Thomas belonged to a family of wealth and status. If he had accepted their plan for his life, he would have become the rich and powerful abbot of Monte Cassino. But he did not. When he was seventeen, Thomas renounced his noble way of life and handed himself over to Dominic's community of begging preachers. In this radical decision, Thomas embraced an entirely new and different kind of life and spirituality from that which he might have pursued as a Benedictine monk: "The Spirit has anointed me to *preach* good news to the poor" (Luke 4:18)! Thomas chose not to isolate himself from the world but to proclaim the good news of Jesus at its heart, in a community of equals and friends who were engaged with the world and its currents of thought. By his choice, Thomas gave his whole life to sharing with others the beauty of the God who filled his mind and heart. And in his decision, he discovered the truth that we ourselves are meant to know by experience: "How beautiful are the feet of those who bear good news to others" (Isa 52:7; Rom 10:15).

Thomas was born *c.* 1226[9] in the family castle at Roccasecca, Italy. Landulf, his father, was a knight and member of the Lombard minor nobility from southern Italy; Theodora, his mother, was a Norman noblewoman from the north. Theodora was Landulf's second wife, and their marriage seems to have resulted in nine children, four of whom were boys: Aimo, a knight-soldier who was captured and held for ransom at Cyprus in 1232 during the Fifth Crusade; Rinaldo, who was executed in 1246 for complicity in a plot to assassinate Emperor Frederick II; Landolfo, about whom we know little; and Tommaso, the youngest of the boys. It seems that Thomas had also five sisters: Marotta, who became abbess of the Benedictine convent of Santa Maria de Capua; Maria, whose daughter, Catherine, helped to supply information for Thomas' canonization process; Theodora, wife of Count Roger of San Severino; another sister who was killed by lightning when she was a baby; and a fifth sister, Adelasia, wife of Count Roger of Aquila.[10]

Thomas' father and brothers were knights deeply involved in the affairs of both empire and papacy and in the ongoing power struggle between the heads of these two institutions. In Thomas' home the rich dimensions of the thirteenth century came to life: the world of Christian, Arab, and Greek learning, Saracen influence, chivalrous love, and strife between papacy and empire. Thomas' grandfather had been lieutenant-general of the empire, and one of Thomas' brothers had with the emperor's forces besieged the Benedictine abbey of Monte Cassino and wrested it from papal power.[11]

Medieval parents often offered their youngest child to God. Thomas was only five when his mother and father presented him as an *oblatus* to the wealthy Benedictine abbey of Monte Cassino. To send the young Thomas there would be a judicious way of making peace with the monks, and of adding to the family fortunes if Thomas were eventually made abbot. In his parents' vision Thomas would grow up with the monks, and after being formed by the monastic way of life would one day rule the rich community as its abbot. With at least three brothers—men who, like their father, made their fortunes on the battlefield—Thomas could be spared to work for the family's wealth in a peaceful setting. The knight Landulf de Roccasecca de Aquino and his second wife, the Countess Theodora, planned for their youngest child a Church career which would augment their own family's wealth and prestige at the same time that it would honor God.

For nine years, from about 1231 until 1240, Thomas lived quietly in this peaceful Benedictine world isolated from the chaos of city life. If all had gone as his parents planned, he would have emerged as the powerful ruler of the affluent abbey. But when Thomas was about fourteen, Emperor Frederick II's troops regained control of the abbey and evicted foreign monks. Thomas, a native of Castello di Roccasecca in Sicily, was forced to leave. But the abbot encouraged Landulf and Theodora to send their son to the imperial school at Naples—rather than the papal school at Bologna—to continue his studies. For three years Thomas led the life of a university student at Naples, feasting on the works of Aristotle that were taught there in defiance of a papal ban. In the summer of 1243, when he was about seventeen, Thomas made a life-choice that rejected all his family had planned for him. He renounced his wealth and noble status. He would not be the powerful abbot of a rich monastery. The young nobleman Tommaso d'Aquino would become a preacher and beggar in Dominic de Guzman's community of mendicant friars.

The Dominican and Franciscan orders had sprung to life as part of the great evangelical movement that swept through Europe in the 1200s. Drawn to a gospel way of life, sons and daughters of wealthy families vowed themselves to poverty and begged for their food in the streets. The Order of Preachers begun by the Spaniard Dominic de Guzman only twenty-five years earlier was already flourishing with communities of preaching "friars" ("brothers") in cities all over Europe, including Naples. Like monks, they gave themselves to contemplation. But unlike monks, they lived where they could spread the gospel, in the heart of the cities.[12] They preached and begged for their food in the streets. Their wisdom was hard-won in study and prayer. They stored up nothing for themselves, and instead trusted God's providence and the people's charity for their daily bread.

Priests jealous of the begging preachers considered them parasites on society. As a young student at Naples, however, Thomas saw for himself the vigor and beauty of the friars' life, their love for Jesus, for one another, and for the people.[13] One of these Dominicans at Naples, Friar John of San Guiliano, befriended Thomas.[14] Brother John began to speak to Thomas about the joy he found in following Jesus in his poverty and preaching mission. Perhaps John told the seventeen-year-old Thomas a story from the life of that other nobleman, Dominic, founder of the preaching friars. Once, when he had no food, Dominic went out to the streets to beg. A compassionate man stopped to help him. Instead of tearing only a piece of bread from his loaf, the man gave Dominic the entire loaf. Dominic, who once could have fed nobility from his own table, fell to the ground before his benefactor; overcome with gratitude, he received the loaf of bread on his knees.[15]

In Dominic, Thomas began to see mirrored both Jesus and him-self. As a nobleman, Thomas could have possessed what his family had planned for him even as a monk: security, power, and wealth. But in the sermon on the Apostles' Creed which he preached to-ward the end of his life, he describes the love which drew him to renounce his status and to join Dominic's community of beg-ging preachers: "The king of kings, the Lord of rulers, in whom are all the treasures of wisdom, was stripped naked, ridiculed, spat upon, bruised, and finally put to death. How falsely, there-fore, are we attached to riches and fine clothes, how falsely to honors, and positions of power."[16]

Thomas longed to "enjoy the *friendship* of charity" with Jesus in his own poverty and preaching mission.[17] He, too, would do as Dominic had done, as Jesus himself had done. He would re-nounce all that he had, even his inclination to lead and govern, and would freely submit himself to others for the sake of Jesus.[18] In Dominic's mendicant community, he would choose, with Jesus, to be ruled rather than to rule (John 6:38).[19] Toward the end of April, 1243, when he was about seventeen, Thomas joined the community of preaching friars at the convent of San Domenico in Naples.

Thomas' choice was not without cost for him. In a work he wrote as a master of theology at Paris, he hinted at the price he had paid in laying aside the privileges of his noble status. "Obvi-ously, begging entails a certain humiliation," he confesses. "To be ruled and obedient *is* less noble than to govern and com-mand."[20] And yet, Thomas continues, a poor and simple life frees us to preach the gospel without restraint. We embrace a radical *love* when we freely choose such humiliations as begging, for we enter into communion with those who are not free to choose, with those who suffer as victims at others' hands.[21]

With Jesus and with the poor, Thomas had decided to lay aside his noble status and to became a person "without social class," a beggar free to share God's Word with people in any station in life.[22]

Thomas' Rich Humanity

At the age of seventeen, Thomas eagerly grasped Jesus' preach-ing mission as his own. In season and out, for his whole life long, with his every word and sense, he would speak of God.[23] But he would "speak of God" in a way that radiated both the Spirit's wisdom and a human richness that have made him a wonderful companion and contemporary to people in every age, especially our own.

The two vital movements of the thirteenth century—one gospel-centered, and the other secular—had pulled many contemporaries of Thomas in opposing directions. The evangelical mendicant movement seemed to pull them away from the world, at the same time that Aristotle's philosophy pushed them to the heart of the world. Many "spiritual" contemporaries of Thomas had opted for Plato's and Augustine's other-worldliness instead of Aristotle's "worldliness," for a gospel way of life in isolation from the world rather than a secular existence at the heart of the world. But Thomas would not be forced to choose between these two dynamic movements. He would have them both.

Thomas chose *both* a gospel way of life centered on Jesus, and a "this-worldliness" inspired by Aristotle, and his choice spread its marvelously rich dimensions in his life and work. He was always the mendicant friar, the intense lover of Jesus, wholly centered on the gospel. Yet he was also and always the deeply "secular" Thomas, friend of Aristotle, open to all the world, drinking in truth wherever he found it. In his own person, therefore, Thomas marvelously combined the two great forces of his times: a vital "secular" interest and sympathy, and a vibrant evangelical Christianity.[24]

This is why, although Thomas was "utterly simple and pure," he was no "other-worldly ascetic." On the contrary, he "was known for his hearty affirmation of all reality, especially of the world of the senses and its beauties."[25] Many of his contemporaries were called to leave the world for the cloister. But Thomas was called to leave the cloister and enter the world, to plumb the depths of God's presence and work in the created universe God has given us. He was not afraid of the beauty of created things, because "the beauty of creatures is the likeness of *God's* own beauty."[26] And so it was utterly typical of Thomas that he "cast his net upon the universe and carried off all things."[27]

Precisely because he was completely a person of his astonishingly vital times, Thomas is a marvelously contemporary person for us. Dominican that he was, Thomas lusted for *truth*. He knew by experience the meaning of Jesus' words: *"I am the truth"*

(John 14:6). And so he was open to all questions and points of view; he read constantly and voraciously; he studied sympathetically and understood the opinions of others who disagreed with his own insights. With all of his soul he believed that "everything that is true comes from the Holy Spirit." And whatever truth he did find, regardless of who said it or where he found it, he incorporated into his own vibrant synthesis.[28]

Each of Thomas' works in this way contributes to the vital debates of his time.[29] He integrated into his writing and teaching the "Italy of the popes, the Germany of Albert, the France of Louis and the University of Paris." His writings contain the treasures of Eastern and Western Christianity, Jewish and Arab learning, and, indeed, the scholarship of the known world available to him.[30]

Yet as a person deeply influenced by the evangelical movement of his time, Thomas always draws his ultimate inspiration from Scripture.[31] To read his homilies as well as his many theological and scriptural works is to be struck by the depth and breadth of his knowledge of Scripture. He quotes Scripture passages constantly in his writings, not as "proof texts" but as the very source of his profound insights. Indeed, his deepest theological insights are simply his penetrating reflections on a truth articulated in Scripture.

In his writings, Thomas is always the Dominican who both continually treasures the Word of God in his heart, and simultaneously claims truth wherever he finds it. In his scriptural commentaries, therefore, he commonly quotes pagan authorities such as Averroes, Avicenna, Porphyry, Pliny, Cicero, Plato, and, of course, Aristotle.[32] And he quotes them, not because they are pagan authorities, but because he finds in specific insights of theirs the *truth*.

Far ahead of his time, Thomas also chooses the literal rather than historical or spiritual sense in interpreting Scripture, even though most of his contemporaries considered the literal sense to be the most primitive level of scriptural interpretation.[33] When he begins his Commentary on Job, for example, Thomas makes it clear that he will not follow the path of previous "spiritual" interpreters. On the contrary, he will propound the book's "literal sense," that is, the meaning the author intended. He knew that only by grasping the human author's intention do we really grasp the Word of *God*. Yet Thomas never displays an arrogant disregard for the value of these other approaches. Gregory the Great, Thomas tells us in his introduction to his Commentary on Job, already had pursued the "spiritual" meaning of this book so well, explaining its "mystical aspects with so much subtlety and learning," that it seemed unnecessary to Thomas to add anything to his work![34]

Accounts like these—of Thomas' perceptive, new, and *fresh* approach to the burning questions of his age—show us why he is so relevant to us today. He himself lived and encourages us to live a life in the Spirit at the heart of the *world,* in the communion and *interdependence* of close friendship with God and one another, sharing the fruit of our prayer and study and love with others precisely as a generous act of friendship. Thomas knew that when we love God, our words cannot help pouring out on others the riches we treasure in our hearts.[35] He himself preached, taught, and wrote from the abundance of his heart. And when he had to defend the very right of Dominican preachers to exist, he voiced his own call in a phrase that has become a motto not only for all women and men formed in the Dominican tradition, but also for each of us who are educated Christians at the heart of the world today: *contemplata aliis tradere*—to let the joy of our faith overflow to others by generously sharing with them the fruit of our own study and contemplation.

Thomas' Relevance for Us Today:
Proclaiming the Good News

In significant, often unassuming ways, Christians throughout the world today are taking seriously their own call to live this mission which Thomas himself followed in his own particular vocation: "Go out to all the world and proclaim the good news" (cf. Mt 2:19-20). The Holy Spirit is inspiring us with a thirst for deeper prayer, for more study and knowledge of the living God, for sharing a committed life together in the Spirit of love. Scripture and prayer groups, as well as renewal, social justice, and evangelization programs, and most especially the Rite of Christian Initiation for Adults (RCIA) based on sharing our faith with others are springing up with great vitality in countless places.

At the heart of this vitality is the Holy Spirit inspiring us to seek an even further step in our journey of faith together. Our prayer, study, and involvement in social justice concerns are leading us to a deeper dimension of our spiritual life at the heart of the world: the challenging, marvelous call to *share* our faith, the fruit of our prayer and study, with others. Many of us feel this call to deeper prayer and study. But we may also shy away from the inseparable call to *share* our faith in interdependence with one another. We may not think that we have the gifts to preach, teach, write, or even simply to speak of our faith with others. Surely, we may think, Thomas proclaimed the good news so powerfully to others because he possessed richer gifts of mind and heart than we could ever claim. If we compare ourselves to Thomas, we can see all too well our own inadequacies, while mistakenly picturing him at his desk, his pen flowing easily in a copious outpouring of wisdom.

And yet the very life and words of Thomas tell us otherwise. His closest friends speak of the great paradox that filled the soul of this remarkable preacher, teacher, and writer—a paradox that has particular relevance for us today. Thomas lived his life simultaneously as a nobleman and as a beggar. He was a nobleman by birth, but in joining the mendicant preachers of Dominic's community, he literally became a beggar. Yet even as a mendicant, Thomas could never stop being who he really was, a person formed in the key virtue of nobility, extravagant generosity with others. As a friend, he learned to lavish on others, however, not the material wealth he renounced for the sake of Jesus, but rather the infinitely greater riches of God's wisdom that filled his mind and heart. Thomas the nobleman poured out on others not the wealth of his now empty purse, but the lasting wealth of his mind and heart.

Here is the other side of the paradox that is Thomas. The untiringly prolific writer, the exquisitely deep theologian, the marvelously clear philosopher, Thomas the nobleman, was for his entire life also and literally Thomas the beggar. But his *real* begging welled up from depths of poverty within him far more profound than lack of the material wealth he renounced. Indeed, after Thomas' death, Reginald, his dear friend and secretary, wept as he spoke of the "secret" he had kept while Thomas lived. All of Thomas' great wisdom had come, not from his own limited mind and gifts, but from the Holy Spirit of love. All that he had ever spoken or written, Thomas literally had begged from God.

This paradox of Thomas, simultaneously nobleman and beggar, is in some sense his greatest gift and relevance for us as educated Christians today. In our being able to read the very words of this book, we show how much Thomas the nobleman is brother to us. We are far from being members of nobility, and yet the great economic, spiritual, and intellectual blessings we enjoy place us squarely in the company, certainly not of the uneducated peasants, but of the nobility of Thomas' day. On the other hand, with all of our rich blessings, we are as much beggars as Thomas was. In spite of our material prosperity, our spiritual and intellectual advantages, we are, all of us, thirsting for something more. As Thomas himself knew—Thomas, who could have been the exceedingly powerful abbot of Monte Cassino or the wealthy archbishop of Naples—we are, all of us, poor, empty, thirsting for *God*. And the source for sharing our faith with others—prayer, study, and friendship with God and one another—is the same wellspring from which Thomas the beggar continually drank, the same wellspring available to us in our own personal spiritual journey today.

Thomas sees our proclamation of the Risen Lord as an act of interdependence with one another. For while he himself was called to a life of scholarship that demanded much time alone, his solitude was not an act of isolation but of communion in friendship with others. This reality of charity as *friendship-love* with God and one another is the very soul of Thomas' person and thought. In giving to others the riches he himself contemplated, therefore, he lived his "spirituality," a life absolutely identical with who he was, drawn at every moment from the Spirit of love. This is why Thomas, "Doctor Communis,"—teacher and friend to us all—opens a mystical path not for an extraordinary few but for every one of us as educated Christians seeking a deeper spiritual life at the heart of the world today. I pray that these chapters may feed us with some small portion of Thomas' profound insights and enable us to taste more and more by experience "how good the Lord is" (Ps 34:8).

In the writing of this book I owe a great debt of gratitude to many people, most deeply to my parents, Michael and Rita Hyzy Fatula, whose constant love, prayer, and encouragement have been a gift greater than words could say. I owe much gratitude to my family and relatives, Sisters and friends, my Dominican congregation of St. Mary of the Springs, the Ohio Dominican College Community and its Faculty Development Committee, and my own Dominican community of St. James the Less Convent, without whose support and prayer I could not have undertaken or completed this book. I am very grateful to those who read and critiqued the manuscript, especially Sisters Mary Michael Spangler, O.P., and Patricia Twohill, O.P., who helped me with invaluable suggestions. I am also indebted to Peter Veracka, director of the library at the Pontifical College Josephinum, who graciously and generously helped me to obtain needed books. I thank, too, Michael Naughton, O.S.B, Mark Twomey, and Colleen Stiller of The Liturgical Press. Finally, I am particularly grateful to Michael Glazier, whose idea this book was, and whose encouragement, scholarship, and spirituality have been a constant inspiration to me.

I pray that this small work may give glory to the triune God, to whose grace I owe whatever may be helpful in it. I pray, too, that readers of this book may be inspired to go to the original sources[36] in order to drink from the fountain of Thomas' own writings. From the abundance of our own prayer and study then, and bound together in charity's intimate friendship-love, may we ourselves share generously the riches of God's intimate friendship with others.

At the end of his life, Thomas—who perhaps had suffered a stroke, but even more, had suffered God's beauty—could only say: "Compared to what I have glimpsed of God, all that I have written is straw." May we enjoy on our own life's journey to God the close friendship of Thomas, of one another, and of all those who have ever found in Thomas' "straw" a magnificent banquet, profound and rich enough to feed us for a lifetime.

Notes

[1]CG III, 134, 4; Rel St 14.

[2]A noted Church historian who was a contemporary of Thomas wrote that Thomas is "supreme among teachers of philosophy and theology. . . . Such is the common view and opinion, so that nowadays in the University of Paris they call him the 'doctor communis' because of the outstanding clarity of his teaching" (HE 23.9; in Kenelm Foster, O.P., trans. and ed. *The Life of Saint Thomas Aquinas: Biographical Documents* [Baltimore: Helicon Press, 1959] 134).

[3]Tocco, c. 38; FVST, 111–12.

⁴Gui, c. 35; Foster, *Life,* 53.

⁵I Can 15; Foster, *Life,* 88.

⁶Gui, c. 30; Foster, *Life,* 48.

⁷Gui, c. 33; Foster, *Life,* 51.

⁸Joseph Pieper, *Guide to Thomas Aquinas,* trans. Richard and Clara Winston (Scranton, Penn.: Pantheon Books, 1962) 30.

⁹For helpful information about Thomas' life, see: Foster, *Life;* James A. Weisheipl, O.P., *Friar Thomas d'Aquino,* rev. ed. (Washington: The Catholic University of America Press, 1983); Simon Tugwell, O.P., trans., ed., and intro., *Albert and Thomas: Selected Writings* (New York: Paulist Press, 1988). Bartholomew of Capua, an important witness at Thomas' first canonization inquiry, testified that Thomas died (in 1274) in his forty-eighth year. On the other hand, Tolomeo of Lucca, a Dominican historian who knew Thomas, said that he was forty-eight or fifty when he died. William of Tocco testified that Thomas died in his forty-ninth year. For a consideration of the various theories about the date of Thomas' birth see Tugwell, *Albert and Thomas,* 291–92. Weisheipl places the date for Thomas' birth in the years 1224–25 (*Friar,* 3–4). I follow Bartholomew of Capua's chronology and date Thomas' birth in 1226.

¹⁰Weisheipl, *Friar,* 6–9.

¹¹Gerald Vann, O.P., *Saint Thomas Aquinas* (New York: Benzinger Brothers, 1940) 37–39.

¹²Michel Mollat considers the amazing growth of the friars' communities during this time an indication of how strongly they spoke to people's deepest needs. Their move away from an ecclesiastical model that was "vertical and hierarchical" to one of fraternity and reciprocity meshed completely with the new movements toward "solidarity with others prevalent in city life" (*The Poor in the Middle Ages: An Essay in Social History,* trans. Arthur Goldnammer [New Haven and London: Yale University Press, 1986] 123–25). Michel Goodich also studies this "move toward democratization" as well as the mobility and engagement with the world characteristic of the new mendicant communities (*Vita Perfecta: The Ideal of Sainthood in the Thirteenth Century,* Monographien zur Geschichte des Mittelalters, vol. 25 [Stuttgart: Anton Hiersemann, 1982] 90–130).

¹³As students, preachers, and teachers, the Dominicans made a tremendous impact in the universities. Charismatic, aristocratic, and learned persons such as Jordan of Saxony and Reginald of Orleans, themselves converted from their rich and worldly way of life to the Dominican mission, used their witness and preaching in the university settings to attract countless others to the Dominican "preaching of Jesus Christ." One particularly influential Dominican who had been a professor of canon law, Reginald of Orleans, preached with such power about the Dominican way of life that he alone drew more than a thousand men into Dominic's preaching community (Goodich, *Vita Perfecta,* 154–55). Four years before Thomas' death there were more than ninety Dominican convents in France alone (Mollat, *The Poor in the Middle Ages,* 124).

¹⁴Gui, c. 5.

¹⁵Dominic's own personality and holiness were themselves extraordinary magnets drawing others to his mission. The influential Ceslaus of Cracow, for example, joined Dominic's preaching community after he witnessed the raising of a young man from the dead through Dominic's prayer (Goodich, *Vita Perfecta,* 154).

¹⁶Ap Creed.

[17]CG III, 138, 5. Emphasis added. Unless otherwise noted, italicized words in this book, including those used in quotations, indicate my own emphasis.

[18]ST II-II, 81, 1, ad 5.

[19]Rel St 10.

[20]CG II, 135, 22; in James F. Anderson, trans., *On the Truth of the Catholic Faith,* vol. 2 (New York: Doubleday, 1955) 188.

[21]CG II, 135, 23.

[22]See Alexander Murray, *Reason and Society in the Middle Ages* (Oxford: Clarendon, 1978) 390.

[23]CG I, 2, 2.

[24]Pieper, *Guide,* 31, 21-23, 30.

[25]Ibid., 124.

[26]Com Div Nom ch. 2, lect. 5; cf. Vann, *Aquinas,* 60.

[27]Jacques Maritain, *St. Thomas Aquinas* (London: Sheed and Ward, 1931) 103.

[28]Vann, *Aquinas,* 177.

[29]Pieper, *Guide,* 15.

[30]Maritain, *Aquinas,* 68.

[31]Thomas used Jerome's Vulgate translation of the Bible (See Weisheipl, *Friar,* 369). In particular, for the psalms, Thomas used both the Gallican and Roman Psalters, as well as Jerome's translation from the Hebrew. What the Vulgate lists as one single "Psalm 10" we today read as Psalms 10 and 11. Thomas' lectures on the psalms, therefore, follow a numbering of the psalms after Psalm 11 that is one less than the numbering in our present versions.

[32]Pieper, *Guide,* 125.

[33]Edward A. Synan, "Aquinas and His Age," *Calgary Aquinas Studies,* ed. Anthony Parel (Toronto: Pontifical Institute of Medieval Studies, 1978) 22.

[34]Exp in Job 2; cf. Synan, "Aquinas and His Age," 23.

[35]In Ps 36:21.

[36]It is from these sources that I have drawn the material for these chapters. (See the select bibliography at the end of this book.) For a tentative listing and brief study of Thomas' authentic works, see Weisheipl, *Friar,* 355-405, 467-87.

In addition to the testimony at the First Canonization Inquiry held at Naples, the key primary sources for information about Thomas' life are the three *Vitae* written between 1318 and 1330 by the Dominicans William of Tocco, Bernard Gui, and Peter Calo. In addition, we have fifteen chapters from the *Historia Ecclesiastica* of the Dominican historian Tolomeo of Lucca, who, as a young student, lived with Thomas at the priory of San Domenico in Naples in 1272. Finally, there are the proceedings of the First Canonization Inquiry at Naples (July 21–September 18, 1319) and the Second Inquiry held at Fossanova (November 10-20, 1321). Most of Gui and the First Canonization Inquiry, as well as some of Tolomeo of Lucca, are contained in an English translation in Foster, *Life.*

The three primary biographies of Thomas originated from the process surrounding the movement in Naples for Thomas' canonization. John XXII had become pope in 1316 and was very favorable to the request of the Dominican province at Naples to have their native son canonized. In 1317 the provincial chapter of Sicily commissioned the Dominican preacher general, William of Tocco—then in his mid-sixties—and a young Dominican friar, Robert of Benevento, to gather materials for Thomas' canonization inquiry. William of Tocco had been a young

Dominican student at the priory of San Domenico in Naples when Thomas lived there in 1272-73 and had been made a preacher general of his Order in 1228. One of the sources used for his account was the anecdotes about Thomas which Lady Catherine de Morra remembered. As a child, Lady Catherine had been present on several occasions when Thomas' mother was caring for her own small child, Thomas, and also had overheard conversations between Thomas' mother and other noblewomen. Tocco also drew much information from Bartholomew of Capua, chancellor and protonotary of the kingdom of Sicily, who knew Thomas and who had gained intimate firsthand knowledge about him, especially from Reginald of Piperno.

When Tocco went to Avignon to present his material to Pope John XXII in July or August of 1318, he met there with the fifty-six year old French Dominican Bernard Gui, who was an excellent chronicler and procurator general of the Dominican Order. He also met there the eighty-year old Dominican Tolomeo of Lucca, who, in March of 1318, had been made bishop of Torcello by John XXII. A canonization inquiry was held at Naples from July 21 until September 8, 1319, and another at Fossanova from November 10-20, 1321. On July 18, 1323, Pope John XXII solemnly canonized Thomas in a grand public celebration in Avignon; King Robert of Sicily, along with many people from Naples, attended. Tocco made two drafts of his *Vita* of Thomas: one in 1319 and a second ca. 1320, in time for Thomas' canonization. Tocco's account represents the Southern Italian stories about Thomas, stories drawn from his family, from his time at Paris and Cologne. His *Vita* is punctuated with pious rhetoric.

On the other hand, Bernard Gui was a Frenchman whose account, though it reproduces much of Tocco, does so more succinctly and with much less rhetorical flourish. His *Vita* was published after Thomas' canonization, somewhere between 1323-25. Tolomeo of Lucca was only twelve years younger than Thomas, and his chapters on Thomas in the *Historia Ecclesiastica* show a familiarity with Thomas absent from the other accounts, which relied much on secondhand information. Tolomeo completed his *Historia* in 1317. Finally, Peter Calo, an Italian Dominican, wrote a *Vita* of Thomas that may be part of a collection of saints' lives published between 1330 and 1342 (Foster, *Life*, 2-15).

Outline Chronology of Thomas' Life*

1215	Frederick II is crowned emperor.
1226?	Birth of Thomas at Roccasecca.*
1231	At the age of five, sent as an oblate to Monte Cassino.
1232	Thomas' brother Aimo, a crusader in Emperor Frederick's army, is held for ransom by Turks in Cyprus. Pope Gregory IX tries to help Thomas' family gain his release.
1233	Thomas' brother Aimo is freed.
1240	Becomes a student at the University of Naples at the age of fourteen.
1243	Enters the Dominicans at the age of seventeen.
1244	Abducted by his brothers and kept at the family castles at Montesangiovanni and Roccasecca.
1245	Thomas is released from confinement at home; spends time at Dominican convent at Naples.
1246	Sent to Paris; studies under Albert the Great. Thomas' brother Rinaldo is executed by Emperor Frederick for complicity in an assassination plot. The pope offers Thomas the abbacy of Monte Cassino at his family's instigation.
1248	Sent to Cologne to study. Serves as assistant to Albert the Great.
1251	Ordained a priest at Cologne.
1252	Sent to Paris to prepare for the position of Master in Theology.

1252–55   Serves as a Bachelor in theology, commenting on Lombard's *Sentences* at the University of Paris.

1256   At the age of thirty, Thomas becomes a Master in Theology at the University of Paris.

1259   Sent from Paris to Naples.

1260   Provincial Chapter at Naples makes Thomas a preacher general of the Dominican Order.

1261   Serves as theology lector at Dominican House at Orvieto.

1264   Composes the Corpus Christi liturgy at Orvieto at the request of Pope Urban IV.

1265   Provincial Chaper asks Thomas to establish a Dominican Studium at Rome.
          Thomas refuses a papal offer to make him archbishop of Naples.

1266   At the Dominican Studium at Rome Thomas begins the *Summa Theologiae*.

1267   Assigned to Viterbo.

1268   Assigned to serve his second regency as Master in Theology at Paris.

1269   Begins his second regency at Paris.

1272   Sent as regent of theology to Dominican convent at Naples.

1273   Preaches Lenten sermons in his native tongue at Naples.
          On December 6, Thomas suffers a breakdown while celebrating Mass.

1274   In February sets out for Second Council of Lyons at the behest of Pope Gregory X.
          Mid-February, brought to his niece Frances' castle at Maenza.
          At the end of February, brought by donkey to the Cistercian monks at Fossanova.
          On March 7, Thomas dies at Fossanova.
          Funeral Mass on March 9 at Fossanova.

1277	Condemnation of 219 propositions at Paris; some of Thomas' supposed propositions are included.
1317	William of Tocco, a Dominican and former student of Thomas, is appointed promoter of Thomas' canonization.
1319	July 21–September 18, the first canonization inquiry is held at Naples.
1321	November 10–November 20, the second canonization inquiry is held at Fossanova.
1323	Thomas is canonized by Pope John XXII at Avignon during celebrations from July 16–21.
1325	Paris condemnation of Thomas' teachings is revoked.
1369	By order of Pope Urban V, Thomas' relics are transferred to the Dominican Priory at Toulouse on January 28. After the French Revolution his remains were taken to the Church of St. Sernin in Toulouse. On October 21, 1974, as part of the celebration in Toulouse of the seventh centenary of Thomas' death, his body was transferred to the restored Church of the Jacobins.

*This chronology is based on Bartholomew of Capua's testimony that Thomas died in his forty-eighth year (FVST, 384).

1

I Have Called You Friends

Thomas, Preacher and Friend

The tender-hearted Dominic de Guzman had imbued his community of preaching friars with his own joy in God's gift of friendship with us and among us. Early Dominicans told stories of friends inspiring their friends to join Dominic's community, and to give themselves as companions to one another in his preaching mission. Twenty-five years after Dominic's death at the age of fifty-one, Tommaso d'Aquino joined his community of friends.

By nature, Thomas was quiet and reserved; much of his day was spent in the solitude of study and writing, away from the crowds who gathered around saints like Catherine of Siena. Given his temperament, we could think that the gift of friendship might have eluded Thomas. And yet, if we look beneath the surface of his story, we find people who loved him dearly and whom he loved with equal devotion. He was especially close to his sister, Theodora, and to his niece, Frances.[1] Thomas was dear friends with his mentor, John of San Guiliano; his beloved teacher, Albert the Great; and, most of all, his secretary and devoted companion, Reginald of Piperno, to whom he disclosed all the secrets of his heart.

In Dominic's community Thomas discovered the profound meaning of the gift of friendship as the deepest symbol of the triune God's closeness to us. Other mystics have used spousal imagery to convey the depth of God's nearness to us. But Thomas began to see that only profound friendship-love, with its dimensions of equality, reciprocity, and mutual self-revelation, forms the heart of all intimacy, even the spousal union.

31

As Thomas reflected on the Gospel of John he found unveiled the God who draws inconceivably near to us in friendship-love: "No longer do I call you servants but friends" (John 15:15). Of ourselves we are only creatures and servants; but in Jesus we have become intimate *friends* of *God*. These glad tidings Thomas could not keep pent up inside himself; this good news he *had* to proclaim from his heart! Thomas the preacher in this way inevitably became again Thomas the friend, and preaching the good news of Jesus became his deepest act of friendship with others.[2]

It was in the context of his friendship with Albert the Great that Thomas first learned to value the theme of friendship as the central symbol of the triune God's intimate love for us. Albert, renowned theologian, philosopher, and scientist of the Dominican Order, chose Thomas as his assistant at the Dominican Studium he founded at Cologne. One of Thomas' responsibilities in this capacity was transcribing Albert's lecture notes on Aristotle's *Ethics*. Despite a papal ban on teaching Aristotle's philosophical works at universities, Albert had devoured Aristotle's newly discovered works and shared the fruit of his study with enthusiastic students at Cologne. It was Albert who introduced Thomas to the theme of friendship, a theme which would eventually form the very soul of Thomas' own theology.

Albert's lectures made a lasting impact on Thomas. As he carefully copied them, he found Aristotle's insights on friendship come to life in Albert's deepening friendship with him. From his own experience, Thomas began to understand the depth of meaning hinted at in the Johannine texts on friendship: "I have no longer called you servants, but friends, for I have told you everything the Father has said to me. . . . There is no greater love than this: to lay down one's life for one's friend" (John 15:15, 13). This motif of friendship as mutuality, reciprocity, equality—a symbol so precious to us today—became so dear to Thomas that he made it central to all of his key theological reflections.

It is true that we can easily overlook Thomas' focus on friendship precisely because, with Aristotle and his own contemporaries, he understood man's biological and sociological make-up as more complete than woman's. Yet we who today are learning to value the rich facets of inculturation will find and appreciate the real Thomas Aquinas if we allow him also to be who he was, a person of his time and culture. In adopting Aristotle's biological principles, Thomas was, in fact, employing the best scientific information available to his time.

And if we look deeper than Thomas' time-conditioned biology and physiology, we will discover his theological focus on the theme of equality which we so value today. For though he adopted Aristotle's biological principles, it is precisely his *theological* understanding of our equality as men and women before God that far surpasses the insights of his contemporaries. Thomas became convinced that all of us, women and men, are called to be *friends* and therefore *equals* with each other through the Spirit's gift of charity. Even more radically, in this same charity, we are called to be intimate friends with *God*. In his focus on friendship as equality, mutuality, and reciprocity, therefore, Thomas is relevant and close to us today. And in considering his reflections on friendship, we begin to understand the depth of his insights on preaching and sharing the fruits of our contemplation as our deepest act of *friendship* with one another.

Thomas' Early Experience of Friendship

Thomas views our Christian call to be mystics as profound and yet simple, beyond us and yet fulfilling our every desire. To be a mystic is simply to be, by God's grace, what we most long to be in our heart: a beloved friend. And since we hold nothing back from one we truly love, we share all that we have and are, even our heart's secrets, with our beloved friend. Thomas found in the Gospel of John this description of our call to be mystics: "I no longer call you servants but friends, for I have revealed to you all that I have heard from my Father" (John 15:15). Thomas knew that to be a mystic is to be the triune God's beloved friend. And he saw that all of us are called to be mystics, the friends who, far from keeping the riches of their beloved God pent up in their hearts, generously share this wealth with others.

Thomas began to understand our great need for friendship in some intuitive way from his own experience even as a child. As a little boy he knew the closeness of a nurse who loved and cared for him.[3] He also had the loving care of a personal tutor. As we have seen, his parents presented him as an oblate at the Benedictine monastery of Monte Cassino when he was still a child. During the nine years of his stay at the Abbey—a stay which his parents hoped would lead to his becoming abbot—he almost certainly had the companionship and care of a private tutor.

As an adolescent, too, Thomas found the comfort of a close friend. When he was fourteen, Emperor Frederick evicted all foreign Dominicans and Franciscans from his territory, and Thomas was sent away from the monastery. But at the advice of the abbot, his parents enrolled him in the university at Naples, his mother's birthplace. Yet even in this large city, with its environment so alien to the warm and peaceful setting of the monastery, Thomas did not find himself alone. The Dominicans had a priory at Naples, and soon Thomas was befriended by the Dominican John of San Giuliano, "who loved him dearly."[4] John began to encourage and support Thomas' increasing attraction to the Dominicans' way of life.

When he was about seventeen years old, Thomas presented himself at the priory of San Domenico in Naples and asked to be accepted as a Dominican. During the following months, as he journeyed perhaps to school at Paris, his brothers kidnapped him, and his family forced him to remain at their castle for about a year. Yet even during this painful time, he was not left without a close friend. Brother John of San Giuliano visited him often and would bring a clean habit for him to wear.[5]

After his family had permitted Thomas to return to the Dominicans at San Domenico in Naples, he was sent as a novice to the convent of Saint-Jacques in Paris in 1246, and at the end of the year he professed his vows as a Dominican.[6] He spent his two years at Paris praying and studying, especially with the lector in charge of studies in the convent. But at Paris he also came to know the most famous Dominican of his time, the learned Albert of Cologne, whom people called "the Great" even in his own lifetime. Albert had been the first German master in theology at Paris. But though he was first of all a theologian, his vast knowledge spanned almost every area of learning, including philosophy and science.

Church authorities had banned the teaching of Aristotle's philosophical works at the universities, judging some of his insights—on the issue of human immortality, for example—to be contrary to Christian belief. This ban, however, did not intimidate Albert, who in his middle-aged years had discovered for himself the depth of Aristotle's philosophical insights. Though other masters in theology at Paris considered it beneath them to lecture in philosophy—viewed as the "handmaid" of theology— Albert's classes commenting on Aristotle's works soon became those most sought after by the students. Albert's audacity in lecturing on Aristotle's philosophy in a theological *studium* is an example, not only of his independence, but also of his conviction that philosophy and science are indispensable for theological studies.[7]

In 1248 Albert's superiors sent him to his native Cologne to start the first general Dominican house of studies or *studium* in Germany. Albert was so impressed with Thomas' work that he decided to take Thomas with him. The young Thomas—he was only twenty-two at the time, and not yet ordained a priest— could hardly have been paid a greater compliment. In the summer of 1248, accompanied by Thomas and others, Albert travelled by foot to Cologne to establish the first general studium in Germany.[8]

Thomas studied under Albert for four years at Cologne. Serving as his bachelor, Thomas responded at Albert's disputations. He lectured, too, on the Bible—his early lectures on Isaiah have been preserved—and assisted Albert in class preparations.[9] Thomas also served as secretary in copying Albert's lectures on *The Divine Names* of Dionysius, and on Aristotle's *Ethics*— a task which would leave an indelible impact on his own theology. Working with, teaching, and advising the young student, Albert grew to know Thomas, and could not help being drawn by his goodness. The two became friends in a bond that would last until Thomas' death and beyond.

After four years at Cologne, Albert convinced his superiors to choose Thomas for the task of preparing as a master in theology at Paris. Thomas tried to refuse the assignment, which he considered above his abilities, but his superiors insisted. In 1252, therefore, at twenty-six years of age and after at least six years of study under Albert, Thomas began studies in preparation for commenting on Lombard's *Sentences* at Paris.

In the last years of his life, after twenty-five years of teaching, writing, and preaching as a Dominican, Thomas himself undertook a commentary on Aristotle's discourse on friendship, just as his teacher Albert had done. Thomas was known for not wasting his time nor writing a superfluous word, yet he took this task on his already heavily burdened shoulders. In the very writing of this commentary Thomas makes a statement of great import about the value of this theme to him.

Though Thomas affirms Aristotle's own teaching, his commentary is not simply an exercise in copying the thoughts of someone else. His own life made him know by experience the truth which as a young student he had learned in copying Albert's notes on Aristotle. As we read Thomas' words, we begin to see the depth of insight that pervades his conviction about our mystical call to be God's beloved *friends,* and to give to others the fruits of our contemplation precisely as our deepest act of friendship with them.

Our Need for Friends

We can find in Thomas' own life the experiences which give personal meaning to his words at the beginning of his commentary: "No one in his or her right mind would choose to live with all other external goods but without friends."[10] Thomas, whose favorite recreation was to walk alone in the garden, and who would quietly escape the companionship of those who tried to walk with him, nevertheless knew the truth of our experience: "A solitary life is a difficult and burdensome life!" We need and want to be close to others because we grow only in communion with other people. To live cut off from human companionship is truly hell for us.[11]

Whether sad or happy, "we need friends in all conditions of life" because true friendship is our greatest gift.[12] Our friends console us when we are sad; they grieve with us, comfort us, and brighten our day. With our friends, Thomas reminds us, we no longer suffer alone.[13] And though we need friends when we are sad, we need them just as much when we are happy. Whatever good fortune we are enjoying, if we have no friends to share it with us, our pleasure in our blessings is greatly lessened.

Thomas thinks of how much happiness being a close friend to someone adds to our own life. For happiness is not a possession but an activity we *do*. We are most alive and content not when we are passively existing, but when we are actively using our gifts and abilities. This is why we have a far happier time when we ourselves are dancing, skating, or playing ball, for example, than when we simply watch someone else have a good time doing the same things. Our desire to be active is especially evident in our need to live a worthwhile life that brings more good into the world. We derive far more pleasure from our life when we are doing something positive and good in the world than when we are simply existing in a self-centered way. And when we live in a worthwhile way, we not only enjoy our life, we also enjoy knowing and feeling how good our life is. We relish not only living a good life but also being *conscious* of the life that surges in us.[14] Our greatest pleasure, therefore, is the joy of making a difference in the world, of creating more good with our life. Not to do this is to live in an isolated way, keeping the potential of our minds and hearts locked within us. We can live stingy lives, meager in love and self-giving, lives that spread little good in the world.

But when we share ourselves with others and become their *friends,* Thomas tells us, we begin to take joy in their good, as well as in their activities and accomplishments, and to love them for their sake and not for our own. And when we love our friends and work for their good, we consider them so much a part of us that they are like our own self. Their virtues and accomplishments in some way become ours, and ours become theirs. Thomas himself had experienced the paradox of true friendship: in loving in this unselfish way, we ourselves gain so much. Loving others deepens our own sense of being loved, and we know we are not alone.[15] It is not only when we are sad, therefore, but especially when we are happy that we need friends. For our friends lessen our sorrow, but even more, they double our joy.[16]

In these insights of Thomas on friendship, we begin to find the heart of the ideas he will develop on sharing the riches we contemplate as our deepest act of friendship with one another. The wealth that fills us through study and contemplation makes us truly rich only in our sharing it in friendship-love with others.

Friendliness and Friendship

Thomas understood from his own experience that we are not born friends; we learn how to become friends. Friendship is a true *virtue,* a *good habit* we develop by giving ourselves. But we achieve friendship-love only by first gaining the simple courtesy that is the virtue of friendliness. We become a friend by learning first how to be friendly. Thomas knew that such friendliness comes naturally to us, if we let it. We are inclined to be pleasant with other people, simply because we live together on this earth as members of the same human race. And we readily show compassion even to strangers who suffer through a tragedy with us. It is true that we reserve signs of real *friendship* for those close to our heart.

Yet our friendliness with others less dear to us is not false, since it expresses the empathy we naturally feel with other human beings.[17]

Thomas found that friendliness is not the intimacy of friendship. But it *is* a true *virtue* which we owe each other in justice. By nature, Thomas himself was reserved and even shy. But he knew the truth of Aristotle's words: "We cannot survive even a day with someone who is sad or joyless."[18] His own experience of community life taught him that if we cannot live agreeably with one another, we cannot live at all. Our being pleasant with one another is not an option or simply the duty of extroverts; it is a virtue each of us is obliged to develop, not in charity but in justice to one another.[19] Just as God's laws are intended only to make us God's *friends,* Thomas tells us, even our own laws are a way we befriend one another.[20] And since virtue always give us pleasure, our friendliness with others not only spreads joy to those who live and work with us, but also makes *us* happy.[21]

Thomas found, too, that the virtue of friendliness can grow into the deeper virtue of friendship. Our pleasantness with others can open our eyes to the real good in them. We find ourselves wanting to be with these certain special people, and immensely enjoying their presence. We begin wanting their good and working to achieve it, for their sake and not our own. We long to have a real "life together" with them by sharing our heart's secrets, and deepening our communion in the virtue of friendship-love.[22] And so we learn from our own experience the depth of the Lord's words to *us:* "No longer do I call you servants but friends, for I have told you all that my Father has told me" (John 15:15).

Thomas agrees with Aristotle that we can and should be friendly with many people, but friends with only a few. True friendship requires *reciprocal* closeness and self-giving, and we are drawn to reveal ourselves only to one, or at most, very few. Thomas himself disclosed his heart's secrets to no one but Reginald, even though many other people had a deep affection for Thomas. We are told, for example, that he spent one Christmas at the home of Lord Richard, the cardinal deacon of Saint Angelo who was "very fond of Thomas and knew him well."[23] But it seems that his relationship with Lord Richard was friendly, rather than one of close mutual friendship. On the other hand, Thomas had a great love for the holy Brother Annibaldo, a Friar Preacher and Master in Theology, "a very humble, sincere, and saintly man whom brother Thomas loved dearly."[24] Thomas clearly chose his friends for their virtue, not for their wealth or status.

Friendship as Equality and Mutuality

Yet we cannot be friends with others unless there is a true equality between us. We wish our friends well when we want their good, for their sake and not our own, Thomas tells us. But without a mutual return, good wishes cannot grow into friendship. Our being true *friends* means becoming consciously aware of each other's esteem and love, and communicating our affection to each other. We may feel love for one another, but unless we speak our love and express it in our actions, we are only mutual well-wishers, not friends.[25]

Both of us, therefore, must want the friendship, and express our love for each other in our actions and also in our words. Thomas learned from experience that affection and inner communion join us to our friends, but it is not enough simply to *want* good for each other.[26] We ourselves know how often we can feel love for someone but not realize it. Or we can hide the love we feel, or fail to voice it by words and actions. This inner but unexpressed love is, for Thomas, only "benevolence," "well-wishing." Our good wishes for one another are not true friendship but only its beginning. We become friends with others not just because we feel an inner love for them, but also because we acknowledge and express our love.[27] On the other hand, friendship is a habit that makes us want to show our love even if sometimes we cannot do so as we would like.[28]

In summary, then, Thomas knew that friendliness makes us kind and pleasant to others, but we are *friends* only with those to whom our heart's affection unites us.[29] However, just as real life means not simply intending to live but actually *living,* real friendship means not simply wanting to be friends, but also expressing our affection.[30] Thomas himself reflects on how a man may "fall in love" with a woman initially because of her beauty, but in friendship-love, his attraction begins to grow toward a "complete love." He wants to be with her more and more, and "begrudges her absence." But if he does not express his love for her in his words and actions, his well-wishing never becomes true friendship-love. Thomas calls this "wishing someone well," unexpressed in our words and actions, a "certain idle friendship," since mere benevolence "does not have any friendly act connected with it."[31]

We can be true friends, therefore, only with someone who is our equal, and who actively returns our love.[32] This is one reason why one who gives and one who simply takes cannot be true friends. As a former member of the nobility, Thomas knew the unbridgeable gulf between masters and servants. A nobleman did not become friends with his servants; he simply used them. But this must not be so with us, Thomas tells us. Only objects, not *persons,* exist for our use. If we simply use another person for our own goals or pleasure, we can never be true friends.[33]

We know from experience that we value little what is cheap to us. This is why Thomas was convinced that a true friendship consists more in giving than in passively receiving love. He saw how even an infant can receive love, but *friends* both receive and *give* love. It is true that friendship is a good *habit,* yet, as Thomas stresses, we are friends not simply by our good intentions but also by our self-giving words and actions. Our friendship deepens, therefore, only when both of us freely commit ourselves to the friendship.[34] Furthermore, while lasting friendship requires real self-giving of us, it also gives each of us much in return. This *reciprocal* nature of friendship-love distinguishes it from any other kind of love.[35]

We can be friends, however, even with those who are not our equals, if we compensate by the generosity of our love. Yet if there is "immense" inequality, there can be no true friendship between us.[36] This is why Aristotle thought that the infinite distance between God and us makes friendship with God impossible. But on this significant point Thomas parts company with his beloved Aristotle. He had discovered the truth of Jesus' inconceivable gift: "No longer do I call you servants but *friends*" (John 15:15). As we shall see, precisely in the gift of the Spirit's charity, we are given the power to love God and each other with God's own friendship-love.

False and True Friendship

With Aristotle, Thomas recognized that we can have two kinds of friendship. Our true and lasting friendships are based on the virtue and goodness in both of us. We love these friends for their own sake, wanting for them the same good we want for ourselves. But in selfish "friendships" based on merely apparent good and not real virtue in each other, we "love" merely what pleases us or is useful to us. We want the "friendship" because we feel dissatisfied with ourselves and our own emptiness, and so we seem to be reaching out to real good. But instead of extending ourselves in generous love, we only appear to be self-giving while in fact we stay centered on ourselves.[37] In such "friendships" based on need or pleasure, we love our own advantage, not our friends' welfare. Instead of *giving* ourselves for our friends' true good, we *take* from them what is useful and pleasant for ourselves. They become a means to our own advantage and pleasure, much the same way that we "love" objects pleasing and useful to us, such as food or clothing.[38]

Thomas knew that selfish friendships are not true but only apparent "love."[39] Since we use someone as an object for our own advantage, such friendships never last. As soon as our need passes, the friendship ends. When our friend stops being useful or pleasant to us, we stop loving him or her: "Once the reason for the friendship dissolves, so, too, does the friendship."[40] But in a true friendship based on virtue in each other, we share in God's *self-giving* love by reaching out to work for our loved one's good.[41] In selfish love, we are drawn to the *apparent* good in another simply as a means to our own ends. But virtuous friendship is different. Just as we love *true* good for its own sake, we love our real friends not because of their usefulness to us but because they are so *good*.[42]

From his own experience, too, Thomas recognized that like attracts like. Similarity is the cause of love, since we are naturally drawn to people with whom we have something in common. Indeed, we begin to love those with whom we are already united in some way because of an affinity we share. Thus, when we have a true friendship based on the good, we love in our friend the very goodness and virtue we are trying to deepen in our own life. And our likeness in virtue with our friend is the very cause of our communion. But selfish love based on our need or pleasure draws us to love not the other person but ourselves. The cause of our union with our "friend" is his or her usefulness to us. And if we are both selfish, our similarity does not unite us, as in virtuous love, but rather disgusts and separates us.[43]

Thomas realized that, as the source in some way for every emotion we feel, love makes us shield ourselves from danger[44] and reach out spontaneously to what seems good.[45] Yet even though we easily desire what attracts us, it may take us a lifetime to learn the difference between selfish "love" and the self-giving friendship which chooses our loved one's good. We begin to learn by painful experience that only the real good that is *virtue*—and not simply beauty or wealth in another—can satisfy our heart: only goodness in others draws us truly to love them,[46] not for our sake but for their own.[47]

Surely, Thomas' own friendship with the extraordinary Albert the Great helped him to understand this difference between selfish love and friendship-love based on communion in the good. Albert had seen beyond the quiet, even silent exterior of the young student Thomas and glimpsed the depth of his soul's goodness. Albert gained this insight not long after Thomas arrived at Cologne, when he was in his early twenties. The only languages Thomas knew were his native Neapolitan tongue and Latin, the language of the schools. His large physique, along with his natural reserve and ignorance of German, soon led the other students to call him "the dumb ox."

One day Albert was conducting a formal disputation for the students on a difficult topic. Thomas had been taking careful notes, and inadvertently dropped them. Another student found the notes and showed them to Albert. As he read them, Albert began to see the extraordinary soul of the quiet student who was their author. He arranged to have Thomas defend a very difficult thesis at the next disputation. Thomas was exceedingly reluctant, and accepted only in obedience. He prepared for this, his first public defense of a thesis, by study and long hours in prayer.

When Thomas did begin speaking, he examined the topic with such subtlety that Albert pressed him further with seemingly irrefutable arguments. Thomas responded so brilliantly to each one that he seemed to Albert to be more like the master than the student. Touched to the heart, Albert later told the other students, "You call Thomas a dumb ox. But I tell you that the whole world one day will hear his bellowing."[48] From that day forward, Albert began to reach out to the young student in what would become a devoted and life-long friendship.

Virtue as the Heart of Lasting Friendship

As Thomas himself learned in his friendship with Albert, the deepest friendship, and the only one that lasts, is based upon our communion in the good. True friends are like our very self; we want their good as if it were our own. Indeed, we want our friends' good for their own sake and not because of anything they can give us.[49] As Thomas himself learned from Albert's unselfish concern for him, we begin to love someone who is good only because we ourselves are good, and both of us are good to one another.[50] True, lasting friendship can be based on no other foundation than virtue in each other. Thomas became convinced that whatever is contrary to virtue in us or our friend is also an obstacle to our friendship. But whatever is virtuous in either of us is also a true benefit to our friendship. If we are friends in the good, we do nothing to harm our friend's true welfare, and we do nothing that will cause our friend to do wrong.[51]

True friendship, therefore, is itself a *virtue*. And virtue, as a good *habit,* is not easily lost. This is why unselfish friendship, based on virtue, lasts.[52] Thomas comments that friendship based on selfish need will always come to an end, but even physical separation cannot damage our friendships based on communion in the good. This kind of friendship inspires us to do good for one another and to live a "life together," in the joy of uninterrupted presence with one another. As Thomas discovered, both these activities are the true acts of friendship. Yet even when physical separation prevents us from doing good for each other in person, we can still deepen our friendship through our readiness and desire to do good for one another. As Thomas emphasizes, "Only the activity of friendship, not the friendship itself, is diminished by distance." And yet, our good habits do die through lack of activity. Since friendship itself is a good habit, just as we "develop habits through repeated activity, we maintain them in the same way."[53]

Thomas points out the great difference between friendship with a good person and with someone who is merely pleasant. We court unworthy people for our own advantage. But we love truly virtuous persons for their own sake, because of the real good in them. Paradoxically, when we love in this unselfish way, not using our friend for our own gratification, our unselfish love gives us great joy and pleasure.[54] And since we grow as persons by giving and not merely passively receiving love, our joy deepens in the measure that we actively give our love.[55] Slowly we learn that our true life's purpose is not only good itself, but also actually *doing* and *enjoying* what is good.[56] In our virtuous friendships based on the good in our loved ones, we are willing even to sacrifice the pleasure of our friends' presence when necessary. This self-giving love is greater than the love that refuses to be separated from our dear ones.[57] For in helping our friends to carry out their responsibilities—even if these responsibilities mean absence from us—we show greater love for them than if we tried always to be with them. We prove that we are seeking *their* true good, and not our own pleasure or advantage. Yet Thomas himself knew the paradox of self-giving love: even in the pain of our separation from our loved ones, our unselfish love itself gives us deep joy. Indeed, we learn to enjoy our friend through love's communion even when we are not physically near him or her.[58] However, Thomas points out that if we are "willingly" and "easily" deprived of our friend's presence, we show that we love our friend only a little, or "perhaps not at all."[59]

The love of friendship thus draws us outside of ourselves, truly to our loved ones' good, so that we love our friends as if they were our own self.[60] Furthermore, God's charity toward us, Thomas never tires of saying, is not simply *benevolence,* but true and intimate *friendship* with us. This friendship-love impels God to unveil to us the secrets of the divine heart, and to work ceaselessly for our happiness, unselfishly and for our sake alone.[61] And when we ourselves want our loved ones' good, not for our sake but truly for theirs, this kind of friendship-love is a share in God's own incomprehensible love for us.[62]

Love for Ourselves and Those Closest to Us

"Love your neighbor as *yourself"* (Mark 12:31). Thomas had experienced the truth of the Lord's words to us; he knew that we are able to befriend others only if we first befriend ourselves. Since our friends are like our own self, we feel toward them what we feel toward *ourselves.*[63] This is why we truly love others only when we are best friends with ourselves.[64] To understand this insight more deeply, Thomas reflects on how we naturally love most the person who most wants our good, the one who is closest to us.

But, he points out, *we* are most closely joined to ourselves. Though we are united to our friends, we are literally one with ourselves. This is why, more than anything else, we naturally long for our own welfare.[65] All the good we desire for our friends, we want most of all for ourselves,[66] since we cannot help caring for ourselves, and seeking what seems to be best for us.[67] We naturally love ourselves and work for our own good even more than we love our dearest friends. Since the Lord commands us to love one another as we love ourselves, therefore, we are *meant* to be our own best friend.[68] And the paradox is that loving ourselves in this way enables us to love others; when we befriend ourselves we can be a true friend to others.[69]

What does it mean to be our own best friend? Thomas knew that when we truly love ourselves, we do not want simply cheap, superficial goods but the best good for ourselves.[70] And since God alone is the best good, we love ourselves best when we love God most. If we let God become our heart's one desire, conflicting wants do not divide our heart, and peace anoints our soul.[71] We might think that self-love is selfishness. But Thomas assures us that this is not so; selfishness is the antithesis of this true self-love. When we love ourselves selfishly, we do not choose the *best* good for ourselves but only illusory goods, and so we have only war within us. Finding no peace in our own company, we certainly cannot find it in others' presence. Thinking that we are unworthy of love, we experience our lives as a great burden and so cannot befriend either ourselves or others.[72]

When we truly love ourselves, however, we find peace in our heart. We *love* to be in our own company, since we find God there. We are filled with contentment and a sense of how good our life is. We recall our past with joy and look forward to our future with trust.[73] And as we value our own company, we value the company of others. In giving of ourselves, we grow more rich in love each day, and cherish virtuous friendships above all other blessings. Our love may grow so deep that we would willingly sacrifice our possessions and even our very lives for those we love.[74] Yet even when we are unable to do all for our friends that we would like, we can still grow in love, Thomas tells us. For a generous heart depends not on how much we give but on how much we *want* to give.[75] Thus the paradox of self-giving love: the more we give, the more we gain. And the richer our own love becomes, the more our love enriches others.[76]

But whom should we love? Are there people to whom we *owe* our love? Thomas assures us that it is natural for us to love most dearly those who are closest to us. And so our self-giving love is meant to enrich first of all our own family. With Aristotle, Thomas was convinced that we should have the deepest, most intimate bond with our spouse and children. They are part of us, and our love for them is inseparable from the very love we have for ourselves.[77]

This is why it is natural for us as parents to love our children with the most intense love, as flesh of our own flesh. Indeed, Thomas comments, our love for our children "comes closest to the love we have for ourselves, from which all friendship is derived."[78] But Thomas also stresses that since our spouse is one with our own self, we are meant to love him or her with our deepest and most intimate *friendship-love*.[79] Because we are joined with our spouse in the most intimate physical union and in the closeness of daily life together, it is with our spouse that we are meant by God to have "the *greatest* friendship."[80]

In this key point Thomas shows how far ahead of his time he was. Again and again, he stresses that friendship is love precisely between equals, love that is reciprocal, mutual in every way. For Thomas, a wife is no appendage to her husband but his equal before God; she is the one to whom he owes his greatest friendship. We know that Thomas does not waste words. He intends us to understand this strong statement in the context of what he says about the essence of friendship as sharing our heart's secrets with one another.

Thomas was not married. But he did have a family whom he dearly loved. And he was convinced from his own experience that, after our spouse and children, we owe our deepest love to our family and relatives. Since our friendships with relatives are the most lasting and stable, our family members have a greater claim to our care in their need then even our dearest friends.[81] He gives an example of our owing someone a huge debt, and then finding that a close family member also is in great need. Our loved one deserves our help first, unless the person to whom we are indebted is in as dire a need as our relative. Yet Thomas agrees with Aristotle (*Ethics* 9.2) that in these matters, "we cannot lay down a general rule;" we need to decide in each particular case whose claims carry the greater weight in terms of our care.[82]

And since we love most of all those who are most good, we cannot help loving best our dear ones who are closest to God. "The more like God a person is, the more he or she is to be loved."[83] For it is charity that makes us close to God, and the greater our charity, the more deeply we love and the more lovable and worthy of love we become.[84] Thomas recalls the proverb, "Forsake not old friends, for the new will not be like them" (Sir 9:14).[85] Love comes from familiarity, and love grows by familiarity.[86] Those who have been our closest friends for the longest time are worthy of our deepest love,[87] since the stronger the bond of friendship, "the more solid and long-lasting it will be."[88]

Communication as "Living Together"

But the real "familiarity" which Thomas sees as the heart of true friendship is the familiarity of "living together": "Nothing is so proper to friends as to live together, for the principal act of friendship is to live with our friends. Even the blessed desire to live with their friends." Yet for Thomas, as for Aristotle, "living together" does not mean simply or even necessarily living under the same roof. Nor does it mean, Thomas comments, surely with a smile, simply eating meals together "as cattle do."[89] We may live under the same roof but never have a true "life together" because we are merely benevolent and polite to one another. What Thomas means by "living together" as friends is a true human life together through *communication,* sharing with each other our thoughts and desires, our fears and goals, and most of all, our heart's secrets. "All friendship consists in *communication,* for friends have everything in common."[90] For Thomas, this precious experience, so well-known to anyone who loves, gives us a small hint of how much God wants, more than we could imagine, an intimacy and life together with us as beloved friends.[91]

Thomas reflects on how we are always seeking good to love, even if we do not always realize it; love is the root of all we feel and do.[92] And, as Dionysius knew, love unites us to those we cherish, so that we want their good as if it were our own.[93] When we truly love, we desire our friends' good for their sake, and not for our own advantage. Love binds us to our dear ones, therefore, and makes them part of us.[94] This is why friendship-love impels us to "have everything in common" with our loved ones.[95] We cannot help wanting to be perfectly joined with those we love, desiring our union in thought and love to be completed by real union. And so we long to have our dear ones with us always, sharing a life together[96] by sharing the activities we most enjoy. Thomas observes wryly that some people love to drink or gamble with their friends. Even without realizing it, they consider these activities a form of "life together," of "communicating" with their friends in what is dearest to them! Furthermore, we do not need always to "live together" in the same building or city with our friends. But we do need to spend time with them, to share our thoughts and secrets in that "life together" which is true communication from our heart.[97]

Not everyone, however, is capable of this "life together" at the core of friendship. Severe, rigid persons "are not suited for the activity of friendship, which is 'living together.' " For critical, bad-tempered people spread misery, not joy. They do not get along with themselves and so cannot get along with anyone else. Unhappy in their own presence, they cannot enjoy anyone else's company; at odds with their own mind and heart, they are constantly warring with everyone else! Such ill-tempered people are incapable of being or having friends, Thomas comments, since they cannot reach out of themselves to communicate with anyone else. Wrapped up in themselves, they do not enjoy conversation with others, and so they cannot "live with" anyone else in the heart's communication that is friendship.[98]

Virtuous persons, however—as Thomas knew from his own experience—"live together" with great pleasure, for they are a joy in themselves and a joy to one another. Friends who love what is good help each other grow even better by their good conversations, by their love, and by their virtuous actions together. Delighting in each other's good example, they live in their own lives the proverb, "We receive *good* things from the *good.* "[99]

And we truly *need* good friends in order to live a good life. Thomas comments that we need to experience real *joy* in living a virtuous life, since we do not pursue any activity that does not give us delight of some kind. If there were no joy or pleasure in living a virtuous life, who of us would want virtue! But one of the deepest joys of living a good life, Thomas tells us from his own experience, is precisely friendship with others who share our ideals, goals, and desire for good. Our virtuous friends give us a joy that encourages and supports us in choosing virtue together with them. When our friendships are good in this way, we ourselves grow even more virtuous, and more pleasing in each other's eyes.[100]

If we love virtue, however, we will relate to many people in a friendly way, and be close friends with only a few. Thomas himself found that people who seem to be intimate friends with everyone are not true friends of anyone. Such people can spend only a little time with each person, and so they become "political" friends, like those in cities where "friendship is judged by such plaudits and familiarities." In reality, however, we need only a few close friends, even for pleasant living. With Aristotle, Thomas agrees that we can have intimate friendship only with "one person, or, at most, toward a very few."[101]

We cannot "parcel ourselves out, so to speak, among many" or have "an immense multitude of friends," simply because we lack the time and energy intimately to "rejoice and grieve with many people." Thomas comments that even "in passionate love, one man does not love several women with intense love, because perfect friendship consists in a certain superabundance of love."[102] Indeed, friendship based on true virtue is a rare and precious gift. If we can find a few such friends, for virtue's sake and for themselves, Thomas writes, "it should be *exceedingly* lovable and dear to us."[103]

Mutual Self-Revelation as the Heart of Intimate Friendship

Thomas was convinced that the surest sign of our having found such a deep friendship is that we reveal our heart's secrets to our friend. For when we truly love, we want the same good for our friend as we want for ourselves, since our friend is our other self.[104] We treat our loved one as we do ourselves; what belongs to each of us belongs to both of us.[105] Most of all, we *want* to reveal our whole heart to our friend, our "other self" (*Ethics* 9.4). And, Thomas assures us, since we have only one heart and soul with our friend, what we tell him or her does not leave our own heart; we keep safe in our own soul the secrets we reveal to our loved one (cf. Prov 25:9).[106] Most deeply, we learn this truth about friendship from the depths of God, for in Jesus, the Father has revealed all of the secrets of the divine heart to *us*: "No longer do I call you servants but friends, for all that I have heard from my Father I have revealed to you" (John 15:15). Through the Spirit's own profound wisdom, we have been made intimate friends of God (Wis 7:27).[107]

Thomas experienced this truth also in his close friendship with Reginald, his Dominican brother. Some time before Thomas' own time as master at Paris, the Dominican community had begun to assign a *socius* to act as secretary and companion to the brothers who were serving as masters of theology there. The Dominicans assigned Reginald as Thomas' *socius*. Though he was not Thomas' intellectual or spiritual equal, Reginald was, nevertheless, a theologian and a deeply spiritual man, with more than ordinary gifts of mind and heart. And what Reginald lacked in terms of equality with Thomas, he made up by the very force of his love and devotion to him.

Through Reginald's love, the naturally reserved scholar gradually learned to open his heart and to entrust its secrets into the gentle hands of his *socius*. What Thomas would tell no one else, he would disclose to Reginald. It was only to Reginald that Thomas revealed the profound mystical experience he had once at Mass, although others present also asked Thomas in vain about what had happened.[108] It was only to Reginald, also, that Thomas told of his brothers' cruelty in sending a prostitute to him after they had kidnapped him from the Dominicans. To Reginald alone the reserved Thomas confessed the temptation, struggle, and grace this outrage had been for him. "To no one would he disclose" such secrets of his soul except to Reginald, his *socius*, "for the love he bore him."[109]

Yet deep friendships like the one Thomas had with Reginald do not happen in a day, as Thomas himself tells us. It takes a long time for us truly to know each other, to communicate our hearts' secrets, and to grow in appreciating each other's virtue. But in these true friendships based on the good, our joy in each other's company only deepens with time. And if we are blessed with such a communion, Thomas assures us, it is impossible for us to love friends like these too much, since our virtue itself will order our affection for one another.[110]

But should we ever end a friendship? For we may find that our friendship is no longer helping us grow in virtue or that we no longer share the same values. Perhaps we have grown in different directions and there is no equality or reciprocity in our self-giving. Perhaps one of us has declined in virtue rather than grown in it, so that we are no longer friends with the same person whose goodness we once loved. Thomas knew from his own experience of becoming a Dominican despite his family's protests that we can begin to value deeply what our loved ones do not cherish. We cannot share our hearts' secrets or rejoice with them in the same good; we cannot "live together" by sharing the same values and goals. Thomas recommends that we first try to work out these difficulties together. But if our efforts fail, or "we cannot bring our friend back to health, we should fittingly abandon the friendship." Yet, Thomas gently urges us, even when we must end a friendship, we should remain friendly toward those we once loved as friends.[111]

Friendship as Union

If our love is based on true virtue, equality, and mutual self-giving, however, we can trust that our friendship-love will endure into heaven itself. When we love someone with true friendship, we are so one in affection that we even seem freely to belong to each other.[112] With Dionysius Thomas stresses that our love so unites us with our beloved[113] that we think of our loved one as our very self. Aristotle himself comments that we seem as inseparable from our intimate friends as knee and tibia! Indeed, we seem to have only one soul; what belongs to one of us belongs to both of us. Furthermore, Thomas adds, since our friend is our other self, we have everything in common.[114]

But from his own experience Thomas became convinced that though we need to share the same values with our close friends, we do not have to hold the same opinions. He points out an experience common to all of us: we can greatly agree with perfect strangers and even enemies about some things, and strongly disagree about other things with our closest friends! Thus we need to have the same ultimate goals, but not the same means to these goals.[115] Moreover, as true friends, we will do what is best for each other even when it is not what *we* want.[116]

Thomas reflected again and again on how friendship-love unites us with our loved one. This union does not occur in selfish love, when we use our "friends" as objects for our own need or pleasure, for there is neither equality in virtue nor reciprocal self-giving between us. But when we love our virtuous friends unselfishly, we are *equals* in virtue and respect, in affection and caring.[117] Thomas gives as an example of "friends returning love for love" our helping a friend even when we are not asked to do so. In such a situation, both we and our friend show unselfish love. For in refraining from asking for our help, our friend shows his or her concern about not burdening us, and we who give help unasked show equal sensitivity to our friend in need.[118]

In this kind of friendship based on virtuous love, our affection makes us seem to have only one soul. In addition, Thomas remarks, our union in affection cannot help drawing us naturally to want a physical union.[119] Thus a man and woman whose love gives them only one heart and soul with each other are drawn to become one body also in marriage. On the other hand, our love for our friends also draws us to give them our tender affection; and even if we are not called to marriage and sexual union, we can have one heart and soul with our closest friends. We can find other ways to become one with our dearest friend, especially by "living together" in the closeness of sharing our hearts' secrets with him or her.[120]

In such friendship-love, Thomas observes, our thoughts are with each other when we are apart, and when we are together we feel a profound contentment. This very contentment makes us experience our friendship as *intimate,* flowing from our inmost heart. Our loved one seems to live in us and we in our loved one; because of our friend, we are never alone. And we are not satisfied with knowing our friend superficially; we hunger to know everything about our loved one, even his or her very soul. Through this intimate knowing of one another, our beloved lives in us and we in him or her. In such friendship-love based on communion in virtue, it is the Holy Spirit, the very person of love, who gives the gift of our "dwelling" in one another through knowledge and love. Friendship makes us live in each other by our mutual love, affection, and contentment, since, as Thomas assures us, true "friends *return* love for love."[121]

Furthermore, we know by experience that we are more intimately united to someone we love than to someone we simply know. The paradox of true friendship in the Holy Spirit is that it so unites us to one another by the "ecstatic" force of love that we are drawn outside ourselves to the true good of our dear one. Thomas was convinced that we draw *into* ourselves what we simply know, but love draws us *outside* ourselves and unites us to the reality of the one we cherish.[122] As self-giving love, every true friendship thus participates in God's own love and draws us out of ourselves in a kind of "ecstasy." In this way, virtuous friendship heals our selfishness, and immeasurably enlarges our heart.[123]

Thomas himself had known this kind of virtuous friendship not only with Reginald but also with Albert, whose love for Thomas could not be broken even by Thomas' death. All who lived with Albert knew how he wept when he heard that Thomas had died.[124] Indeed, he would shed tears whenever Thomas' name was mentioned. His constant grieving distressed his brothers, but they were even more concerned when they found out that the old man wanted to go to Paris. Thomas' Aristotelian focus had made him unpopular with followers of the more "spiritual" Augustinian theology.[125] Albert was determined to defend him publicly against his attackers.

When Albert's Dominican brothers heard about his plan to travel to Paris—by foot, as the friars were obliged to do—they feared he might die on the way. They were also concerned that Albert would make a fool of himself, "since he was now in decline and his memory and general intelligence were not what they had been."[126] When they talked with him, they succeeded initially in changing his mind. But he grew so insistent that they eventually had to give in to him. Brother Hugh accompanied Albert as his *socius.*

When Albert arrived in Paris, he addressed the assembled Dominican community with a fiery speech defending Thomas. "What praise can the *dead* give to one living?" he began. Among the "dead" assembled here, Albert cried out, Thomas alone lives! He then delivered a moving panegyric on Thomas, his beloved student and friend. At Cologne, too, during a solemn assembly of the Dominicans, Albert gave an impassioned tribute to Thomas. And for as long as he lived, "Albert could never hear Thomas named without shedding tears."[127]

After Thomas' death, Albert began to have all of Thomas' works read to him in a particular order. Surely, one of the most precious of these writings for Albert was Thomas' Commentary on Aristotle's *Ethics,* especially books eight and nine on friendship. In this commentary Thomas had written that virtuous people's love can grow so deep that they become willing to give even their life for their friends. In their very death, they show the greatest love not only for their friends but also for themselves. For virtuous people choose to delight for a short time in a great work of virtue rather than to take meager pleasure over a long period of time in commonplace works. They prefer to live in a wonderfully excellent way for one year rather than in a mediocre way for many years. It is true that those who die for the sake of good may live a shorter time. But because they do more good in one action alone, in which they sacrifice themselves for their friends, than in many other mediocre actions, they truly live a *long* life.[128]

Thomas himself died when he was only forty-eight years old, and in his prime. Albert, therefore, surely recognized in Thomas' words a description of his student's own life and death. For Thomas had made his preaching, teaching, and writing his deepest act of love not only for Jesus, his beloved friend, but also for all the people throughout the ages whom Jesus had given him to befriend.

Notes

[1]A monk of the abbey at Fossanova where Thomas died recalled that Thomas often came to visit Frances at her castle at Maenza (I Can 15).

[2]CG III, 134, 4; Rel St 14.

[3]Gui, cc. 1-2.

[4]Gui, c. 8; Tocco, c. 11; I Can 76.

[5]Ibid.

[6]Weisheipl, *Friar,* 38.

[7]James A. Weisheipl, O.P., *Thomas d'Aquino and Albert His Teacher,* The Etienne Gilson Series 2, March 6, 1980 (Toronto: Pontifical Institute of Mediaeval Studies, 1980) 9.

[8]Ibid., 6.

[9]Ibid., 8

[10]Fr 8:1.

[11]Fr 9:10.

[12]Fr 8:1, 2.

[13]ST I-II, 38, 3; Fr 9:13.

[14]Fr 9:10.

[15]CG III, 153, 2.

[16]Fr 9:10.

[17]ST II-II, 114, 1, ad 2.

[18]ST II-II, 114, 2, ad 1.
[19]Ibid.
[20]ST I-II, 99, 2.
[21]ST II-II, 114, 2, ad 2.
[22]Fr 9:14.
[23]I Can 86; Foster, *Life,* 115.
[24]HE 22:23; Foster, *Life,* 130–31.
[25]Fr 8:2.
[26]Fr 9:4.
[27]Fr 8:2; 8:9; 9:5.
[28]Fr 8:5.
[29]ST II-II, 114, 1, ad 1.
[30]Fr 8:2.
[31]Fr 9:5.
[32]Fr 8:5.
[33]Fr 8:3.
[34]Fr 8:8; 8:5.
[35]Fr 8:5.
[36]Fr 8:8; 8:7.
[37]ST I-II, 28, 3.
[38]Rel St 13; Char a 8, ad 16; ST I-II, 27, 3.
[39]ST I-II, 26, 4, ad 3.
[40]Fr 8:3.
[41]ST II-II, 23, 1; II-II, 25, 1.
[42]Fr 8:3.
[43]ST I-II, 27, 3.
[44]ST I-II, 28, 4.
[45]ST I-II, 28, 3.
[46]ST I-II, 27, 1.
[47]ST I-II, 26, 4.
[48]Gui, c. 10.
[49]ST I-II, 26, 4.
[50]Fr 8:3.
[51]Fr 8:8.
[52]Fr 8:5; 8:3.
[53]Fr 8:5.
[54]Char a 11, ad 6.
[55]ST II-II, 26, 12.
[56]ST I-II, 3, 2, ad 1.
[57]Char a 11, ad 6.
[58]Rel St 18.

[59]Char a 11, ad 6.

[60]In Jn 15, lect. 2; ST I-II, 28, 1; Fr 8:5; 9:11.

[61]Char a 8, ad 16; ST II-II, 23, 1.

[62]ST II-II, 25, 1.

[63]Fr 9:4.

[64]ST II-II, 25, 4.

[65]ST I, 60, 3; Fr 9:8.

[66]Fr 9:4.

[67]ST II-II, 25, 7.

[68]ST II-II, 25, 4; II-II, 25, 7; Fr 9:8.

[69]Fr 9:4.

[70]Ibid.

[71]ST II-II, 29, 3.

[72]Fr 9:9; 9:4.

[73]Fr 9:4; ST II-II, 25, 7.

[74]Fr 9:9.

[75]ST II-II, 117, 2, ad 1.

[76]Fr 9:9.

[77]ST II-II, 26, 9.

[78]Fr 8:12.

[79]ST II-II, 26, 11, ad 2.

[80]CG III, 123, 6.

[81]ST II-II, 26, 8, ad 1.

[82]ST II-II, 31, 3, ad 3.

[83]ST II-II, 26, 9.

[84]ST II-II, 27, 1, ad 1.

[85]ST II-II, 26, 9; Fr 9:5.

[86]Fr 9:5.

[87]ST II-II, 26, 9; Fr 8:12.

[88]CG III, 123, 6.

[89]Fr 8:5; 9:11.

[90]Fr 8:9.

[91]CG I, 91, 6.

[92]ST I, 20, 1.

[93]CG I, 91, 4; ST I, 20, 1, ad 3.

[94]CG I, 91, 3.

[95]Fr 8:9.

[96]CG I, 91, 6.

[97]Fr 9:11; 8:9.

[98]Fr 8:5; 8:6.

[99]Fr 8:5; 9:14.

[100]Fr 9:14.

[101]Fr 9:12.

[102]Ibid.

[103]Fr 8:3; 9:12.

[104]Fr 8:10; 9:11; ST I-II, 26, 2, ad 2.

[105]CG IV, 21, 7.

[106]In Jn 15, lect. 3.

[107]Ibid.

[108]Gui, c. 26.

[109]I Can 61; Foster, *Life,* 100.

[110]Fr 8:3; 8:6.

[111]Fr 9:3.

[112]ST II-II, 27, 2.

[113]ST I-II, 26, 2, ad 2.

[114]Fr 9:8.

[115]Fr 9:6.

[116]Truth q. 23, a 8, ad 2.

[117]Fr 8:7.

[118]Fr 9:13.

[119]ST I-II, 28, 1, ad 1.

[120]Cf. ST I-II, 25, 2, ad 2; In Jn 15, lect. 3.

[121]ST I-II, 28, 2.

[122]ST I-II, 28, 1, ad 3.

[123]ST I-II, 28, 3.

[124]I Can 67.

[125]The source of the animosity toward Thomas lay in his use of Aristotle and, ironically, his great charity in helping the young Arts faculty at Paris by writing commentaries on Aristotle's philosophical works for them. There were four faculties in the University of Paris: theology, law, medicine, and arts. The trivium and quadrivium, the seven liberal arts, were the foundation for all other studies. The Arts course of studies lasted six years; the students were primarily teen-age boys (Thomas himself was about fourteen when he enrolled at the University of Naples) and the faculty were young men in their early twenties. Since the Arts faculty had the most members, the head of this faculty became in effect the president of the entire university.

On March 19, 1255, the Arts faculty had published a syllabus requiring the study of Aristotle's metaphysics, ethics, psychology, natural science, and logic. The seven arts in this way became auxiliary to philosophy rather than theology, and philosophy was established as an academic discipline in its own right. The young Arts faculty thus evolved into a philosophy faculty.

But there emerged in the faculty of Arts a tendency to rationalism which manifested itself in an excessive adherence to pagan authorities, contempt for Christian insights based on faith, and an animosity toward the theology faculty. This rationalistic crisis was a key reason for Thomas' being called back to Paris from Italy in 1268-69. In the late 1260s, the leader of this rationalism, called "Latin Averroism" (Averroes had been a Muslim commentator on Aristotle) was Siger of Brabant, a brilliant master in the Arts faculty. It was Siger's brand of rationalist Aristotelianism that Bonaventure tried to assail in his university sermons and that Thomas counteracted in his *De Unitate intellectus.*

During his second regency as a master in theology at Paris, Thomas began to realize the urgency of commenting on Aristotle's philosophical works in order to help the young Arts faculty avoid the heretical propositions that flowed from Averroism. Thomas' charity in helping these young teachers explains much of his fevered output of commentaries on Aristotle's philosophical works in the precious last years before his death.

In 1277, three years after Thomas' death, Bishop Tempier of Paris issued a condemnation of 219 rationalistic propositions denounced by Augustinian theologians. His prologue lashed out at people "who are studying in Arts at Paris and who have overstepped the limits of their faculty." Supposed propositions of Thomas himself were included in this condemnation, without naming Thomas directly. This was a cruel irony (Foster, *Life,* 155-56).

[126]I Can 82; Foster, *Life,* 112.

[127]Foster, *Life,* 113.

[128]FR 9:9.

2

Jesus, Our Beloved Friend

We have already alluded to a significant incident from Thomas' early adulthood which spoke with special force of the love for Jesus, his Lord and beloved *friend*, which would claim Thomas for the rest of his life. When he was seventeen years old, he presented himself to the Dominican community of preachers at Naples and asked to receive their habit, a simple tunic they wore in communion with the poverty of Jesus. His family was not pleased. The prospect of finding Thomas dressed as a beggar in the streets of Naples, birthplace of his mother, Countess Theodora, was not a happy one for them. Theodora set out with a retinue for Naples to "speak" with her son.

But before Theodora could get to him, the Dominicans sent Thomas on his way to begin his Dominican studies at Paris. Theodora in turn sent his brothers to abduct Thomas and to bring him to her forcibly. Seizing their youngest brother, they ordered him to take off his offensive "rags." When Thomas refused, they attempted to tear them off. But though they were strong men, used to killing, they could not wrest his habit from him.

Thomas had been raised as a Benedictine oblate, and peace had become a way of life for him. Unlike his brothers, he had no experience in the ways of violence. Yet Thomas "put up such a resistance that, for fear of wounding him," they had to let him keep on his habit. Even after they confined Thomas in the family castle, his brothers kept trying to rip his Dominican tunic from him. They hoped that, "by the shame of being seen in rags, their brother might be induced to put on the clothes [of nobility] they wished him to wear." But Thomas fought them so fiercely that they had to relent.[1] During the entire year that he was confined at home, Thomas continued to cling to his "rags" as if to his very life. And indeed, in one sense, these Dominican "rags" *were* Thomas' life, for they symbolized the One to whom Thomas belonged, the person with whom he had clothed his whole being: "Put ye on the Lord Jesus Christ and make no provision for the desires of the flesh" (Rom 13:14).

Thomas' family fiercely loved him, but they just as surely did not understand him. That Thomas would choose a beggar's life did not make sense to them. He could not make them see that he was cleaving not to his beggar's rags but to the *person* whose humble love these rags bespoke. Thomas loved his brothers, but these knights valued their noble status and wealth; violence was their way of life. They could not be his intimate friends by receiving the secrets of his soul, nor give him the heart's home for which he longed. It was precisely this ache for intimate friendship that Jesus, his God and Lord, satisfied beyond all that Thomas could have desired. His brothers saw for themselves the love for Jesus that consumed Thomas, a love far more intense than even their fierce love for him. "The love of *Christ* compels me" (2 Cor 5:14); "for his sake I have suffered the loss of everything" (Phil 3:8). It was *Jesus* whom Thomas found as his most intimate friend, *Jesus* for whom he would forsake all else. Thomas would spend his life lavishing on others, not his own riches as noble lord but rather the riches of *Jesus,* his Lord and intimate friend.

The Incarnation as an Act of Intimate Friendship

Thomas was an intense person, yet his feelings often are hidden behind his terse writing style. But when he writes about Jesus, the force of his love shatters his usual reserve. If we "earnestly and devoutly" contemplate Jesus, God the Word made flesh for us, "we find such depth of wisdom that it exceeds our human knowing. In our prayerful reflection, more and more wondrous aspects of this mystery are unveiled to us."[2] Indeed, in all that Thomas writes of Jesus, we find him speaking of his most intimate *friend;* the Incarnation, the life, and the death of Jesus are acts of God the Word's deepest *friendship* with us.

In his own person Jesus shows us the infinite ache of the triune God to be close to us. We know how we ourselves can never seem to get near enough to one we love. For Thomas, this intimate experience, so familiar to anyone who loves, hints at the depth of love that consumes the triune God. Nothing could satisfy God the Word's longing to be near us, nothing except becoming flesh of our own flesh. In this radical kinship with us, we would know God's heart in a way we could never have known otherwise: "God wished to draw *near* to us by taking our flesh."[3]

Thomas discovered in Jesus, God the Word made flesh, the Father's intimate *friendship* with us in person. We know from experience that only a person who is in some way our "equal" can love us with the reciprocal, mutual love of a friend. "Since friendship means a certain equality between friends, those who are greatly unequal cannot be friends." And since there is an *infinite* inequality between God and us, we could never become equals with God. Yet we are, by nature, friends with other human beings. So, in order to become close to us in intimate *friendship,* God the Word, in unbounded humility and tenderness, has become one of *us.* God the Word's becoming flesh for us has brought us the inconceivable gift of a more deeply *"familiar friendship* with *God."*[4]

Thomas found unveiled in the Gospel of John the ache of God to be close to us. And whether we realize it or not, we, too, ache for this closeness to God. We long for a God who is totally for us, a God who is always close to us. But the very distance between God's unbounded love and our own emptiness is so infinite that, without Jesus, "in our search for happiness, we would grow cold, held back by our very desperation."[5] Such familiar closeness with God would be an empty dream for us; our weakness and sin would keep us far from the God for whose closeness we ache. And so, in an act of inconceivable friendship-love, God the Word, Lord of the universe, "willed to become small," and to fill us with his own glory "by taking to himself our littleness."[6] Like "a bridegroom coming from his bridal chamber," the Word espoused us to himself by becoming flesh of our flesh.[7]

The second divine Person, our dear friend, "did not come to us and become flesh for any trivial reason, but for *our* exceedingly great advantage." The Word made an exchange with us, and "became human that *we* might become divine."[8] When Thomas reflects on this "exchange of love," he thinks of our own experience. We cannot help wanting to give all that we have and are to the friend we love with all of our heart. Everything that belongs to us belongs also to our friend: "All that is mine is yours" (John 17:10). And Jesus is our true friend, giving us in friendship-love all that is his, and lovingly taking upon himself all that is truly ours. In his union with us, Jesus takes what is ours alone—our weakness—and because of his union with the Father, gives us all that belongs to the Father.[9] But since Jesus himself belongs to the Father, Jesus now belongs also and irrevocably to us. Jesus is not only our intimate friend but also our mediator, uniting us in unspeakable closeness with the Father.[10] This is a gift about which we could never have dared even to dream. We "could never imagine, understand or ask that *God* become one of *us,* or that *we* become *God* and a sharer in divinity. But God has done this in the incarnation."[11]

Thomas sees how deeply our own desire to belong completely to our beloved friend pales before the triune God's ache to be close to us.[12] Jesus is the Father's gift to us, the triune God's friendship with us in person. In Jesus, the depths of the Father's love meets the depths of our need and raises us in our weakness to the very heights of God's glory: "The glory which you have given me, I have given to them" (John 17:22).[13] Jesus makes us "divine" through our union with him in love: "God was made human, that we might be made God. And so we are taught how great our dignity is."[14] In Jesus we find our own deepest meaning and dignity as human persons: "We who reflect on this exaltation of our nature and are ever conscious of it, should scorn to cheapen ourselves by sin."[15]

In Jesus, therefore, Thomas discovered not only our value but also our destiny. For the incarnation does not simply inspire us in an external way to love God in return. Rather, in uniting himself to us, Jesus gives us all that *he* is, becoming in his person *our* own fulfillment. "By the incarnation, our human nature is raised to its highest perfection," Thomas tells us,[16] for Jesus lifts us from our emptiness to the very heart of God.

Jesus is our fulfillment in person. But he is also "the very *way* we *reach* our fulfillment."[17] In sharing with us the riches of his divinity, Jesus not only raises us to glory at the end of time,[18] but also fulfills us *now* in our intimate union with him. In the humanity and divinity of Jesus, our Lord and friend, we there-fore find not only "the most powerful help to us in our search for happiness,"[19] but also "the very way we gain happiness."[20] "Nothing in all of creation is greater than the incarnation, which has brought us our salvation." And the salvation Jesus gives us is nothing less than "perfectly *enjoying* God, infinite goodness itself."[21]

Thomas sees that God wanted true friendship with us, but friendship means reciprocity. We needed to be allured, attracted by the fascination of God's love, therefore, in order to freely want to love and enjoy God's presence. Only being loved would make us want to give our love in return. "Nothing so draws us to love someone as experiencing his or her love for us, since love unites us with our loved one as closely as possible." And "God's love for us could not be shown more forcefully than this," Thomas assures us, "that God willed to be joined to us in person."[22]

We know by experience how happy we feel to be truly loved; many things delight us, but union with our beloved makes us happiest of all. And our very joy makes us love to say the *name* of our loved one. Thomas knew the joy of Jesus' name in his heart, the name that is our hope and the very power of our salvation.[23] But Jesus is power for us because he is not only the mystery of God's closeness to *us,* but even more the mystery of the intimate closeness *within* God. "No one has ever seen God. The only-begotten Son, in the Father's heart, has revealed God to us" (John 1:18).

Thomas pictures the Word in the intimate depths of the Father's heart, whom the Father has cherished from all eternity. We know how we ourselves carry a "word" or thought of our loved one in our heart. Our secret considerations of our beloved are not simply in our mind but also in our heart, Thomas tells us, for these sweet thoughts are hidden deep within us. But the time comes when love itself pushes us to voice the love we have carried secretly in our heart. Love presses us to speak our "heart's word" aloud. This experience, so familiar to anyone who loves, hints at the profound mystery of Jesus. The Word made flesh is the very secret of the Father's heart, and love alone has impelled the Father to speak this beloved Word "aloud" to us in the incarnation.[24]

Thomas contemplates how the Gospel of John pictures God the Word as the shining light, the intellectual splendor of the Father (John 1:1-3).[25] It was especially fitting for God the *Word* to become flesh for us, therefore, since in the very beauty of our gift of reason, we are "kindred" to this beloved Word.[26] Thomas could not restrain his awe before the depths of love in God the

Word whose closeness to us in our intellect has compelled him to seal that nearness to us in our very flesh.[27]

But in becoming flesh of our flesh, God the Son has become intimately one in some way with *all* of creation, healing and perfecting the whole material universe through us.[28] The incarnation "re-creates" all things in Christ! We human beings alone are body and spirit, standing at the boundary of the physical and spiritual universe. And because we are the summit of the material universe, the incarnation completes the triune God's great work in the universe. Christ's saving grace in us, his home, thus heals not only us but also the entire universe. Since everything is made for us, "everything in the universe is re-established" and made new through Jesus.[29] Through Jesus we and the entire universe return in love to God our source.[30]

We and the whole cosmos have been created and continue to draw our existence at every second only in and by this Word dear to the Father's heart. Thomas thinks of Origen's beautiful analogy. Origen pictures us speaking only the words that we already are saying silently in our mind. If we would stop thinking these thoughts, we would also cease speaking the words that express these thoughts. Our experience hints at how we ourselves are the beautiful "words" spoken aloud in time only because we have been created in the beloved eternal Word. The first chapter of John's Gospel shows how we and all of creation exist only in the infinite loveliness of God the Word. And if for even a second we ceased existing in the beloved Word, we would cease to exist at all.[31]

Not only have we been created and sustained in this Word; we have also been *saved* by God the Word whom friendship-love has brought utterly close to us. Only the Father's intense love has bestowed on us Jesus, the Word made flesh for us (John 3:16).[32] This is why Thomas is convinced that Jesus has been given to us only through the Holy Spirit, the very person of love.[33] We know that we ourselves give presents as a way to bestow our love; in every gift of ours, we share our love most of all. Our own experience hints at why Scripture attributes every gift of God to the Holy Spirit, the very person of love. Thomas assures us, "No greater gift has ever been given us than *union with God in person.*" This is why the entire mystery of Jesus is marked as the Spirit of love's own work.[34] The Holy Spirit has caused the incarnation of God the Word and also the great *effect* of the incarnation among us: our deepened love for the God so near to us. This "great gift" of the incarnation, therefore, cannot help filling us with intense love for the God who has become so close and familiar a friend to us.[35]

Jesus, Our Compassionate Friend

Thomas knew that our union with someone dear to us is proved most of all when times become difficult, when we pass through the crucible of suffering together. Our own experience teaches us that compassion means "suffering with" anyone in pain, but most especially with our loved ones. Thomas himself had "suffered with" his family as they endured the kidnapping of his brother, Aimo, when Thomas was young,[36] and the tragic execution of still another brother, Rinaldo, after Thomas had become a Dominican. Rinaldo had been in the service of Frederick II, but when the emperor was excommunicated on July 17, 1243, the Aquino family turned their allegiance from the emperor to the pope. After an assassination plot against Frederick was uncovered in 1246, Rinaldo was accused of complicity and executed as a traitor. Along with the pope, Thomas and his family believed that Rinaldo was a martyr. Thomas was even granted Church funds for the support of his other brothers when they became fugitives in the Campagna in order to escape Frederick's wrath.[37]

From experiences like these Thomas learned that even though we naturally reach out to *anyone* who is in pain, nothing equals the compassion we feel for our loved ones when they are suffering. Indeed, the older and wiser we grow, Thomas comments, the more we empathize with others in their pain, since we know more deeply our own weakness.[38] Thus we naturally feel empathy even for strangers in trouble, especially if they are suffering a heartache we ourselves have endured. We pity them because our own experience makes us feel their pain as ours. Even more, when we do treat each other with compassion, we enflesh God's own mercy toward us.[39] But we cannot help feeling the deepest compassion for our loved ones who are united to us through love's affection; we feel our dear friends' pain as if it were our own.[40] Indeed, "with those so closely united to us that they are part of ourselves, such as our children or parents," Thomas tenderly comments, we do not simply *pity* their distress, but also "suffer as for our own sores."[41]

Thomas himself knew what it was to suffer with his loved ones "as for his own sores." We cannot help feeling the ache in his heart when he tells Reginald that the Lord had answered his pleas for assurance that his murdered brother was in heaven. Thomas' prayer surely expresses not only his pain at his brother's death, but also his grief at his brother's violent way of life.[42]

As Thomas suffered these "sores" of his own brothers, he grew to see the depth of the Father's compassion for *us* in Jesus. Our own heart reaches out and suffers the pain of those who "belong to us" in love. But our compassion as spouse or parent or friend for one who "belongs to us" can only hint at the depth of the Father's compassion for us, his beloved children. Those of us who are parents know that we would give our own lives before we would see our children harmed in any way. Who of us does not know stories of a parent dying in an attempt to save his or her own child from death? But when Thomas writes that "with those so closely united to us that they are *part* of ourselves, such as our children, we do not simply *pity* their distress, but *suffer* as for our own sores,"[43] he is thinking of the infinitely greater love our own beloved Father has for us. Our Father "takes pity on us through love alone, since he loves us as *belonging to him*."[44]

Precisely because we "belong to him," the Father reaches down to the depths of our sores with incomprehensible mercy. When we ourselves show mercy to others, we "grieve for their distress"[45] and reach out to help them in their need. But our infinitely compassionate Father has loved us in our *deepest* need, in the places in us that deserve no love, in the depths of our weakness and sin. The Father has given us his own beloved Son precisely because our need was so great.[46] Jesus is the Father's compassion and mercy for us in person,[47] who literally suffers our sores as his own. In Jesus our sores have become God's sores. Before such unfathomable love Thomas can only fall down and adore. That God the Word would "assume our flesh, so far removed from God's simplicity," Thomas writes, is not simply compassion but "incomprehensible compassion."[48]

Thomas in this way experienced Jesus as inseparably the Father's intimate *friendship* with us and his unspeakable *compassion* for us. Thomas knew that we often experience our own closest friends as God's sheer mercy to us. Their unconditional love helps us to know the infinite compassion of our Father for us. But Jesus is the Father's compassion for us in person. In becoming flesh of our flesh, Jesus has drawn us irrevocably close to himself and to the "enchantment of his way of life."[49] And because God showers mercy and compassion precisely on "those who have no claim to it," Jesus has loved us to the limit of death itself only through the most incomprehensible grace and mercy.[50] This is why Paul cries out, "Where our sin abounded, God's grace abounded even more" (Rom 5:20)! The triune God's love for us is stronger than even our most grievous sin, stronger indeed than the sin of the entire world. Thomas recalls how in blessing the paschal candle at the Easter Vigil, we cry out in joy, "O happy fault, that merited so great a Redeemer!" Our hymn at this vigil assures us that God allows evil only because God's infinite love can bring even greater good for us from it. "We have been raised by God's love to something even *greater* after our sin."[51] The sin of the whole human race is "as perfectly healed in each one of us as if it were healed in us alone. For through the union of charity, what is given to all of us is counted as our own by each of us."[52] Even in the most heinous crimes we could ever commit, we find mercy and healing in Jesus. "The more grievous our sin," Thomas assures us, "the more particularly did Christ come to heal it."[53]

Even in the length of time we unknowingly waited throughout the centuries for the gift of Jesus, Thomas finds only God's infinite compassion. We know how often we are able to reach out for healing only after we have sunk to the depth of our helplessness. In our own experience we find the reason why Jesus did not come to us at the very beginning of our history, at the very first moment and source of our sin. Growing more helpless with time, we waited for our healing not because God was indifferent to us but precisely because God was so compassionate toward us. The triune God "did not give us the remedy of the incarnation at the beginning of time, lest we should despise this gift through pride by not recognizing our sickness."[54]

Thomas knew that before we could truly receive God's mercy in Jesus, we needed to feel the depth of our own weakness.[55] Seeing ourselves unable to "trust in our own wisdom and power, we would not consider Christ's coming as unimportant." Experiencing our weakness would make us all the more eagerly desire Jesus, our healer.[56] Thomas comments that the triune God *seemed* to abandon us to the full consequences of our weakness, only so that we could see how truly "we were not equal to our own salvation. In our helplessness, and not relying on ourselves, we would then put our hope all the more in God, who alone can heal our sin."[57]

Jesus' Death for Us as Unbounded Friendship-Love

Jesus culminated his life in a cruel death which he suffered with infinite love for us as his beloved friends: "Greater love than this no one has than to lay down his life for his friends" (John 15:13). As he reflects on these depths of Jesus' friendship-love for us, Thomas cries out, "Christ's death for us is so tremendous that we can scarcely grasp it! In no way can our reason understand the meaning of his death for us. God's grace and love are so immense that we cannot comprehend what God has done for us in the death of Jesus."[58]

From his own experience of suffering with his knight-brother who was tortured before his execution, Thomas reflects on how even those unafraid of death fear being tortured to death. But it was precisely to *this* kind of death that Jesus freely surrendered himself through incomprehensible friendship-love for us.[59] As a nobleman, Thomas had seen how pride can make us love worldly glory. But he found in Jesus' passion not only a tortured death but also a *humiliating* death to which Jesus freely gave himself. Jesus' death was "not just any sort of death, but a death abject in the extreme." And since "there is no greater dignity than being God, the humility of Jesus was praiseworthy in the extreme when Jesus bore the abjection of his death for our salvation."[60] For Jesus did not *have* to suffer this death; he freely *chose* it out of infinite love for us. The Father inundated Jesus' human heart with this infinite love and desire to suffer for us.[61] "The Father did not force one who was unwilling," Thomas assures us, but delighted in Christ's unbounded charity in *embracing* his death.[62]

Thomas saw that Jesus' death saves us not because it was full of pain, but because it was full of love.[63] He reflects on how, by our sin, we choose to make the all-good God our enemy. But Jesus has reconciled us to our Father by *healing* our hatred with his incomparable love in suffering for us.[64] "Jesus' love infinitely surpassed the hatred of his murderers."[65] Indeed, precisely because of the unbounded love that filled Jesus' heart, his death is infinitely more than enough to heal and satisfy for all the sins that have ever been committed. For "sin is not wiped out by sin";[66] love alone has the power to heal our sin. And love so unimaginable that it suffers even the most excruciating death for us has the greatest power of all.[67]

Thomas urges us, therefore, to look upon Jesus crucified if we long for healing. "If you seek an example of charity," he tells us, "look at the wounds of the one who said, 'Greater love than this no one has than to lay down his life for his friends.' If you seek an example of humility, look upon the one who is crucified."[68] Thomas finds it incomprehensible that Jesus, *God* the Word, would suffer such excruciating torments for us precisely when we were most estranged from God. It is significant that Thomas locates the first and deepest of Jesus' sufferings in his dearest friends' betrayal: "Christ suffered from his friends abandoning him; in his reputation, because of the blasphemies he endured; in his honor and glory, from the mockeries and the insults heaped upon him; in things, from being despoiled of his garments; in his soul, from sadness, weariness, and fear; and in his body, from wounds and scourgings."[69] Yet though Christ was poor and of no honor, his very person inspires us to despise what the worldly desire, for "without secular power Jesus has changed the whole world for the better."[70] Indeed, Thomas tells us, if we lovingly contemplate Jesus' passion, our lives will be completely reformed.[71]

Most of all, it is the *blood* of Jesus which gives us the power for a whole new way of life in closeness to the triune God: "You who were once far off have been brought near in the blood of Christ" (Eph 2:13). Christ pours out nothing less than his blood as a laver washing us clean from our sin;[72] the blood of God the Son is the "infinitely great" price of our redemption.[73] Thomas could not help being touched by the depth of meaning in the Johannine passage, "And I, if I be lifted up from the earth, will draw all things to myself" (John 12:32). It is the blood of Jesus which irresistibly draws us to him because in it we find "his vehement love most forcefully revealed." As we gaze upon Jesus' blood, poured out with such unrestrained love upon us, we have the irrevocable proof that these words of God's heart are the final truth about each one of us: "I have loved you with an everlasting love" (Jer 31:3).[74]

The cross itself displays vividly how Jesus' blood is healing for the whole universe. The cross-beam's *breadth* to which Jesus gave his wrists to be nailed shows us the love that "stretches out" even to his enemies, to those who hate him. The *length* of the cross against which Jesus' body leans shows us love that is infinitely faithful and enduring. The *height* of the cross on which Jesus rests his head speaks to us of a love that reaches to heaven itself. And the cross' *depth* resting unseen in the ground symbolizes the depth of the triune God's invisible love which sustains us. As we gaze on the cross, therefore, we see the power of Christ's love, and the feebleness of ours. The truth of his love surpasses our human understanding. Indeed, the plans of God's heart for us are "beyond our comprehension."[75]

Jesus, Our Savior

Thomas had found Jesus as his heart's closest friend. Precisely for this reason, he experienced Jesus as his Savior. We know from our own experience that someone who truly loves us in some sense saves us, for the unconditional love of our friend rescues us from our isolation. And yet, even in our experience of human friendship, we learn, too, that not even our closest friend can be always with us and for us, or "save" us completely and forever from our aloneness. From his own experience Thomas found that only God can be for and with us at every moment, in our every need. In *Jesus,* God the Word made flesh, Thomas discovered his heart's closest friend, the one who is always *with* us, the one who rescues us from the pain of our aloneness, from the prison of our self-centeredness. In becoming our intimate friend, in loving us without condition or limit, to the point of death itself, Jesus saves us.

"Christ's passion was of such value that it was enough to expiate for all the sins of the whole world, even of a hundred thousand worlds," Thomas assures us.[76] In his saving death, Jesus returned to his Father infinitely more love than the hatred the entire human race has directed against God throughout all of history. Jesus saved us because of the "boundless love from which he suffered."[77] As we have seen, therefore, it is not Jesus' suffering but his *love* that binds us to the triune God, Jesus' *love* that is the very content of our salvation.[78] Love so great has filled him that he himself is "the price paid for us; Christ saved us by giving *himself*."[79]

For Jesus has given a human yes of infinite love to his Father, a love he pours out on us through his death on the cross. And if we truly gaze on this love symbolized in the blood of Jesus, Thomas finds it impossible to think that we could turn away. We cannot help wanting to give all of our love to the God who so treasures us. In his passion Jesus shows us "how much we are loved," and "so stirs us to love God in return." For Thomas, therefore, salvation is not an external paying of a debt, but the re-creation of our inmost self, the healing that radically changes our heart. Now we can respond with love to the God who so cherishes us. This is "salvation": that we freely love God in return.[80] The love which filled Jesus, therefore, truly becomes *our* love, which we freely give back to the Trinity. But how do we gain Christ's love as our own? Thomas finds the answer in Jesus' intimate union with us through the love which has made us one body, even one "person" with him. Thomas assures us, "When two people are one in charity, the one can atone for the other. Christ, our head, and we, his members, are as one mystic person. And so his saving love belongs to all of us as his members."[81] The love Jesus poured out in his passion saves us precisely because we are "his members." His charity that "gains pardon for our sins" now becomes ours. Thomas thinks of our own experience of hurting someone and then seeking to heal the harm we have done by an act of kindness. For example, we may try to repair a sin we commit with our tongue in lying about someone by doing something kind for that person. The loving action we do with our hands in some way makes reparation for the sin we have committed with our tongue. So, too, Thomas assures us, "just as our body is one, though made up of diverse members, the whole Church, Christ's mystic body, is in some way one person with its head, who is Christ."[82]

Thomas knew that Jesus died for every one of us, and is now true *power* for us both in his divinity and humanity.[83] But his death can heal us only to the extent that we are willing to "cleave to the incarnate God by faith and love."[84] We are saved, filled with love and made whole by being born anew through cleaving to Jesus. For the sin of our first parents has filled our human birth not only with life, but also with the prospect of sin and death. Jesus' death, however, has brought us unquenchable life through our new birth in baptism. It is this sacrament that joins us to Jesus, making us "one person" with him,[85] enabling us to "cleave" to him through love.[86] Thus, through the *sacraments,* especially baptism and the Eucharist, we cling to Jesus in his healing death.[87]

We know what it is to suffer the pain of a broken relationship, to feel like a stranger or even enemy of a person with whom we once had "one heart and one soul." But if we have ever experienced the miracle of seeing such a broken relationship healed, of having estrangement turned into even deeper closeness, we know what Thomas means when he says that *friendship-love* is our *salvation.* God has never drawn away from us; it is we who can pull away from God's closeness, and treat the triune God as a stranger and even enemy. It is we alone who can make God's love for us unrequited. We can cut ourselves off from the very love that we most need and want, the love that alone can heal our heart's ache for intimacy. And in our estrangement from God, it would indeed be a miracle to have our heart completely "turned around," to allow the triune God to draw close to us. To be changed in this radical way would indeed be love "saving" us. We would know in our own life the miracle of unrequited love being transformed into the reciprocal love of true friendship, love that we return.

From our own experience we know that what we most need and want is to be loved not as self-chosen strangers and enemies, but rather as intimate friends. For Thomas this is precisely what "salvation" means. The love that fills Jesus' heart pierces the barriers in our heart and changes our "no" into a great "yes!" The love of Jesus for us transforms our resistance into surrender, our enmity into intimacy. Salvation is the miracle of the triune God's unrequited love for us being turned into love that we freely return. This alone is salvation, our *reciprocal* friendship-love with God, our *freely* loving God in return.[88]

When Thomas preached his Lenten sermons to the people of Naples, he could not restrain his tears as he contemplated a love so great that it can and does shatter the barriers of our own resistance. Thomas pictures the gate of paradise being flung wide open as Christ's side is pierced and torn open with the soldier's spear. With this outpouring of Jesus' sacred blood, Thomas says, *our* guilt is washed away, *our* infirmity is healed, and we exiles are called back to the kingdom! As an assurance of the power of Jesus' blood for each one of us, the thief receives from Jesus the promise of *immediate* salvation: *"This day* you will be with me in paradise"* (Luke 23:43). Never before was this spoken to anyone, "not to Adam, not to Abraham, not to David; but this day, having asked for pardon, the thief received it."[89] Thomas was convinced that Jesus wants to lavish on us the pardon he gave to the thief. "The more we conform ourselves to Christ's passion, the greater the pardon and grace *we* gain."[90] The saving effects of his death become ours in an intimate union with him through faith and love,[91] a union so intimate that whatever is done to us is done to Jesus. This sense of the inseparable union between Jesus and us makes Thomas hear even in the cry, "My friends have deserted me" (Ps 38:11), the psalmist's foreshadowing not only of the passion of Jesus, but also of us, his members, who suffer in any way.[92]

In Christ's passion, therefore, Thomas contemplates his most intimate act of *friendship* for us; the salvation that Jesus brings is not only our healing but also the deepest intimacy with him. When Thomas reflects, for example, on our creedal confession that "Jesus descended into hell" he comments that Jesus longed to "perfectly deliver all his *friends.*" "Christ had his friends both in the world and in hell. And his disciples on earth were his friends because they already possessed charity and believed in Jesus present among them." Thomas pictures the good people who lived before the coming of Jesus as awaiting him eagerly in the depths of the nether world—among them Abraham, Isaac, Jacob, Moses, David—and all those who departed this life with charity and faith in the Redeemer who would come. "Since Christ had dwelt among his *friends* in this world and had delivered them by his death," Thomas reminds us tenderly, "so he wished to visit his *friends* who were detained in hell and deliver them also."[93]

Jesus, Risen Lord and Giver of the Spirit

Jesus has suffered for us, his friends, and died our death; his death, however, has brought us an astounding reversal! In a beautiful image Thomas pictures Christ's resurrection as an astonishing "re-flowering" of a dead blossom, a re-flowering that surges with infinitely deeper life and beauty.[94] In his glorious resurrection Jesus' human existence is transformed into a life full of the Spirit's glory, incapable of suffering and death.[95] Thomas finds in the words of Jesus to his Father, "all that is mine is yours," the promise which Jesus speaks in friendship-love to us (John

17:10). Through his passion, death and resurrection, Jesus becomes our intimate friend and mediator, exchanging what he shared with us, our capacity to suffer and die, for what he shares with the Father and Holy Spirit, infinite *life*. Uniting us to the Father, Jesus makes the triune God's own glorious life now ours![96] In baptism we are joined to Jesus' resurrection, the pattern and cause of our resurrection.[97] And so, Thomas assures us, Christ's resurrection is the very source of our own because his risen body is united to the Word of life.[98] God the Word, the very "fountain of *life*,"[99] is now also risen Lord, the cause of life for us even in his risen body (John 5:21).[100]

Thomas was struck by Paul's contrast between our Lord, fountain of *life,* and our first parents who simply lived. The source of their life was simply their human soul, which could never *give* life to us. Likewise, even as members of Christ's body we ourselves cannot *cause* each other's resurrection; only Christ our head can be the pattern and source of our resurrection. The human perfection of Jesus, risen Lord, is drawn from the divinity of God the Word and also from the Holy Spirit, giver of life. Through the Holy Spirit, Thomas tells us, Jesus received in his very humanity the power not only to live but also to become "life-giving spirit" and giver of life to us![101] Thomas contemplates how Jesus' passion merited our resurrection by healing our sin. But his *resurrection,* "the beginning and exemplar of all good things," actually *causes* our own.[102] Even now, baptism joins us to Jesus' resurrection, giving us power for a whole new way to live. When we are fully united to his resurrection at our own death, we, too, will gain a resplendent "spiritual" body—a "Spirit-filled," "glorified body subject to the Holy Spirit" (cf. 1 Cor 15:44).[103]

The wonder of Jesus' resurrection drew Thomas to the mystery of Pentecost, for Christ's paschal mystery is inseparable from the outpouring of the Spirit through the Word made flesh and through whom the Spirit renews the world.[104] Glorified in his resurrection and ascension, the risen Lord has lavished his Holy Spirit on all of us.[105] Christ performs marvelous works in this outpouring, not only in our bodies but even greater ones in our hearts. If we call on the name of Jesus, Thomas tells us, we see among us even today the miracles of "hearts inflamed by the affection of God's love, people suddenly filled with knowledge of the things of God, and the tongues of unschooled people made skillful in speaking of God's truth to others!''[106]

For Thomas, then, the saving work of Christ for us is inseparable from the Holy Spirit: Jesus gives every good gift to us through the Spirit of love.[107] Thomas finds in our own experience an analogy for the relationship between Jesus, the Holy Spirit, and us. A part of our own body—an arm, a leg, a finger—cannot live if it is severed from our head;[108] life flows only to the parts of our body which are joined to our head. Likewise, only those who live in Jesus our head through faith and love can receive the Holy Spirit of life. We cannot receive the Holy Spirit without belonging to Jesus. On the other hand, however, we cannot belong to Jesus without the Holy Spirit;[109] as Paul tells us, if we do not possess the Holy Spirit, we cannot be members of Christ (Rom 8:9). But when we do believe in Jesus, we belong to the new covenant of God with us.[110] For Thomas, this new "law" of the gospel is the very person of the Spirit as well as the Spirit's grace, which we receive through Jesus.[111]

From His Fullness We Have All Received

To understand more deeply the inseparable union between Jesus, the Holy Spirit and us, Thomas thinks of the intimate relationship between our head, our heart, and the rest of our body. Our head exerts its influence over our body in a visible way, but our heart is hidden within us. Yet it is our heart that is the secret source of the life-blood flowing within us. Like our heart, the Holy Spirit is the "hidden center of life" in the whole body of the Church. "The Spirit gives life to the church and *invisibly* makes us one." But Jesus is our head in his concrete, visible humanity; "the one who is *human* is set over us" visibly as our Savior and Lord.[112]

Yet because Jesus is not only our head, but also the Father's beloved Son, our union with him gives us the unimaginable gift of living as members of God's own family. Thomas compares us to material that blazes with light only when lit with fire. Of ourselves we are only creatures, infinitely distant from God's beauty and goodness. But Jesus is the only beloved Son, God from God, the fire of intimacy with the Father. *This* is the gift we could never

imagine or deserve: the triune God loves us not simply as creatures, but as members of God's own family![113]

Thomas thinks of how love joins us not only to the one we love
but also to anyone dear to our loved one. "When I love someone
very much," he writes, "I also love whoever *belongs* to my
friend." This is the amazing reason we ourselves are loved so irrevocably by the Father, not just for who we are in ourselves—
helpless and faithless—but even more deeply for who we are in
Jesus, the Father's beloved Word. By the incarnation we belong
irrevocably to Jesus, who has become forever flesh of our flesh.
We are loved from all eternity in Jesus, the Father's beloved Son.
Jesus "is beloved before all else and essentially; he is naturally,
and in a most excellent way, loved by the Father."[114]

We, who are only *creatures* of God by nature, become in Jesus,
true *daughters* and *sons* of the Father, and the more so, the more
we grow like him. With Paul, Thomas sees the amazing influence
of Jesus upon us as similar to the way our own head gives life
to the rest of our body. The rest of our body can live and grow
only if joined to our head. Jesus is the "head" of his living body,
the Church. "In his entire humanity, body and soul, Christ influences every one of us, both in soul and body."[115]

Thomas recalls the beautiful words of Genesis 2:10: "A river
flowed forth to water paradise." For Thomas, Jesus himself is
this river of graces pouring out his own gifts on us, the members
of his body. "In the Church, Christ alone has all graces, which
he lavishes upon his members." And the "river of graces"—the
wonderful gifts each of us has as members of Jesus—flows forth
to "water paradise." The Church is that paradise, and our rich,
diverse gifts bring to full blossom Christ's own gifts in this paradise. The gifts of each one of us in this way fill the Church with
the splendor of Christ's own gifts.[116] For Jesus receives every gift
of the Holy Spirit "without measure" in his humanity, and we
share in Christ's fullness through the unique gifts the Father gives
to each of us.[117]

Since Christ is our head, therefore, he pours out on us what
the Father has given him.[118] As our own body draws its life from
our head, we draw our life from Jesus: "From the fullness of *his*
grace," Thomas tells us, "he bestows all grace on us:"[119] "Of
his fullness we have all received" (John 1:16). Thomas never tired
of contemplating this text as he reflected on the meaning of Jesus
for us. We receive every grace only "through him and in him,"

for Jesus is the "original font of all grace."[120] Indeed, he is the firstborn, whose grace is the first and highest, poured out now on us, his brothers and sisters, members of his own body.[121] Jesus was anointed by the Spirit on *our* behalf, for the sake of all of us, members of the Church, who would be filled with the Spirit. All that we have of the Spirit's anointing and grace we gain only from the overflowing abundance of Christ.[122] As the very source of "grace or the Holy Spirit" in his divinity, Jesus pours out the Spirit of love on us.[123]

In his humanity, therefore, Jesus is the mediator between the Father and us (1 Tim 2:5), for "of his fullness we have all received, grace for grace."[124] Christ's grace is so unbounded precisely because his humanity is united to the person of God the Word. And from his own infinite grace, Christ pours out the Spirit's grace on all of us.[125] This is why the Father delights in Jesus' asking for what belongs to him by inheritance: "Ask of me and I will give you the nations as an inheritance" (Ps 2:8). *We* are his inheritance, Thomas tells us, since we *belong* to Jesus. By his intense prayer for us (John 17:20), and, most of all, by his great love for us in his passion, Jesus has "asked" for us as his inheritance. And his asking has not been in vain; Hebrews 5:7 tells us, "In everything he asked he was heard." Jesus, therefore, is not simply like the prophets or apostles who were *ministers* to the nations; Jesus is *Lord* of all the nations! Moses was faithful over the house entrusted to him as a minister, but Christ was and is the true Son in his own home (Heb 3:5-6). And *we* are that home, Thomas assures us.[126]

John's Gospel shows us the Word whose own intimate "home" from all eternity is the Father's heart. But in becoming flesh for us, God the Word has forever "pitched his tent" also with us: Jesus is God the Word who is also at "home" now with us. "There is no clearer proof of God's love for us than that God, Creator of all things, would become a creature, that our Lord would become our *brother.*"[127] Before the mystery of Jesus Thomas can only fall down and adore.

Yet more than any words that Thomas wrote, his own life speaks to us about the depth of his love for Jesus. One incident in particular stayed in his Dominican companions' own hearts as they recalled the kind, intense face of their beloved brother. Shortly before his death, when Thomas was at Naples, several of the friars noticed how Thomas often would get up before Matins and go down to the church to pray alone. At the time he was writing the last part of the *Summa Theologiae* on the incarnation, birth, suffering, and resurrection of Christ. One night a brother quietly followed him and watched him pray in the chapel of Saint Nicholas. Thomas was gazing at the crucifix when the brother heard these words: "You have written well of me, Thomas; what reward do you desire?" The once wealthy Thomas, the nobleman who could have asked for power and honor, for riches that would have made him lord over nations, answered with tears, *"Yourself,* Lord." Soon after this, Thomas fell sick and never wrote again. Within a short time he was dead.[128]

Very early in his life, Thomas had chosen to spend his energies pouring out on others, not the wealth of the possessions he had renounced, but the riches of Jesus, his beloved friend and Lord. He himself once had said that when we think of Jesus, no other response remains than to let "our love burst into flame."[129] Thomas *did* let his love for Jesus burst into flame. And with its fire he has warmed and illumined countless people throughout the centuries until our present time.

Notes

[1]Gui, cc. 6–7; Foster, *Life,* 28–29. Jacques Le Goff notes, "Clothing was of even greater social significance" than sumptuous eating, since clothing was the means of showing one's social class. Ostentatious dress was "flaunted" by the rich; the beggar in rags was treated with disdain (*Medieval Civilization 400–1500,* trans. Julia Barrow [London: Basil Blackwwell, 1988], 358.)

[2]CG IV, 54, 1.

[3]ST III, 1, 2, ad 3.

[4]CG IV, 54, 6.

[5]CG IV, 54, 3.

[6]Comp Theo I, 1.

[7]In Ps 18:3.

[8]Ap Creed.

[9]ST Supp, 90, 2.

[10]ST III, 26, 1.

[11]In Eph 3, lect. 5.

[12]ST III, 1, 2, ad 3.

[13]ST III, 5, 2, ad 3.

[14]ST III, 1, 2.

[15]Ap Creed.

[16]ST III, 1, 6.

[17]ST III, 1, 6, ad 2.

[18]ST III, 1, 6.

[19]CG IV, 54, 3.

[20]ST II-II, 2, 7.

[21]CG IV, 55, 10; IV 54, 5.

[22]CG IV, 54, 5.

[23]In Ps 39:2.

[24]Ap Creed; CG IV, 46, 2.

[25]ST I, 39, 8.

[26]In Jn 1, lect. 5.

[27]CG IV, 42, 1; IV, 42, 2.

[28]CG IV, 55, 5; IV, 55, 7.

[29]In Eph 1, lect. 3.

[30]CG IV, 55, 5.

[31]In Jn 1, lect. 5.

[32]In Eph 1, lect. 3.

[33]CG IV, 46, 4.

[34]CG IV, 46, 5.

[35]CG IV, 55, 14.

[36]In 1233, when Thomas was about five, his brother Aimo, who had been on the Fifth Crusade in Emperor Frederick's army, was held for ransom in Cyprus. Pope Gregory IX helped to gain his release (Weisheipl, *Friar,* 48).

[37]Edward A. Synan, "Saint Thomas Aquinas: His Good Life and Hard Times," *Thomistic Papers,* III. Ed. Leonard A. Kennedy, C.S.B. (Houston: Center for Thomistic Studies, 1987) 44.

[38]ST II-II, 30, 2, ad 2.

[39]ST II-II, 30, 4.

[40]ST II-II, 30, 2.

[41]ST II-II, 30, 1, ad 2.

[42]Gui, c. 22.

[43]ST II-II, 30, 1, ad 2.

[44]ST II-II, 30, 2, ad 1.

[45]ST II-II, 30, 3.

[46]ST I, 20, 4, ad 2.

[47]In Ps 47:6.

[48]In Jn 1, lect. 7.

[49]Ibid.

[50]In Eph 1, lect. 2.

[51]ST III, 1, 3, ad 3.

[52]ST III, 1, 4, ad 3.

[53]ST III, 1, 4.

[54]ST III, 1, 5, ad 1.

[55]ST III, 1, 5.

[56]In Eph 1, lect. 3.

[57]CG IV, 55, 12.

[58]Ap Creed.

[59]CG IV, 55, 20; IV, 55, 22.

[60]CG IV, 55, 20.

[61]ST III, 47, 3; III, 47, 3, ad 1; III, 47, 3, ad 2; CG IV, 55, 19.

[62]CG IV, 55, 19.

[63]CG IV, 55, 25.

[64]ST III, 49, 4, ad 2; III, 49, 4, ad 3.

[65]ST III, 49, 4, ad 3.

[66]CG IV, 55, 25.

[67]CG IV, 55, 20; IV, 55, 22.

[68]Ap Creed.

[69]ST III, 46, 5.

[70]CG IV, 55, 15.

[71]Ap Creed.

[72]Ibid.

[73]In 1 Cor 6, lect. 3.

[74]In Eph 2, lect. 5.

[75]In Eph 3, lect. 5.

[76]Ap Creed.

[77]ST III, 48, 2.

[78]Ibid.; ST III, 48, 3.

[79]ST III, 48, 5.

[80]ST III, 46, 3.

[81]ST III, 48, 2, ad 1.

[82]ST III, 49, 1.

[83]ST III, 8, 2.

[84]CG IV, 55, 30.

[85]CG IV, 55, 29.

[86]CG IV, 55, 10.

[87]ST III, 52, 8, ad 2.

[88]ST III, 46, 3.

[89]Ap Creed.

[90]Ibid.

[91]CG IV, 55, 29.

[92]In Ps 37:7.

[93]Ap Creed; *The Catechetical Instructions of St. Thomas Aquinas,* trans. Joseph B. Collins (New York: Joseph F. Sagner, Inc., 1939) 31.

[94] In Ps 27:7.
[95] CG IV, 55, 14.
[96] ST III, 26, 2.
[97] ST III, 54, 2.
[98] In 1 Th 4:2; ST III, 56, 1.
[99] ST III, 5, 3, ad 2.
[100] ST III, 56, 1.
[101] In 1 Cor 15, lect. 7.
[102] ST III, 53, 1, ad 3.
[103] ST III, 54, 1.
[104] ST II-II, 2, 8.
[105] ST I-II, 106, 4, ad 2.
[106] CG IV, 55, 11.
[107] ST II-II, 14, 3, ad 3.
[108] In Rom 8, lect. 2.
[109] In Rom 8, lect. 1.
[110] ST I-II, 106, 1, ad 3.
[111] ST I-II, 108, 1; I-II, 106, 2; I-II, 106, 4; I-II, 107, 1, ad 2.
[112] ST III, 8, 1, ad 3.
[113] In Eph 1, lect. 2; In Eph 1, lect. 1.
[114] In Eph 1, lect. 2.
[115] ST III, 8, 2; cf. III, 8, 6.
[116] In 1 Cor 12, lect. 1.
[117] In Jn 1, lect. 10.
[118] ST III, 58, 4, ad 1.
[119] ST III, 8, 5.
[120] In Jn 1, lect. 10.
[121] ST III, 8, 2, ad 1.
[122] In Ps 44:5.
[123] ST III, 8, 1, ad 1.
[124] ST III, 7, 1.
[125] ST III, 7, 9; III, 8, 5, ad 1.
[126] In Ps 2:6.
[127] Ap Creed.
[128] Gui, c. 23.
[129] Ap Creed.

3

Life to the Full: God's Provident Mercy

As we read Thomas' writings, we cannot help being struck by his great largesse. There is nothing rigid or dour, nothing mean or small-hearted about him. Thomas was a big person in every sense of the word. As one commentator points out, the young, enthusiastic Arts faculty at Paris dearly loved Thomas, and they certainly would not have heaped on him their devotion had he been simply a "dusty academic technician."[1] The fact that he most certainly was not a "dusty academician" shines, as we shall see, in charming stories like the one about his good cheer at the healing of his dear friend and *socius,* Reginald of Piperno, through the intercession of St. Agnes. Thomas, then in charge of the young Dominican students at Naples, was so delighted that he threw a party in honor of Agnes and announced that the event would be an annual one,[2] celebrated with special festivities, and a really "good dinner!" As Chesterton notes, this engaging story has "quite a convivial sound!"[3]

Indeed it does. But Thomas could be so "convivial" precisely because he had experienced in his own life the largesse of the Father who has given us through Jesus life to the full. From his own experience Thomas discovered the God who enfolds our freedom in lavish mercy, and providently turns everything, even our missteps, to our good. It was the merciful love of this God that filled Thomas and spilled out to others in his teaching, preaching and writing.

God's Mercy Enfolding the Universe

Thomas the nobleman knew the meaning of mercy. He had seen servants and slaves beg for mercy, and from his own experience he had learned that justice gives us what we deserve, but mercy lavishes on us good that we could never deserve. Yet in his heart he knew that we are all servants, begging for mercy from God. Of ourselves, we could never *deserve* anything good; our very existence is God's sheer mercy, God's undeserved gift to us.[4]

As he does so often, Thomas reflects on our experience of friendship to understand more deeply the meaning of God's mercy. Mercy can be poured out only where there is *need,*[5] and every one of us knows what it is to be in need. Now, when we are in trouble, when we have any need, where do we turn but to a loving friend? But the triune God is our dearest friend to whom our great neediness cries out for mercy.[6] The more helpless we are, the more the divine Persons are drawn to shower mercy on us. Especially on the little, the weak, the poor—and we are all weak and poor—the triune God pours out nothing but mercy.[7] "A friend is known in sorrow," the biblical proverb tells us (Prov 17:17). Yes, Thomas adds, it is especially in times of pain that we prove our love for our friends. Jesus himself showed his mercy in the most touching way when he wept over the death of his beloved friend, Lazarus: "See how he loved him" (John 11:36).[8]

But in our own human mercy, we can only suffer with and comfort our loved ones in their pain. Our mercy cannot of itself heal their pain; our tears of compassion cannot reverse a tragic accident or bring a loved one back to life. Far less can we enter into the hidden places of our friends' souls and give them peace when they are suffering the anguish of sin.[9] For it is not misfortunes like poverty or sickness that most torment us and our loved ones, but sin alone that exposes the depths of our need and brings us to the brink of despair. Sin alone robs us of the peace that makes other sufferings in our life bearable.[10] In the prison of our sin, our addictions, our bitterness and unforgiveness, we and our loved ones experience our deepest need, and it is precisely here that we are powerless to heal ourselves and them. Regardless of the love and compassion and mercy we feel, *we* cannot give either ourselves or them peace.

But God's mercy can enter into our very soul and into the depths of our own and our loved ones' pain to heal our misery. God's mercy does not helplessly stand by, or even merely suffer with us, as we ourselves must do when our friends are in pain; God's love truly cures our sin and pain.[11] God alone lavishes on us a mercy that heals us and cares for us in our every need.[12] Jesus is the beloved friend who does not walk away from us even in our sin, our beloved friend who says these healing words to our soul: *"My* peace I give you" (John 14:27). For Jesus loves us not in spite of but *in* our sin, and speaks these words of Jeremiah to every one of us: "In everlasting love I have loved you" (Jer 31:3).[13]

Thomas cannot hold back his wonder at this mercy of God showered on us in Jesus, given to us even before we could know how or even dare to ask for him. God's love answers our need even before we ask, recklessly pouring out mercy on us, not simply in answer to our prayer, but even before we beg for it in prayer.[14] And it was at the time when our need was the greatest, when we were in the depths of our sin, that Jesus came to us as the outpouring of the Father's infinite mercy. The Father, who "loves Christ more than the entire universe" did not hold back from us even his beloved Son but gave him to us precisely because our need was so great.[15]

Yet sometimes we may think that, in our need, God has forgotten or abandoned us. We cry out for help, but no one, not even God, seems to hear. Thomas is convinced, however, that God never refuses our prayer for mercy. When everyone and everything else fail us, when we have nowhere else to turn, the triune God showers the *deepest* mercy on us. Then, when we have no other recourse but to God, we find ourselves most open to God, most ready to receive and to put our whole trust in the God who is our dearest friend.[16]

From his own experience, Thomas found that God's *mercy* may allow disappointments and even tragedies in our life, only as a means of showing us even greater mercy. It was in bitter times like the torture and murder of his brother Rinaldo that Thomas learned how truly God's mercy permits sufferings in our life. Loving parents give small things to their little ones, Thomas tells us; but to their older children they give more important gifts. This is what God does with us. When we are "small," the triune God gives us little things—temporal gifts and only sunny skies. But when we are more mature in Christ, God gives us deeper spiritual gifts, gifts of the heart and soul which often take root in us only through difficult times.[17]

Thomas is convinced that God's mercy can and will turn to our
good any misfortune that may befall us, for Jesus himself has
entered into the depths of our misery and brought us the mercy
of God.[18] Indeed, Jesus *is* God's mercy in person, given to us from
the wellsprings of the Father's tenderness. In Jesus, risen Lord
of the universe, the Father's mercy stretches out to the ends of
the earth: "All of the earth's vast riches spring only from the
mercy of God."[19] This mercy fills the earth certainly through the
created goods which bless our lives. But most of all God's mercy
fills the earth through the deeper blessings of heart and soul
lavished on us through Jesus. In pouring out on us the Holy Spirit,
the risen Lord has bathed the entire universe in God's mercy.[20]
If we praised God's wonders forever, Thomas assures us, we still
could not begin to tell of all the miracles God's mercy has worked
in our lives.[21]

But the greatest marvel of all is that God's mercy enables us
to love God in return. Of its very nature love is meant to be
reciprocal,[22] yet we know that regardless of how much we may
want another person to return our love, we cannot force any one
to love us. God's love, however, is infinitely stronger than ours.
In the depths of our being God's mercy lures us to return the love
God pours out on us. Unlike our own helpless love, God's love
for us *causes* us to love God in return.[23] As John tells us, we are
not loved because we love; we love God because we are loved by
God.[24]

The words of Psalm 36:5-6 helped Thomas to voice his own
wonder before the depths of God's mercy. The psalmist sings
about the justice of God that rises like the mountains, and God's
truth that is like the clouds, which are higher still. But God's mercy
is like the heavens, which reign over all the earth! While God's
justice would give us what we deserve, God's truth gives us the
far greater good God has promised us. Yet God's mercy lavishes
on us in Jesus far more than we were promised, far more than
we could ever deserve. Indeed, Thomas exclaims in wonder, God's
mercy, source of all our good, reigns over all the universe![25]

Thomas had experienced in his own life the truth that God's
every work toward us is unbounded mercy.[26] Mercy alone is the
source even of God's infinite love for us.[27] "In every work of God,
viewed at its primary source, mercy shines forth. In everything
that follows, the power of God's mercy works with even greater
force. Out of the abundance of the divine goodness," God works
so bountifully![28] Thomas turns to the psalmist's beautiful prayer,

"Have mercy on me, O God, according to thy abundant mercy" (Ps 51:1). When he comes to the words, "According to thy *abundant* mercy," he abandons his usual restraint: "These are words of *great sublimity.* God's mercy *fills* the universe!"[29]

The more deeply we know this beautiful truth, the more God's mercy to us makes us givers of mercy to one another. In his own mercy toward us, Jesus implores us, "Be merciful as your Father is full of mercy" (Luke 6:36). Envy makes us sad over others' good fortune, but mercy inspires us to grieve with and to help them in their misfortune.[30] From his own experience Thomas assures us that the mercy we give to others heals our own sin. For in giving God's mercy to one another we learn what it means to live as the children of God.[31]

God's Mercy in *All of Creation*

These thoughts drew Thomas to the mystery of our very existence poured out on us by God's sheer mercy. Thomas contemplated how the triune God alone is unbounded life and be-ing itself. As fire spreads its heat and light to others, the Trinity alone is the infinite fire of life igniting nothingness and making us and the entire universe burst into existence.[32] Yet we *continue* to live only from the wellspring of life that God *is.* The triune God's mercy, therefore, does not simply reign *over* the universe; God's mercy so intimately embraces us that we live and move and have our being *in* the mercy of God.

Thomas reflects on what it means for us just to live. We are alive when we move and direct ourselves in some way, at the least by the beating of our heart. The more we can direct our own life, the fuller our life is. Though animals are led only by natural instinct,[33] we can understand and choose our own goals.[34] Yet even with such blessings, we only *have* life. Perfect life, however, means not simply *having* teaspoons of life but *being* the unbounded ocean of life.[35] The triune God *is* this infinite ocean of life and be-ing itself. God does not merely exist; God is the fullness of existence itself![36]

This is why the author of John's Gospel pictures each of us and the entire world springing to life only through God the Word, the very fountain of life: "All things were made through the Word and without the Word nothing was made. In the Word was *life*"

(John 1:3-4). If God the Word's loving presence were withdrawn from us for even an instant, we would cease to exist. For God the Word is life itself, acting in our inmost depths to give us life.[37] Thomas knew that, of ourselves, we are infinitely distant from God; compared to God's fullness, we have more nonexistence than existence. Yet in the very existence the triune God gives us, we are *like* God, the fire of be-ing itself. And the closer we come to God, the more fully we live, while the more fully we live, the closer we come to God.[38]

To illumine the depths of this profound truth, Thomas reflects on how the triune God brings all of us into existence. Wherever anything truly exists, God dwells.[39] Absolutely nothing in the universe can be distant from God,[40] since God creates and preserves us not from outside ourselves, but from within our inmost depths, as our very source.[41] Dwelling in us as the giver of our existence,[42] the triune God is more deeply within us and all of creation than even what is most intimate to us, our own existence. "Because existence itself is inmost in us, God alone is *in* all things, and innermostly."[43]

But though the triune God lives in us, even more truly, we live in God. We and the whole of creation not only come *from* God and strain *toward* God as our perfect fulfillment; we also exist only *in* God.[44] Thomas thinks of how physical realities contain what exists in them; our bodies, for example, enclose our hearts, and the whole universe encircles us. But spiritual realities, which greatly surpass anything material, contain *us*. We may say, for example, that our soul is "in" our body, but in reality, our soul enfolds *us*.

Nothing, therefore, holds or contains the triune God, who is the fullness of life itself. Rather, Thomas tells us, we and all of creation are contained within God.[45] By lavishing its inmost existence on everything, the triune God enfolds and fills all that is. God is "in" us by enveloping us.[46] We are known by God through our existence *in* God.[47]

Furthermore, Thomas was constantly allured by the beauty of all that our loving God has created. The world is filled with myriads of different creatures, unique in their loveliness. He was convinced that the closer they are to God, the more beautiful they are. Indeed, our beauty pours forth the fragrance of our Creator's beauty (Wis 13:3-5).[48] But Thomas was even more convinced that God the Word is the reason for the infinite variety and beauty we see in all of creation. As a work of art shows us its artist's soul, the whole universe displays the magnificence of the Father's Wisdom, God the Word.[49] No mere creature serves as the model for the creation of any of us; each of us is made in the infinitely rich and lovely image of God the Word.[50]

Because none of us can perfectly mirror the beauty of this Word, all that exists imitates the charm of God the Word in different ways. Each of us and all of creation draw our unique beauty from our archetypes in the infinite loveliness of God's own being.[51] Every one of us and all of creation thus spring as magnificent works of art from the eternal art who is the second divine Person.[52] This is why we exist more truly in the Word than in ourselves. And we and all of creation are truly ourselves only insofar as we image our unique idea or archetype in God the Word's infinite beauty.[53]

Thomas' fascination for our loveliness and that of the created world grew not only from his Christian but also from his Aristotelian perceptions. It was because Thomas found Aristotle deeply akin to Christian sensitivities[54] that his theology is so uniquely open to the beauty of creation.[55] This "vigorous acceptance of the natural world"[56] permeates his theology, and highlights the originality of his thought. Albert and Bonaventure, his two great contemporaries, described the seven sacraments, for example, as cures for specific sins. But Thomas compares each sacrament to a way our human body is healed and grows to its full maturity.[57]

Yet even more, the source of Thomas' "resolute worldliness" is his theology of creation.[58] Thomas was convinced that since God is the fullness of be-ing itself, "the first fruit of God's activity in things is existence itself." Whenever we encounter anything real, therefore, we encounter something that has "flamed up" from God; every created reality confronts us with God![59] Indeed, the reason that Thomas loved the created beauty of this world is that it has come from the God who is be-ing itself, the God who makes creation not only good but also *holy*.[60]

Thomas was opened to the beauty of the created world also by his theology of the incarnation. As Chesterton notes, Thomas believed with all of his heart that through the incarnation, God the Word has forever "entered the world of the senses." When Thomas "walked in the steps of Aristotle," therefore, he was, "if you will, taking the lower road." But, Chesterton adds, because of the incarnation, "So was God."[61] By its loveliness, all of creation, therefore, is meant to lure us to God's own goodness (Rom 1:20). We can certainly abuse the created beauty that surrounds us. But Thomas is convinced that if any of God's creation leads us away from God, the fault lies in our own misuse of God's gifts, not in their God-given charm.[62]

The Gift of Our Human Sexuality

One of the remarkable facets of Thomas' world-affirming outlook is his theology of our human sexuality as one of these wonderful gifts of God to us. Indeed, as one commentator points out, Thomas' treatise on sexuality and chastity in the *Summa Theologiae* "strikes us as a breath of fresh air."[63] We have already considered the charming story of Thomas' celebration in honor of St. Agnes. Thomas was devoted to this martyred girl honored for her virginal purity. He even wore around his neck a relic of hers which he had obtained when he was at Rome, the same relic that he placed on Reginald to heal his fever.[64] And, as we have seen, when Reginald suddenly got better as a result, Thomas decided to host a party for the community every year on Agnes' feast![65]

This spontaneous desire to "throw a party" in Agnes' honor is the same life-affirming attitude that permeates Thomas' insights on sexuality and chastity. His treatment of our human emotions in the *Summa Theologiae* is filled with a depth of psychological insight that still strikes us today as wonderfully whole and sound.[66] For Thomas, a healthy sensuality is not only not evil but positively good, and "unsensuality" is not simply a defect, but a vice.[67] Thomas considers as "unreasonable" the opinion that our human procreation in paradise was nonsexual! Sexuality is not an expression of our weakened condition because of sin, he assures us, but belongs to the very goodness of our human nature.[68] This is why "our soul *united* with our *body* is more like God than the soul separated from the body, for in being united to our body, our soul possesses its own nature more perfectly."[69]

Yet we might ask what weight these statements of Thomas have in the light of a comment made by one of his biographers that Thomas seemed to "avoid women."[70] Thomas certainly was very close to the women in his own family—his sisters, cousins, and nieces. But it does seem that he chose to guard his virginity, which he had consecrated to Jesus, by avoiding relationships with women outside the context of the loving relationships familiar to him from his home environment. His choice may become more understandable to us in the light of several significant factors in his childhood and adolescence.

As a child Thomas was raised by a nurse, and at a young age, was sent to live with the monks of Monte Cassino. For the rest of his life he lived in environments that lacked a consistent womanly influence. In addition, his biographers speak of an extremely traumatic incident which Thomas suffered in his late adolescence. As we have seen, soon after he had entered the Dominicans, Thomas was traveling, perhaps to Paris, to begin his studies as a Dominican student. On the way, however, his brothers accosted the group and abducted Thomas. Sometime after this, he suffered a cruel attempt of his brothers to force him to change his mind. In an extraordinary account, which surely comes from Thomas' confidante, Reginald, Bernard Gui tells of the experience: to break Thomas' resolve, his brothers sent a prostitute to his room to seduce him.

Bernard Gui writes that the teen-age Thomas could not help feeling the force of the woman's allure.[71] In another remarkable account, Thomas' first biographer, William Tocco, discloses that after ''seeing her and feeling the first effect of her presence in himself,'' Thomas suddenly seized a log from the fire and drove the woman out![72] He matched the violence of his brothers' affront to him—he was about seventeen years old at the time, and a virgin—by the violence of his own refusal to be seduced.

After he had driven out the prostitute, Thomas marked the sign of the cross on the wall of the room with the charred tip of the log, fell to the ground and began weeping. He begged God for the gift of a virginal chastity, for the grace to keep for the rest of his life the same resolve he had been given that night to consecrate his virginity to the Lord. Praying and weeping, Thomas then fell asleep. As he slept, he dreamed that two angels came to him, assuring him that God had answered his prayer. In the dream, they bound his loins with what Thomas interpreted as the gift of a lifelong virginal chastity. Gui comments that after this, Thomas seemed to avoid the company of women.[73] Thomas told no one of his experience at the time. But at the end of his life, he revealed this and other secrets of his heart to his dear friend Reginald ''for the love he bore him.''[74]

It is true that Thomas' solution in dealing with his attraction to women differs from that of Dominic, the founder of the Order he joined. The joyful Spaniard saint fostered close friendships with women to whom he was not related. In an extraordinary public confession on his deathbed, he acknowledged both that he was still a virgin—obviously a virginal life was not the rule but the exception in Dominic's time—and that he could never quite overcome the "fault" of preferring the company of younger women! But Dominic had a deep relationship with his mother and was keenly influenced by her warmth and holiness. He lived in a close-knit family and had a wonderful father, as well as a virtuous brother who was very dear to him.

Thomas came from a very different family environment. But if he had a father and brothers given to a violent way of life, and if he was deprived of a tender and holy mother's affection, he nevertheless most certainly did not hate women. He was, in fact, very loving to women in his family. He treasured his sisters, and they cherished him. He was very close also to his niece, Frances (Countess Francesca di Ceccano), at whose castle he not infrequently stayed. It was this same niece whom he visited before his death, and from whose castle he was taken to the nearby Abbey of Fossanova to die. Frances was prevented from attending the funeral since women were not permitted in the monastery. But she wept so uncontrollably at the monastery gate that the monks had to bring Thomas' body to her so that she might see him one last time. This kind of deep attachment to Thomas certainly was not elicited by a man who hated or avoided women!

In choosing the path of virginal chastity for his life, therefore, Thomas surely was not motivated by fear of women. Rather, he had discovered in his own heart the call and truth of Paul's words, "The virgin is free for the things of the Lord" (1 Cor 7:34). Those who knew Thomas spoke not only of the depth of his insights but also of the simplicity and purity of his heart and life. Indeed, toward the end of his life, he described this intimate connection between contemplation and purity of heart. He wrote that we know from experience how our sexual struggles can cause in us an especially intense inner war (Gal 5:17). But the Spirit's charity gives us a purity of heart that heals our inner divisions and fills us with peace. Indeed, a heart full of peace is a chaste life's special gift in us.[75]

Growing toward Chastity as a Means
of Living Life to the Full

It is part of the gift of Thomas that the compassion and wisdom of his insights on chastity still speak with power to us today. Indeed, his psychological insight shines with special force when he writes about the value of our growing toward chastity in our own way of life and precisely as a means of living "life to the full" (John 10:10). Thomas was convinced that a fully rich and beautiful human life is not only possible but also *enhanced* in a chaste lifestyle. He saw that we are all called to the freedom and joy of this chaste life in whatever vocation is ours. For married people, a chaste life means loving fidelity to their spouses; for unmarried people it means a celibate way of life. But for Thomas, such a chaste life, lived in different ways by married and unmarried people, is a path not to a deprived life, but rather to human life to the *full*.

It is true that sex can have a whole range of meanings—from merely satisfying a natural craving to the Christian view of sex as the radical self-giving that seals our marrriage covenant in God. Many people today are finding that with God's grace they *can* make the liberating choice for this latter meaning. Our own experience is teaching us that outside the context of the marriage covenant, far from liberating and healing us, sex far too often enchains and denigrates us. We are discovering by our own experience the truth that Thomas himself found: a chaste way of life, far from being inhuman and unhealthy, is, in fact, full, rich human life.

It is true that Thomas was a person of his own thirteenth century, with no access to the kind of rich psychological and theological understanding of the meaning of our sexuality that is available to us today. And because his insights were the fruit of his own experience of virginal chastity, Thomas says little about the meaning of sexuality in marriage; he concentrates instead on the struggles of those who are called to grow in a celibate way of life. Yet even married people experience times when they must refrain from the full sexual expression of their love. This is why Thomas' compassion and wisdom in reflecting on our struggle to grow more fully *human*, precisely in living a chaste life, remain helpful for us in any state of life.

Thomas himself discovered that purity of heart and life can concentrate our emotional energies at a profound level and channel them in rich expressions that can give birth to a profoundly fulfilling way of life and a more intense spirituality. He found that purity of heart and life focused his own energies in an extraordinary way and freed him, as he himself tells us, for the profound work of his theological and philosophical endeavors. Indeed, he discovered by his own experience that virginal chastity fosters the peace and freedom to contemplate and to share with others the things of God in a powerful, undistracted way.[76]

This is why Thomas' insights on purity of heart and life speak with special force to those who are learning by their own experience the freedom and beauty of a chaste way of life. Thomas knew that we are capable of greatly wounding ourselves and others by our sexual sin. Yet he also knew that God's merciful and loving grace can and wants to give us as a gift the very chastity that we cannot attain by our own strength alone. He also knew from experience that nothing precious is gained without cost: purity of life is not possible without prayer and sacrifice. His reflections, therefore, offer encouragement and hope to those who are trying to grow in that purity of heart and life which is life to the *full*.

Of all our trials, Thomas comments in one of his homilies, our struggles to channel our sexual drives in a virtuous way seem particularly strong precisely because we are always in our own company.[77] We may sometimes feel as if we are contending with someone in our own household[78] and that we are being besieged where we feel most vulnerable.[79] Thomas knew, too, that the attraction of sexual satisfaction outside of marriage is especially strong for us because its pleasure is so alluring. Sin always holds out to us the offer of some good, and so satisfies some of our desires—otherwise we would never sin. Thomas quotes Augustine's saying that of all our struggles, the most difficult ones involve chastity, for the fight is a daily one, but the victory is rare (Sermo 293) since the allure of sexual sin is so strong.[80]

Because we are choosing what only *appears* to be good, but what can never fulfill our deepest longings, sinful satisfactions leave us troubled and unpeaceful.[81] Thomas gives a perceptive description of the way sexual pleasure outside marriage seduces us. When we sin the first time, we feel sure that we will never repeat this mistake; and yet, as we soon find, our sin makes it easier for us to succumb again.[82] Sexual pleasure begins to deceive, then betray, and finally enchain us.[83] Our unpeace keeps us from spiritual things and leaves our soul troubled,[84] until we may feel like someone at the bottom of a well, unable to be freed without help.[85]

It is at this point that the depth of Thomas' wisdom and compassion shines with particular force, and offers encouragement for all who are engaged in the day to day struggle of trying to live a chaste lifestyle. Thomas reflects on how our succumbing to sexual satisfaction outside of marriage may be a matter of momentary weakness rather than the malice of mortal sin. When we are preoccupied, not feeling well, or weighed down with pressures, he tells us, it is very easy for us to forget what we know habitually and in the back of our minds, so to speak. In fact, he comments, sometimes when our passions are intense we are not following our reason at all. We do not pay attention to what we know when we are away from the sway of passion. We may know in general, for example, that illicit sexual satisfaction cannot be ultimately healing for us, but we may not know that we should not engage in this specific sexual relationship or activity. Or we may know both in general and particular that this action is wrong, but not actually be aware at this moment of what we know. Then it is easy for us to act against what we know but do not actually avert to.[86]

This is why Thomas considers sexual sins as often far less grievous than other sins, for many times they result from our human weakness, from the lure of sexual pleasure or a momentary passion. The sins we commit with knowledge and malice can be far more serious than our sexual missteps[87] and the sins we commit under the sway of momentary passion.[88] Thomas agrees with Aristotle that only our freely chosen actions are human in the fullest sense of the word. In terms of morality, then, *why* we do something is even more important than *what* we do.[89] And the more our reason and will do anything of their own accord, and not through the impulse of a passion, the more free our actions are.[90]

Thomas recalls how Socrates considered every virtue to be a kind of knowledge, and every sin to be a kind of ignorance. Socrates was partially right, Thomas tells us, because we are always seeking what is good, or at least what *appears* to be good in some way. We would not choose evil if we could truly understand the damaging nature of our choices.[91] Thomas knew that the cause of our sinning lies in our reason, not our emotions or passions. We sin mortally only when, with our whole consent, we knowingly reject God in our sin.[92] Because sexual pleasure is so addictive, and our sexual impulses are "very difficult to overcome," Thomas comments,[93] our passions can sometimes overcome our reason at a given moment. Sins we commit through passion, therefore, are sins "of weakness,"[94] precisely because our passions keep us from freely choosing our *truest* good. However, as Thomas recognizes, we are usually responsible in some degree for our missteps, even when acting under strong emotions,[95] for our impulses do not suddenly overtake us without our permitting and encouraging them. And if, with God's grace, we would use our reason to anticipate the consequences of our impulses, the growing force of our passion could be calmed.[96]

Thomas comments that virgins can be tempted by curiosity to experience sexual pleasure, which, he notes, often appears greater than it is in reality! In contrast, those who are not virgins can be tempted more frequently not by curiosity but by the remembrance of sexual pleasure.[97] Yet Thomas was convinced that chastity as a "virtue is not concerned with the amount of pleasure we experience in our senses, because this depends on our body's disposition. What does matter is how much our interior desire [for God] is affected by this pleasure."[98]

Though we have many obstacles to chastity, Thomas assures us, we also have many means to help us. Most of all, we need to recognize that only God can give us the gift of purity of heart and life. Thomas himself had discovered by experience that the Spirit's charity is not only the opposite of unchastity but also the very heart of true chastity. Thomas pictures the Spirit's charity as binding us to God in an irrevocable love full of tenderness and delight: *"charity* alone is true chastity—the charity that weds us to God."[99] It is the Spirit's charity that heals our unchastity, and the Spirit's own delight that frees us from addiction to the pleasure of sexual sin.[100]

Thomas finds particular wisdom in the advice of John Chrysostom: we can, with God's grace, find the purity of heart and peace of soul we want so much if we are careful about what fills our thoughts. Because Scripture delights our heart with the "sweetness of God's Word," prayer, contemplation, and meditating on Scripture help us greatly in living a chaste life.[101] Thomas urges us, therefore, to fill our mind and heart with thoughts of God's love and beauty. He reminds us of Paul's own encouraging words: "Whatever is true, modest, just, holy; whatever is lovely, of good fame; if there is any virtue, anything praiseworthy, think on these things" (Phil 4:8). Thomas also is convinced that prayer to Mary, whose purity is "greater than that of the angels," also greatly helps us. For she who is "purity itself" is also our dear mother, with great power to gain the gift of purity for her beloved children.[102] And above all, this is the most powerful way of attaining a chaste heart and life, Thomas tells us, surely from his own experience: "Do not presume on your *own* strength, but trust in *God's* grace"![103]

God's Merciful Providence Enfolding Our Freedom

Thomas' wise, compassionate insights on our growing toward chastity as a way of living "life to the full" were inseparable from his sense of how good our human freedom is. He knew by his own experience that even our mistakes and missteps are enfolded by God's merciful providence. "How great are the Holy Spirit's blessings, making everything work together unto good for us."[104] Thomas thinks of how we ourselves cannot help wanting to care for our loved ones. Yet our own experience gives us only a small hint of God's immense care for us in our every need,[105] for what God loves, God cares for.[106]

Since the triune God draws all of creation toward its completion by a wonderful plan of love, everything in the universe falls under God's tender providence. God's love has a beautiful plan for *our* good, gently but surely carrying each of us toward our fulfillment by this loving providence.[107] Indeed, those who are closest to God most deeply experience God's care for them.[108] For God has created us as free persons, to direct ourselves to our own goals. But Thomas also discovered that God's love is great enough to embrace and care for us even in our freedom, enfolding us in our missteps and mistakes as well as in our good and wise decisions.[109]

If sometimes we think that God is far away from us, that God is not caring for us especially in our smallest needs, we are immensely mistaken, Thomas assures us.[110] For though many things might seem to happen by accident, God's providence over the whole universe means that absolutely *"nothing* results from chance." We *can* experience God's providence deep at work in our own life, since many times we see that situations turn out far differently than they should have. As Thomas points out, when we least expect it, "the powerful fall," and circumstances in our life change radically for the good.[111] And God can do what no one else can do, change even what we freely want, by gently and powerfully working in our heart.[112] As the very source of our freedom, the triune God can influence us from within more powerfully than even we ourselves can do. If we can change our own mind from one moment to the next, how much more surely can God change what we want and cause us to desire what we did not want before![113]

Because God is more powerful than even our free will, God can influence us gently, without force.[114] The triune God can make us spontaneously want what we did not want before, or give us a virtuous habit that makes us want the good.[115] Yet it is not that God is partly responsible for our free choices and that we also are partly responsible for them. Rather, we completely cause our own free choices, and God also causes them, yet in a wholly different way, as the ultimate source of our freedom.[116]

From his own experience, therefore, Thomas became convinced that we conquer in difficult times only through God's loving care for us.[117] He envisions God's way of love for us not as a heavy burden but as a lightsome path, full of life for us. As the Lord himself tells us, "My yoke is sweet and my burden is light" (Matt 11:30).[118] The Lord's power can free us from our chains and raise us up new and whole. Thomas' optimism—the fruit of his great trust in Christ's grace and care for us—shines in his encouraging words, "Before Christ's passion few lived without falling into mortal sin; but afterwards *many* have lived and *are* living without mortal sin."[119] Therefore, he assures us, God's tender providence should be a source of immense hope for us.[120]

God's Providence Enfolding Us in Difficult Times

Thomas believed with all of his heart that God cares for us *even* by allowing sin in our life, and evil in the world. It is true that when tragedies happen to us, we can think that our life is sense-less and unfair. If we see good people suffer and evil people en-joy good times, we begin to doubt God's providence. But God knows how to use even misfortunes, indeed even wicked people, for our good.[121] Thomas gives the example of a doctor who pre-scribes special medicines for each patient. In our ignorance we could think that the doctor chooses the medicines at random, when the physician in fact knows exactly which prescription is needed for each patient's good health.[122]

God is like this wise, loving physician. The triune God knows what we need, what healing remedies will make us strong and whole. The medicine that would destroy one person is exactly what another one needs to get well. Thomas was convinced that God allows difficulties in our life only because God's loving care can enter into our pain and bring even greater good for us from it.[123] Even out of tyrants' evil, Thomas comments, God can bring forth infinitely greater good, such as the power of martyrs' love.[124] We are foolish, then, to doubt God's providence for us just because we do not yet know God's loving reasons for permitting all that happens to us.[125]

Thomas was convinced that if God would erase all evil from the world, we would be deprived of even greater good. Indeed, he assures us, "the *good* is stronger in its goodness than evil is in its malice."[126] God permits evil only because God's love can bring still greater good from even the most heinous crime and transform our tragedies into healing for our wounds.[127] Thomas urges us to think of how willingly we endure a painful operation in order to save our life. In the same way, let us trust in God's love which sometimes permits us to suffer one sorrow only to save us from an even deeper one.[128]

Even in tragedies, therefore, we need to believe that God is em-bracing us in a mercy whose plan we will one day understand and rejoice in. God sometimes permits us even to sin only because God can bring from our fall even deeper benefits for us. God's love desires a greater good for us even more than the absence of a lesser evil. And while all sins are hateful in themselves, some are more destructive for us than others. We may commit a sin of weakness which humbles us greatly, Thomas comments, but which also saves us from a more serious sin of pride or malice. And in our weakness, we can gain the greater good of humility and trust in God's mercy and power.[129]

As we learn from our own experience time after time, it is just when we think we are standing by our own strength that God allows us to fall on our face! But even when we do fall, it is God who tenderly picks us up, embraces us, and sets us gently on our feet again.[130] This is why, even and especially in our weakness, we must never give up hope. Because despair itself drives us into still greater sins, we need to trust always in God's forgiveness and power to heal us. For this reason, Thomas encourages us never to tire of praying the "Our Father," especially the plea, "Forgive us our trespasses." Each time these words well up from our heart, our hope in God's mercy and healing power is deepened. And, Thomas adds, "it helps us greatly to be always full of hope."[131]

Thomas thinks of how God's tender mercy sometimes permits even very holy people to fall into sin just to bring them to deeper trust and intimacy with God. The triune God permits saints to sin, sometimes even seriously, as David did in committing adultery and murder, so that we might learn from them not to trust in our own strength but in God's. This is why Gregory the Great tells us that we have profited more from the apostle Thomas' *unbelief* than from the other apostles' *faith*.[132] Even our weakness and sin can become the means of our sharing good with others.

Generously Sharing Our Good

For Thomas, possessing "life to the full" means that we can and must share this life with others.[133] Only *things* are meant to participate in God's goodness merely by existing; *we* are meant not simply to exist passively but actively to live![134] Indeed, God's immense goodness wants us to cause more life and good in the world as true co-creators with God.[135]

Thomas turns again to our experience of friendship to understand more deeply how the triune God's goodness invites us to life so full that we can share it with others. Our love for our friends grows more intense in the measure that we are united to them in what is most deep and intimate in us. But this experience can only hint at how intimately and intensely God loves us, since God's own *goodness* is most intimate in the heart of God. God loves us, therefore, "not only with a true love, but also a most perfect and most enduring love."[136]

From all eternity, God has loved and willed each one of us into being,[137] loving us only for our own sake and good.[138] But God lavishes on us our *own* being, not a shadow existence and goodness simply mirroring God's being.[139] The triune God's unbounded love gives us our own proper autonomy, our own unique existence and good. And if, in order to give more glory to God, we disparage the inherent value of what God has made, we in fact disparage God's infinite goodness.[140] We and all that God has created are *exceedingly* good,[141] good with our very own being and goodness,[142] which the triune God intends us to share with others.

In order to develop this wonderful insight, Thomas reflects on how we ourselves love the good we already find in our friends, and how we love them because their goodness is *worthy* of our love. But God's love is infinitely more creative than ours. God does not love us because we are good; God loves us into existence and by this love *makes* us good! Indeed, the only reason we exist is that God loves us.[143]

Each one of us has been willed into being by the kindness of God, who gives life to what is not.[144] Since God's graciousness is the source of all that God does, we exist only because God is so good.[145] Furthermore, since we are created in the infinitely lovely Word, we ourselves cannot help wanting what is good and beautiful. Yet whether we realize it or not, when we desire anything good, especially that of our own completion, we are in fact thirsting for God,[146] who is goodness itself.[147] The triune God, therefore, is our source and goal, our truest good,[148] the fulfillment of our every desire.[149]

Moreover, the closer we are to God, Thomas assures us, the more God cares for our every need. This is why, of all creation, we persons share most deeply in God's providence. We do this by receiving God's care, as all creation does, but also and especially by our concern for one another.[150] In this way God's love provides for us not only through natural causes, but also through our own care for ourselves and for each other.[151] We are meant to be co-creators with God, causing more true life for others. For in our concern for one another, especially the most poor and weak, we become most like God, who gives life abundantly to others.[152]

Just as God lavishly pours out life on us, therefore, God also gives us the capacity and call to pour out our good on others. Thomas believed that this vocation is built into our very make-up as human persons through the gift of our freedom. God lavishes life on us not only to make *us* rich and full, but also to make us a source of life to others.[153] Thomas thinks of how the best source of light does not simply shine for itself but also to give light to others.[154] The sun, for example, does not hoard its light, but generously floods the whole earth. It lights up other heavenly bodies so that they can shine with their own light, and spread it to others. We, too, participate most deeply in God's largesse when we share our good with others, enabling them to give their bounty to still others.[155]

This is how Thomas spent his own life. He could have embraced the values of his father and brothers, exerting his energies to amass more and more wealth for himself. But he wanted to live in communion with Jesus, as Jesus himself had lived, giving lavishly to others the good news of the God he treasured in his mind and heart. Thomas believed with all of his soul that the triune God wants us to pour out our good on others, in the very way that God does, not through force or instinct or need but freely, generously, lavishly.[156]

This is why Thomas urges us to let God's goodness to us become our own pattern for relating to one another. We are meant so to participate in the triune God's bounty that we become, in God and like God, generous givers of life to others.[157] By sharing not only our resources, but also our own inner riches with others, we become a means of helping them to grow in their own fullness. In this way, Thomas assures us from his own experience, we find our most noble way of imitating God, and our own fulfillment as persons created for "life to the full."[158]

Notes

[1] Vann, *Aquinas*, 58.
[2] HE 23:10.
[3] G. K. Chesterton, *St. Thomas Aquinas* (Garden City, N.Y.: Doubleday Image, 1957) 131.
[4] ST I, 21, 3.
[5] In Ps 37:2.
[6] In Ps 40:3.
[7] In Ps 40:1.
[8] In Jn 11, lect. 10.

[9]In Ps 24:5.
[10]In Jn 11, lect. 10.
[11]In Ps 50:1.
[12]In Ps 24:6.
[13]In Jn 11, lect. 10.
[14]In Ps 40:1.
[15]ST I, 20, 4, ad 2.
[16]In Ps 24:11.
[17]In Ps 43:1.
[18]In Ps 40:7.
[19]In Ps 47:6.
[20]In Ps 32:4.
[21]Cf. In Ps 39:3.
[22]ST III, 46, 3.
[23]CG III, 151, 2.
[24]In Jn 14, lect. 4.
[25]In Ps 35:2.
[26]ST I, 21, 4.
[27]In Eph 2, lect. 2.
[28]ST I, 21, 4.
[29]In Ps 50:1.
[30]In Ps 36:1.
[31]In Ps 40:1.
[32]ST I, 8, 1.
[33]ST I, 18, 3.
[34]ST I, 18, 3, ad 1.
[35]ST I, 4, 2, ad 1.
[36]ST I, 4, 2; I, 6, 3; I, 18, 3; CG I, 97, 3. Plato had envisioned "being" as archetypes and pure essences. But Thomas views being as "be-ing," as "existence." For Thomas, God is "sheer Be-ing, existence itself." The Jewish philosopher Moses Maimonides had formulated this concept of being and God almost one hundred years before Thomas, but Thomas pursued Maimonides' line of reasoning to its limits (Pieper, *Guide,* 138).
[37]In Jn 1, lect. 5.
[38]Truth q. 2, a 3.
[39]CG III, 68, 47.
[40]ST I, 8, 1, ad 3.
[41]In Jn 1, lect. 5.
[42]ST I, 8, 1, ad 3.
[43]ST I, 8, 1.
[44]Com Div Nom ch. 13, lect. 3.
[45]Pot 1, 2.

⁴⁶ST I, 8, 2; I, 8, 1, ad 2.

⁴⁷Truth q. 2, a 3, ad 2.

⁴⁸Ap Creed.

⁴⁹In Jn 1, lect. 5.

⁵⁰Truth q. 4, a 4, ad 5.

⁵¹Truth q. 2, a 4, ad 2; q. 4, a 4, ad 4.

⁵²Truth q. 4, a 4, ad 5.

⁵³Truth q. 4, a 6.

⁵⁴Chesterton, *Aquinas,* 41.

⁵⁵Pieper, *Guide,* 133.

⁵⁶Ibid., 125.

⁵⁷See ibid., 124–25.

⁵⁸Ibid., 131.

⁵⁹CG III, 68, 4; Pieper, *Guide,* 142, 143.

⁶⁰Pieper, *Guide,* 130, 143.

⁶¹Chesterton, *Aquinas,* 42.

⁶²ST I, 65, 1, ad 3.

⁶³Pieper, *Guide,* 123.

⁶⁴I Can 60.

⁶⁵HE 23:10.

⁶⁶See ST II-II, qq. 22–48; I-II, qq. 77–79.

⁶⁷ST II-II, 142, 1; II-II, 152, 2, ad 2; II-II, 153, 3, ad 3.

⁶⁸ST I, 98, 2.

⁶⁹Pot 5, 10 ad 5.

⁷⁰Gui, c. 7.

⁷¹Ibid.

⁷²I Can 61; Foster, *Life,* 100.

⁷³Gui, c. 7.

⁷⁴I Can 61; Foster, *Life,* 100.

⁷⁵In Ps 36:8.

⁷⁶ST II-II, 152, 3.

⁷⁷Our Father.

⁷⁸Ten Com.

⁷⁹Our Father.

⁸⁰ST II-II, 154, 3, ad 1.

⁸¹ST II-II, 29, 3, ad 1; II-II, 29, 2, ad 3.

⁸²Ap Creed.

⁸³Our Father.

⁸⁴In Ps 37:2; In Ps 37:3.

⁸⁵Ap Creed.

⁸⁶ST I-II, 77, 2.

[87]ST II-II, 154, 3, ad 2; II-II, 154, 3, ad 3.
[88]ST I-II, 78, 4.
[89]ST I-II, 7, 4.
[90]ST I-II, 77, 6.
[91]ST I-II, 77, 2.
[92]ST II-II, 35, 3.
[93]ST II-II, 154, 3, ad 1.
[94]ST I-II, 77, 3; I-II, 77, 3, ad 2.
[95]ST I-II, 77, 7.
[96]ST I-II, 77, 8.
[97]ST Supp, 96, 5, ad 1.
[98]ST II-II, 153, 2, ad 2.
[99]ST I-II, 70, 4.
[100]In Gal 5, lect. 7.
[101]Ten Com.
[102]Hail Mary.
[103]Our Father.
[104]In Rom 8, lect. 6.
[105]ST I, 20, 2, ad 1.
[106]CG III, 90, 6.
[107]ST I, 22, 2.
[108]CG III, 90, 6.
[109]ST I, 22, 2, ad 4.
[110]In Ps 46:2.
[111]Truth q. 5, a 5, ad 5.
[112]Truth q. 22, a 9.
[113]Truth q. 22, a 8.
[114]ST I-II, 6, 4, ad 1; I-II, 10, 4; Truth q. 22, a 8.
[115]Truth q. 22, a 8.
[116]CG III, 70, 8.
[117]Truth q. 5, a 5, ad 5.
[118]Ten Com.
[119]Ap Creed.
[120]In Ps 20:5.
[121]Truth q. 12, a 5, ad 5.
[122]Ap Creed.
[123]Ibid.
[124]In Ps 10:24; CG III, 71, 6.
[125]Ap Creed.
[126]CG III, 71, 6; Anderson, *Catholic Faith,* 239-40.
[127]ST I, 22, 2, ad 2.

[128]In Ps 38:1.

[129]Truth q. 5, a 5.

[130]In Jn 20, lect. 5.

[131]Our Father.

[132]In Jn 20, lect. 5.

[133]CG III, 69, 15.

[134]Truth q. 5, a 8.

[135]CG III, 70, 7.

[136]CG I, 91, 4; *On the Truth of the Catholic Faith,* trans. Pegis and others (New York: Doubleday, 1955-57) 278; ST I, 20, 2, ad 2.

[137]ST I, 19, 3, ad 1.

[138]CG I, 91, 3.

[139]ST I, 6, 4.

[140]CG III, 69, 16.

[141]Truth q. 21, a 5, ad 1.

[142]Truth q. 21, a 2, ad 1.

[143]ST I, 20, 2; In Eph 2, lect. 2; In Jn 5, lect. 3.

[144]ST I, 19, 2.

[145]ST I, 19, 2, ad 3; I, 19, 4, ad 3.

[146]ST I, 6, 1; I, 6, 1, ad 2.

[147]ST I, 6, 3; Truth q. 2, a 8.

[148]Truth q. 21, a 5.

[149]ST I, 6, 1.

[150]Truth q. 5, a 5.

[151]ST I, 22, 4.

[152]ST I, 22, 3.

[153]Truth q. 9, a 2; CG III, 21, 8; III, 69, 16.

[154]CG III, 21, 6.

[155]Truth q. 5, a 8.

[156]Ibid.

[157]CG III, 19, 2.

[158]Truth q. 9, a 2; CG III, 24, 9; III, 21, 6; III, 21, 8.

4

Spirit of Love

Thomas' Experience of the Holy Spirit

Thomas' father and brothers were knights, soldiers formed in the values of war. As Thomas watched how they lived, he knew that he would have to choose a way of life in radical opposition to all that they held dear.[1] Years after he had become a Dominican friar, he described the heart of his own call. Those formed by the world's "spirit," he tells us, live harsh, oppressive lives. But those fashioned by the Holy Spirit live gracious lives full of the Spirit's sweetness.[2] It was in the gentle strength of this Spirit that Thomas learned to live "life to the full."

Those who knew Thomas could see how the Holy Spirit had filled him with a peace and prayerfulness that set him apart from his brothers even as a child. The Holy Spirit had led him first to Benedict's monks, and then to Dominic's community,[3] where he learned to give himself fully to the Holy Spirit's guidance. Among his companions dedicated to proclaiming the good news, Thomas' own words began to radiate the Holy Spirit's "sweet graciousness." His hearers saw in him the mind and heart not of an arrogant intellectual, but of a humble friar filled with God's Spirit.[4] This same "sweetness" of the Spirit began to overflow into Thomas' writings. Indeed, one distinguished contemporary of his, James of Viterbo, doctor of Scripture and archbishop of Naples, acknowledged how difficult he found it to read the works of other authors after tasting the "sweetness" of Thomas' writings.[5]

After Thomas' death, his close friend Reginald wept as he told the "secret" of Thomas' profound insights and productivity: all that he had said and written he had drawn not simply from his own intelligence but far more from the Holy Spirit's anointing.[6] Thomas had learned from experience that friends reveal their heart's secrets to their friends; since only the Spirit of love makes us "friends of God," this Spirit alone unveils to us the secrets of God's heart (1 Cor 2:9-10).[7] Thomas' hunger to know the heart of his beloved God had led him to drink from the Spirit's loving wisdom, and from this font to pour out on others, through his preaching, teaching and writing, the Holy Spirit's own sweet graciousness.

Spirit of Jesus

"The love of God is *poured* forth in our hearts by the Holy Spirit, who is given to us!" (Rom 5:5). In these wonderful words of Paul, Thomas finds a hint of the unrestrained torrential flood of the Spirit whom the risen Lord lavishes on us, for "not by measure does God give the Spirit" (John 3:34).[8] But the risen Lord can pour out the Holy Spirit so recklessly on us only because, as Thomas assures us, God the Word, the inexhaustible wellspring of the Holy Spirit, is *forever* "breathing forth love," the very person of the Spirit.[9] Both in his divinity and humanity, Jesus possesses the Holy Spirit without measure.[10]

The Gospels show that the Holy Spirit marvelously filled Jesus' humanity from the first moment of his conception. The Holy Spirit is the love between the Father and the Son,[11] and only love impelled the Word to become flesh in Mary's womb. Since every gift and grace flows from this Spirit of love (1 Cor 12:4), the incarnation itself is the Spirit's gift to us.[12] Luke thus depicts the entire life of Jesus as *"full* of the Holy Spirit" (Luke 4:1).[13] Indeed, Thomas stresses, the Holy Spirit *is* the "fullness of Christ."[14] Jesus' humanity is healing for us not only because of its union with God the Word, therefore, but also because of its anointing with God the Holy Spirit. Without the Word and the Spirit, Christ's human flesh, Thomas tells us, "has no more power for us than any other flesh." But united to the Word and filled with the Spirit of love, Christ's humanity has wonderful power to heal us.[15] For at the fulfillment of his life, Jesus offered his death for us as his supreme act of love inspired by the Holy Spirit.[16]

Jesus was so perfectly receptive to the Spirit's guidance precisely because the Spirit filled his humanity in an unsurpassable way; he received the Spirit's gifts to overflowing in his humanity, and in his divinity he now pours them out on us.[17] Yet Jesus is filled not only with the Spirit's gifts but also with the person of the Spirit in an unsurpassable way. "Not by measure does the Father give the Holy Spirit to Jesus," Thomas reminds us (John 3:34).[18] And now, through his resurrection, Jesus has become the risen *Christos,* the Christ lavishly anointed with the invisible oil of the Spirit.[19] We share in Christ's saving death and resurrection through our baptism, which draws its healing power not only from Christ's passion but also from the Spirit's love.[20] Both in his divinity and humanity, therefore, the risen Lord possesses the Spirit beyond measure and lavishly pours out this Spirit of love into our hearts.[21]

Spirit of Love

"The love of God has been poured into our hearts by the Holy Spirit given to us" (Rom 5:5). In company with Augustine and Gregory the Great, Thomas discovered in these words the beautiful name of the Holy Spirit as "Love" itself. He had found the Holy Spirit hidden in this most precious and delightful of our human experiences, that of loving and being loved. He saw how the very word "Spirit" hints at love's own tender impulse, for our beloved seems to live within our heart, drawing, pulling, and impelling us in some way outside ourselves to our beloved in person.[22]

In the very word "Spirit," Thomas found an allusion to the gentle drawing that our beloved exerts on us. The name "Spirit" reminds us of love's allure, attracting us to our beloved, delighting our heart like a tender kiss, or a breath of love. Love always has this dimension of a sigh, an "ahh" pulling us in the direction of our beloved. This is why the third divine person, "God proceeding by way of *love*" is called "Spirit," for the Holy Spirit is the Father and Son's "breath of love," their very "impulse of love"

toward one another. From all eternity, the Father and Son love each other with an impulse of love so intense that their love is *someone,* the Holy Spirit who forever springs forth from them as their Spirit, their "breath of love" in person.[23]
Thomas thinks of how, in loving someone dear to us, we also feel our own love "abiding" in the depths of our heart;[24] love seems to leave a tender "impression" or "seal" of our beloved in our heart.[25] This suggests for Thomas how intimately the Holy Spirit lives in the Father as the "beloved dwells in the one who loves."[26] The Spirit is the Father's love for his beloved Word; and the Holy Spirit abiding intimately in the Father's heart is this very love in person. Yet we know from our own experience that our love does not dwell only in *our* heart but also in the heart of our beloved. This precious experience is a pale reflection for Thomas of how the Spirit of love abides not only in the Father but also "rests" in the Father's beloved Son. The Holy Spirit, the Father's and Son's love for one another in person, thus intimately dwells in the Father who loves,[27] and in his beloved Word whom he loves.[28]

Our own experience shows us still another side of love's paradox. Love not only "pulls" us *outside* ourselves to our dear one; it also draws us deep *within* ourselves where our beloved dwells through love's affection. For Thomas, our experience hints at the Spirit of love intimately dwelling *in us.* And when their Spirit lives in us, the Father and the Son also dwell in us through their Spirit: *"We* will come and make our home with those who love" (John 14:23).[29] The First Epistle of John continues, "Those who abide in love dwell in God, and God in them" (1 John 4:16). Indeed, we live in the triune God because we have been given the Holy Spirit (1 John 4:13).[30] Deep within us, the Holy Spirit makes us God's home, and through this same Spirit, the triune God becomes our home.[31]

"The Holy Spirit *is* the Father's and Son's love for each other and for us."[32] Thomas found from his own experience that the Father and Son give us their Spirit precisely so that we can love the triune God in return, in mutual *friendship-love.* By sharing intimately in the Holy Spirit, who is their own love in person, we become "lovers of God."[33] Our love for God in this way reflects a far deeper tenderness—God's love for us.[34] Our love for God comes not from ourselves, therefore, but from the Spirit of love (Rom 5:5)[35] who dwells in us through charity.[36] And in our loving God, the Holy Spirit fills us more and more with the love that the Spirit *is*.[37]

Lavished on us by the risen Lord, the Holy Spirit now lives in us, gently drawing and "goading" us to love the triune God in return. Even our very desire for God, Thomas tells us, comes from God. The Holy Spirit within us strongly, gently inclines us to God, filling us with desire for the Trinity as the God of our heart.[38] Through grace, therefore, the Spirit of love dwells in us, inspiring and protecting us,[39] drawing us into loving relationship with the triune God.[40]

In this way the Holy Spirit makes us God's intimate *friends,* whose lives are filled with forgiveness. Thomas recalls the words of Jesus in the Gospel of John: "Receive the Holy Spirit. Those whose sins you shall forgive, are forgiven" (John 20:22-23). Thomas had found from his own experience that friendship-love nurtures forgiveness at its very heart. And since the Holy Spirit makes us "friends of God," our sins are forgiven and healed through this same Spirit of love. The Spirit of love, therefore, is the very *cause* of our being forgiven.[41]

Furthermore, the Holy Spirit is the source not only of our forgiveness but also of our union in love with one another. Every Sunday in the creed we proclaim our belief as a community in "one, holy, catholic, and apostolic Church." But in these words, Thomas reminds us, we are proclaiming our faith ultimately in *someone,* the Spirit of love making us holy.[42] Moreover, since the "Spirit of the Lord fills the whole *world*" (Wis 1:7), the same Spirit who permeates Christ fills his entire Church, joining us to one another, making us one in faith and love (Eph 4:3-5).[43]

Thomas finds this wonderful work of the Spirit expressed in a beautiful way in the symbol of the dove. This gentle creature, Thomas tells us, loves only one spouse, ardently and faithfully. And so too does the Holy Spirit love us.[44] Furthermore, it is by guarding the Spirit's unity even in our unique differences that we follow the Lord's command, "Love one another as I have loved you" (John 15:12). For while the Spirit's love joins us to one another in an unbreakable bond, the Spirit also causes our wonderful diversity as members of one body, giving us different gifts and ways to serve each other in charity.[45] Our love shares in the Holy Spirit's tenderness, therefore, when we love each other selflessly and because we and they are holy, or so that we and others may become holy.[46]

Holy Spirit, Gift

As Thomas reflects on our experience of love, he thinks of how we cannot help wanting to give gifts to our loved ones. But we impart a true gift only when we bestow it out of love, freely, irrevocably, and with no intention of its being returned. Loving parents cherish their little ones, conferring gifts, especially their own love, with no expectation of return. And all unselfish love is like this. We bestow our love *freely* because the very nature of love is wanting our dear one's good, not our own advantage. In this way our love is the source of every other gift we confer on those we cherish; what we really impart in our gift is our love. Thomas finds in this experience of love as gift a hint of how the Holy Spirit, the Father's and Son's love in person, is their most precious *Gift* to us.[47]

For Thomas, the Spirit's very name is not only "Love," therefore, but also "Gift." We know from our own experience that we confer as a gift only what is first ours to bestow; and we impart it precisely so that it will belong now to our loved one. Our gift in this way becomes irrevocably related both to us and to our beloved. And thus we have an intimation of the triune God who loves us. The Holy Spirit is the Father's and Son's beloved Gift to us in person, belonging in love both to them and now also and irrevocably to us.[48]

For a gift we bestow belongs first to us; but after we confer it, our gift truly belongs to our loved one. Our experience hints at how the Father and Son give us their Holy Spirit to belong now also to us. As the Father and Son's intimate love in person, their Spirit is their first and ultimate Gift to us, and the source and reason for every other good gift in our life.[49] Because they impart their Spirit to be our Spirit also, their Spirit now belongs also to us.[50]

Thomas was struck by Paul's beautiful words, by love "we *belong* to one another" (Rom 12:5). Anyone who loves knows how we need and desire freely and in our own autonomy to "belong" to our beloved. Thomas finds in this experience a trace of the profound mystery of God who in love chooses to "belong" to us. *We* belong to the God who loves us; but even more radically, through love, *God* truly belongs to *us*. The love that is ours in the Holy Spirit allows us to *possess* the divine persons who give themselves to us precisely so that they will "belong" to us in love.[51]

We know that what truly belongs to us is *ours* to freely use and enjoy. But more than anything else, we enjoy the one we love. Thomas finds in this a reflection of how we are meant to enjoy the Holy Spirit, and in their Spirit, the Father and Son as well. For the Father and Son love us so deeply that they give us as their most precious gift their own intimate love for each other, the person of the Spirit. And they give us their Spirit so that we might freely use the Spirit's gifts as well as enjoy the Spirit's own delightful presence. For of all creatures, only we persons can "possess" and "enjoy" the Spirit through love.[52] In his younger years, Thomas had written that we possess the Spirit as one "whose *resources* we enjoy."[53] But in his maturity, Thomas knew that, through grace-filled knowledge and love, we are meant to enjoy the very *person* of the Spirit.[54]

The Holy Spirit, therefore, is inexhaustible gift to us. But a gift is given to us freely, not because we deserve it.[55] Nothing of our own power, therefore, can draw down the gift that is God to us. Of ourselves, we cannot merit the Holy Spirit, nor even prepare our hearts to receive this gracious Person; the Spirit's outpouring in our lives is sheer gift to us (Rom 5:5).[56]

The Spirit Making Us the Father's Own Beloved Children

The Holy Spirit is not only gift but also the compelling power of love within us. For Thomas, the word "Spirit" hints at this impelling force, like a gentle breath or wind, inviting, "pushing," "pulling" us toward our beloved. The Holy Spirit is like this impulse of love, drawing our hearts to the beauty of Jesus, the Word made flesh, and joining us to him.[57] For Jesus is the Father's beloved Son, God the Word who became human through the Holy Spirit of love.[58] In uniting us to Jesus, therefore, the Holy Spirit forms each of us, in him, into the Father's own beloved child, an intimate member of God's own family.

Just as the Father's beloved Son became human only through the Spirit of love,[59] we become God's adopted sons and daughters, intimate members of God's family, through this same Spirit (Rom 8:15-17).[60] Jesus lavishes on us the Spirit of love precisely to make us members of God's own family.[61] A deepening, tender affection for our Father is the very sign that we are becoming more and more the Father's beloved child, since only the Spirit of love can fill our hearts with the love (Rom 5:5) that inspires us to cry out, "Abba, Father!" (Rom 8:15).[62] Paul tells us, "You have not received the spirit of slavery to return to fear again, but you have received the spirit of adoption as sons and daughters" (Rom 8:15). Thomas himself learned from his own experience the truth of Paul's words: "Where the Spirit of the Lord is, *there* is freedom" (2 Cor 3:17).[63] Yet we are free, Thomas assures us, only if we do good—not because a law tells us to, but because we truly desire it. And since we do freely only what we do out of *love,* only the Spirit of love makes us truly free.[64]

The Holy Spirit, therefore, empowers us to live as noble, free daughters and sons, living in love, and not in fear as slaves do. Thomas himself knew what it was to have the freedom of a nobleman. He experienced his life not as a bondage to another's will and pleasure, but as the creation, in God's grace, of his own decisions. *All* of us are meant to live as free persons, he tells us, as "nobility," from our *own* will, and not as slaves submitted to the will of another.[65] Yet whenever we stay enchained to our sin and fear, we act like slaves, rather than as "members of the family." We live under a sense of coercion rather than in the freedom of God's children. On the other hand, when we love, we are free, indeed, "noble" people, for God's sons and daughters are meant to live not as slaves, but as liberated women and men.[66]

The "law" we are meant to follow is not a powerless system outside us, but the very person of the Spirit who is power within us, transforming us from creatures and slaves into God's own beloved children.[67] As we draw our life more and more from this Spirit, we begin to experience the wonderful paradox of the Spirit's charity taking root in us: by love we serve one another, and yet nothing makes us more free. For everything we do out of love we do willingly, not because we are forced to. Thomas himself experienced how "Christ's charity urges us" to do all that we do for God's love (2 Cor 5:14). The Spirit of love, therefore, not only inspires us to want what is good, but also gives us the power to do what is good.[68]

Paul tells us that the Spirit cries out within us, "Abba, Father" (Gal 4:6), not with a loud voice, but with intense love. Indeed, the Spirit's "cry" within us is our very desire for God, desire inspired by the Spirit.[69] Scripture also tells us that the Son prays *for* us to the Father, but the Spirit prays *in* us to the Father. By inspiring us to desire God, the Holy Spirit gently draws us to ask for all that is good.[70] In this way the Spirit of love "prays *in* us," inspiring us to pray,[71] and drawing us to ask for the very blessings the Father longs to give.[72]

Thomas thinks of how well-loved children have no fear of boldly asking their dear parents for what they need and want. Indeed, loving parents would be hurt if their children approached them with fear and caution in their need, expecting from them only the most miserly help. Since the Holy Spirit has made us the children of God, we are to have the bold confidence of beloved children in our own prayer (Rom 8:14-17). The Holy Spirit is the Spirit not of caution and fear but of boldness, since God's own confident, familiar love is "poured forth in our hearts by the Holy Spirit given to us" (Rom 5:5). The Spirit therefore "prays in us" by inspiring us to pray boldly, indeed to cry out to our Father. The more we realize how loved we are, the more bold we grow in our love and prayer.[73]

We experience for ourselves how such familiar, confident love leads us to prayer. For love makes us want to spent time with our dear ones. Thomas finds in this experience a reflection of how the Spirit of love inspires us to enjoy the presence of our beloved God in contemplative prayer. The more we love God, the more we want to relish God's company in prayer (cf. 2 Cor 3:18).[74] And just as love makes us good friends with our beloved, the Holy Spirit makes us close friends of the triune God. But friends not only love to spend time with each other; they also love to work for each other's good; so the Spirit of love inspires us not only to pray, but also to live a life of charity as the Father's beloved children.[75]

Consoler

Thomas' experience of friendship made him see how sweet it is for us to have friends who truly love us. "We delight in our friends' presence," he tells us; "their words and actions make us happy, and we find in them a security against all our anxieties. Especially in our sorrows we run to our friends to be consoled."[76] In this comforting experience of friendship, Thomas finds an intimation of the Holy Spirit, our consoler, who makes us God's dear friends. Because of the Holy Spirit of love we dwell in God, and God dwells in us. Such intimacy cannot help greatly comforting us. "Through the Holy Spirit we have joy in God and security against all the world's adversities and assaults," Thomas assures us. This is why the Gospel of John calls the Holy Spirit the "Paraclete"—a name which Thomas interprets as "Comforter" (John 14:26).[77]

In this name "Paraclete" Thomas hears allusions to the infinite sweetness of the Spirit as our dearest "consoler." He thinks of how comforting we find it to be truly loved for our own sake and not because of our usefulness; this is the kind of generous love the Holy Spirit lavishes on us.[78] Since being loved in this unselfish way cannot help being sweet to us, Thomas pictures the Holy Spirit as feeding us with the Trinity's own tenderness, healing our sadness, and filling us with joy (Gal 5:22).[79] For Thomas, the Holy Spirit is the Father's and Son's love in person, filling our hearts with this sweetness.[80] Thomas himself experienced the Holy Spirit's consolation as joy and contentment in tasting how good the Holy Spirit makes our life feel. Jesus consoles us by giving us his Spirit in our heart, but the Holy Spirit consoles us as the very person of love within us.[81]

Paul speaks about the sweet fruit of the Spirit in our life, as delicious to our soul as luscious fruit tastes in our mouth (Gal 5:22). As Thomas reflects on this charming insight, he thinks of how God has placed natural "attractions" in our heart that make what is good for us also very sweet. He knew that the triune God has made us free, able to reach out by our own inclination to what is good for us. Thus, for example, we *need* to eat if we want to live. But to ensure that we will *want* to eat, the good God has given us a natural attraction to food, so that we are inclined to eat when we are hungry. In this way, Thomas tells us, love—desire for a good that attracts us—is the very first of our "natural" inclinations and the reason we do anything.[82]

Thomas finds in this experience an intimation of how the Spirit's very first fruit in our life is love. The Spirit's charity "attracts" us to God's loveliness, and permeates all the other fruits of the Spirit— peace, joy, patience, kindness, chastity, mildness, goodness. We know from our own experience that our love is incomplete without joy. We can love someone yet be sad because he or she is far away or seems far away from us. But the fruit that crowns our love and makes it perfect is joy in our loved one's actual presence. And since we "possess" the triune God's intimate presence through the Spirit's charity, it is the Spirit who causes true joy to well up within us.[83] Even in times of temptation, the Spirit calms our desires by satisfying our deepest hunger for joy.[84]

Yet Thomas knew by experience that we feel the Spirit's contentment within us especially when we contemplate the things of God. Augustine had written that God the Word comes to us not in simply any kind of knowledge, but in a "sweet" knowing of God by experience (De Trin 4.20): "The word we speak is knowledge with love" (De Trin 9.10). Yes, Thomas assures us, this is what true wisdom is, a "sweet" knowledge of God. For the Father's Word is not simply any kind of word, but the Word who endlessly breathes forth the love who is the Holy Spirit. It is not simply when we know anything at all that the Word comes to us in our knowledge, but only when our knowing is filled with the Spirit's love.[85]

Thomas relished how comforting the Spirit's wisdom is in our hearts, and how much joy it gives us to study and contemplate the things of God. We, too, can experience how turning our thoughts often to God deepens our love and therefore our joy. For our beloved God is *always* close to us, and the joy of this closeness can often inspire us even to break into song! Paul encourages us to sing and make melody to God with all of our heart (Eph 5:19). Yes, Thomas adds, singing our praise to God is a great consolation to our spirit; it fills us with joy and gives us new energy to praise God with the good works of our life.[86] Even when we are besieged by temptations, the Holy Spirit can calm our desires in this way with deep inner contentment.[87]

Paul himself found such great joy in the Spirit that he urges us, "Be *filled* with the Spirit!" For he knew that the Holy Spirit makes us happier than any wine could (Eph 5:18) and far more bold (Acts 4:13-20) in spreading God's joy.[88] Like a river that wears down the resistance of even the hardest stone, the Holy Spirit can soften and touch our heart even when it feels like stone. But unlike a river's action that takes long years, the Spirit can powerfully, quickly fill us with love and joy, like the sudden outburst of a mighty storm. The people gathered at Jerusalem for Pentecost (Acts 2:1-42) experienced how unexpectedly the Spirit can touch our hearts with love and joy.[89]

Yet though the Spirit's joy can fill us suddenly, it is not merely a momentary joy. For the God of love is always present deep within us when we love: "Those who abide in love, abide in God" (1 John 4:16). Just as our beloved's presence cannot help delighting us, the presence of the triune God which the Holy Spirit effects in us imparts a deep contentment.[90] Even in our weakness and sin, the Spirit, our comforter, frees us from pleasures that cannot satisfy us and anoints us with God's sweetness. The Spirit who is the person of love thus heals and consoles us by filling us with joy in our beloved God.[91]

Thomas thinks of how Jesus himself was anointed with the Spirit's "oil of gladness" (Ps 45:7; Acts 10:38). Thomas considered oil a precious liquid, but the Spirit's "oil of gladness" is the most treasured gift of all. We know how spilt oil is impossible to contain; it spreads everywhere. The *Holy Spirit* is the "oil of gladness" poured out everywhere, in our hearts and in the whole world! As oil spreads fire, heat, and light with it, the Holy Spirit fills our minds with light and our hearts with love.[92]

The Lord in this way has abundantly fulfilled his promise to give us the sweetest of all consolers, the Spirit of love poured out on those who love (cf. John 15:26). Like water that quenches our body's thirst, the Holy Spirit slakes our soul's thirst: "Whoever drinks the water I give will never thirst again" (John 4:14). Yes, Thomas adds from his own intimate experience, the Spirit flows as the inexhaustible font of living water welling up in us, a font that never fails.[93] Since unbounded mercy streams from the Spirit of love, Thomas encourages us to let the Holy Spirit reign in our heart, and to live each day in the Spirit's consoling sweetness.[94]

Fountain of Life

Every Sunday, we confess our belief in the Holy Spirit, "Giver of life" (cf. John 6:63).[95] Thomas experienced the power of these words in his own life. He learned to plead for the Spirit as a dying person begs for water and to savor the invitation of Isaiah 55:1: "Come to the waters, all you who thirst." We ourselves may know what it is to crave water, to long for a cool drink in scorching heat. But the physical water that refreshes our parched throat can only hint at the consoling, refreshing life-giving "water" that the Holy Spirit is. The scriptural authors at times compare the Holy Spirit to fire because the Spirit warms our heart. But John also compares the Spirit to the water without which we literally cannot live, the water that not only refreshes and washes us clean but also gives us life.[96]

"Let those who thirst come to me and drink; as Scripture says, out of their hearts shall flow rivers of *living* water" (John 7:37-38). These rivers are the very person of the Spirit who is the fountain and river of life.[97] Thomas had discovered the great difference between "still" water—collected from another source and placed in ponds and cisterns—and "running," "living" water. In his travels, Thomas and his companions, hot and tired and thirsty, would find the wonderful gift of "living" water, water flowing freely and lavishly from its source and welling up to slake their thirst. He could understand why the author of the Gospel of John calls the Holy Spirit *"living* water!" "The love of God is *poured* out into our hearts by the Holy Spirit, who has been given to us" (Rom 5:5). The Spirit flows as the unfailing fountain of life, pouring out on us all other gifts of grace. And the Spirit's grace lavishes on us the inexhaustible source of all grace, the very person of the Holy Spirit.[98]

Thomas considers another dimension of our own experience. Regardless of how thirsty we are, we can physically drink only a limited amount of water at any one time. Also, our supply of water is limited, since the water we drink comes from a source outside us. But when by faith we drink from Christ, an unending fountain of living water springs up in us: "The water that I give will become a fountain within them welling up to eternal life" (John 4:14). The Spirit is the spring of life[99] from whom we drink, the font whose supply can never be exhausted.[100]

The intimate relationship between the Holy Spirit and the Eucharist became more and more evident to Thomas. Paul tells us that we were baptized into one Spirit and that we drink of the one Spirit's overflowing water (1 Cor 12:13). Thomas found in Paul's words the wonderful gift of the Spirit who refreshes our hearts with contentment, and the sacrament of the Eucharist which the Holy Spirit himself makes holy.[101]

As we drink more and more from the Eucharistic cup, the words of the psalmist begin to take root in our heart, "My soul *thirsts* for God, the *living* God" (Ps 42:2). Furthermore, as our longing for God grows, our desire for material things recedes. Thomas the nobleman himself experienced this truth as his appetite for other things faded before his increasing desire for God. When Thomas describes the difference between how material goods and spiritual blessings make us thirsty, therefore, we can glimpse his own soul's experience. The delight that material goods and physical pleasures gives us can be only a momentary slaking of a superficial thirst. In wanting material possessions, Thomas tells us, we always think that what we do not yet have will satisfy us. But after we get what we want, we find that it is not as great as we thought. Regardless of the wonderful things we have, we always want something else that seems even better.[102]

Thomas found that the opposite is true of spiritual blessings like peace and joy and love. They bring us such delight that we want more of *them,* not of something else. We begin to lose our thirst for other things, and to know the ache of the psalmist: "My soul thirsts for God, the living God!" (Ps 42:2). The Spirit's joy and peace which we taste only partially now then begin to make us thirst for heaven's perfect joy where our every desire will be satisfied to overflowing.[103]

"Do not grieve the Holy Spirit of God with whom you were *sealed* unto the day of redemption" (Eph 4:30). In this baptismal imagery Thomas found the mystery of the Lord marking us with the Spirit as his own "seal," setting us apart as his beloved people. Cattle owners brand their herd to mark them as their own. But our care for our animals is only a minute hint for Thomas of how the Spirit guards and sets us apart as God's own. The Lord marks us with his own seal and sign, the Spirit who is love itself, and tells us, "By *this* shall all know that you are my disciples, if you have love one for another" (John 13:35). The Holy Spirit himself is the sign, the seal setting us apart as God's own beloved family.[104]

Even more, this seal forms us into a new creation.[105] In baptism the Spirit's love wipes out our sins and makes us as fresh and innocent as newborn babes; we are born again, in the image of Jesus, as the Father's own beloved child (John 3:3, 5-6). The Spirit's grace in our heart in this way contains heaven's joy for us even now, just as the seed contains in itself the whole tree. Indeed, by grace the Holy Spirit dwells in us as the cause of life everlasting, the "pledge of our inheritance" (Eph 1:14).[106]

A "pledge," Thomas tells us, is an indispensable part of what we are promised as our inheritance. For Thomas, this pledge is first of all the Spirit's charity within us, a created sharing in God's own love that will be made perfect in heaven.[107] The Spirit's grace, containing our entire happiness, in this way is the pledge and first payment of heaven's joy even now.[108] For we receive a pledge as the absolute certitude of our one day possessing the entire reality. In this sense, not only the Spirit's charity, but even more the very person of the Spirit is our pledge of heaven, and indeed, its very wealth and content. Though we have this Spirit now as our certitude of attaining heaven, in heaven we will possess the Spirit as our very inheritance.[109] This is why Thomas joins Paul in urging us not to "grieve the Holy Spirit" with whom we have been sealed, but rather to cling to this font of life.[110]

For in heaven, our thirst will be quenched by living water so delectable that it will gladden us like exquisite wine: "You give them to drink from the river of your delights!" (Ps 36:8). Yet if we "drink" of this Spirit here on earth, we will find abundant "rivers" of the Spirit's gifts flowing from us even now (1 Cor 12:7-11). They will abound as true "rivers of living water," however, only if we pour them out, sharing with others the gifts God has lavished on us.[111]

Spirit of Truth

Thomas himself shared with others all that the Spirit of God had spoken to his heart in study and prayer: "We speak not in words taught by human wisdom but by the Spirit" (1 Cor 2:13). As a member of Dominic's community of preachers, Thomas had discovered the act of preaching as a sweet sword which the Spirit uses to pierce our hearts. But he also had found that only preaching filled with the Holy Spirit's anointing can touch others' hearts in this way (cf. Mt 10:20).[112] Anyone whose preaching or teaching has fallen on deaf ears knows the truth which Thomas learned: we truly hear the Word not with the ears of our body, but with those of our heart, ears which no preacher or teacher, regardless of how eloquent, can open. Only the Spirit of God can touch the heart of the preacher as well as the hearts of those who hear the preacher's word.[113]

Thomas wanted to move people's hearts in his preaching, teaching, and writing. He longed to speak and write of God's depths as the scriptural authors did, with a tongue that flowed "like the pen of a skillful scribe" (Ps 45:1). But through his study of Scripture, Thomas saw that the prophets had preached[114] and the scriptural authors had written with power only by the Spirit's sweet instinct and inspiration.[115] He learned that he himself could speak and write a life-giving word only through the Spirit's anointing in his mind and heart, for the Spirit alone "searches the depths of God" (1 Cor 2:10) and guides us into all truth (John 16:13). Only the Spirit of God could unveil to Thomas those depths of God's heart which he longed to share with others. This is why he turned to the Spirit of love to inspire him in all that he preached and wrote. From his own deep friendship with Reginald, Thomas had discovered that only our love draws us to reveal our heart to our friend. Even more, he found in the Holy Spirit the person of love who unveiled to him the heart of God.[116] In this Spirit, the person of love, Thomas encountered the wellspring of every truth we know or speak. This is why he assures us that only the Holy Spirit inspires truth in us,[117] teaching and forming us into the Truth whose Spirit he is.[118] Most intimately of all, the Spirit gives us the light to understand and speak the wonderful truth about God.[119] For this Spirit of the Son who is truth itself teaches us through love what our minds alone could never know.[120]

The Holy Spirit, Our Interior Preacher and Teacher

The First Letter of John tells us, "The anointing you received from God abides in you; you have no need for any one to teach you. God's anointing teaches you everything" (1 John 2:27). We know by experience that teachers and preachers can say words that our ears hear, but only the Holy Spirit can truly teach us interiorly, enlightening our mind and opening our heart to receive what we hear.[121] As a preacher and teacher, Thomas learned that the Holy Spirit speaks to us with two voices. One voice is the preached word of Scripture which we hear with our ears, and everyone, even sinners and unbelievers, can hear this "external" voice of the Spirit. But the Spirit also speaks interiorly to our hearts, and only believers and holy ones hear this voice.[122]

Every preacher in this way learns that only God can convert hearts. The Lord uses preachers' words to invite us to God, but it is not their words but rather God's voice in our heart that draws us to believe.[123] Thomas knew from his experience as a preacher that unless we hear this "inner voice" of the Spirit in our heart, we cannot truly hear the words anyone else speaks to us.[124] Their words will move us only if the Spirit within us opens our heart.

Thomas saw that even the words of Jesus touched others only by the Spirit's anointing in his heart and in theirs: even when he preached, the Holy Spirit had to give understanding to the minds and hearts of those who listened, or they could not have believed and surrendered to what they heard.[125] This is why Jesus himself assures us, "The words I speak are *spirit* and life" (John 6:63).

If the Holy Spirit does not teach us, therefore, our attempts to hear and learn are in vain. Thomas compares our being without the Spirit's anointing to a person who is not well. Sickness makes us lose our sense of taste; when we are ill, good food does not taste good to us. In the same way, Thomas tells us, without the Holy Spirit, we lose our taste for God's sweetness, and we long simply for passing goods that can never satisfy our soul's hunger.[126]

Only the Holy Spirit, therefore, can lead us to Christ. Paul himself assures us, "No one can say Jesus is Lord except in the Holy Spirit" (1 Cor 12:3). Yet, as Thomas knew, we proclaim Jesus as Lord not only with our mouth but also with our heart and actions. The Spirit alone enables us not only to confess Jesus as Lord with our words and to revere him as Lord in our heart, but also to obey him as Lord in our actions. Thomas adds that not all who *say* words, even beautiful words like, "Jesus is Lord" say these things "in the Holy Spirit." He was convinced that no one speaks any truth unless through the Holy Spirit's influence. Even Caiaphas (John 11:49-52) spoke about Jesus only because he was moved by the Holy Spirit to speak. But his words were not "in" the Holy Spirit, that is, *anointed by* the Holy Spirit.[127]

Only the Spirit of God, therefore, can open the secrets of God's heart to us.[128] Just as the Son unveils the Father, the Spirit unveils the Son to us.[129] Whenever our preaching is fruitful, we know that the hidden source of its power is the Spirit's outpouring by the risen Lord: "He ascended above the heavens and filled everything" (Eph 4:8). As risen Lord, Christ fills the whole earth by sending the Spirit to inflame our hearts with the Spirit's own love. Thomas applies to the Holy Spirit the beautiful words of the Song of Songs: the Spirit's "flashes of love are flashes of fire, a vehement flame!" (Cant 8:6).[130]

If so many of us have received the Holy Spirit, however, why isn't the whole world on fire from our preaching? Thomas finds the answer in an image of the Spirit's fire burning like the sun's heat. The sun shines on all of us, but we can hide ourselves from its heat. And though the Holy Spirit is poured out lavishly everywhere and wants to be received by all of us, we can "hide" from the Spirit of God. Preachers and hearers alike, we can close ourselves to the Holy Spirit's anointing in our lives.[131] Yet the Spirit of God will *not* be conquered even by our resistance. The words of Psalm 22 come to mind for Thomas: "My heart is like wax, melted within my breast" (Ps 22:14). We know how easy it is for us to close ourselves even to our dear ones when they open their hearts to us. But Thomas pictures the Scriptures as Christ's "breast" opening his heart to us, and the Spirit of love as the fire melting even our resistance with his love.[132] This Spirit melted even the stubborn heart of Paul. This is why Paul himself described the Holy Spirit as "leading" and "driving" us tenderly to God: "Whoever are led by God's Spirit are children of God" (Rom 8:14). Paul knew the tender force of the Spirit's love urging and pushing him to proclaim the good news of Jesus to others: "The love of Christ impels us!" (2 Cor 5:14).[133]

This same experience of being "driven" by the Spirit's love inspired Thomas to see in the very word "Spirit" an intimation of love's wonderful force, its "unyielding energy."[134] Thomas' friends watched in amazement as they saw the Holy Spirit's "unyielding energy" drive him to produce great works, one after another, in remarkably short periods of time. Though "always scrupulous in his recitation of the divine office and in reading and prayer," Thomas produced an incredible amount of writings for one whose life spanned only forty-eight years. Indeed, the depth and volume of his output seemed beyond mere human ability. James of Viterbo, doctor of Scripture and archbishop of Naples, testified that it did not seem possible "for a person using merely human powers to have written so many great works in so short a time."[135]

Toward the end of his life, Thomas would dictate "to three secretaries, and even occasionally to four, on different subjects at the same time." His Dominican brothers knew that such activity was impossible without a special grace.[136] The Dominican historian Tolomeo of Lucca could not contain his amazement at Thomas' accomplishments: "What an output it all was! What a marvelous abundance of work produced in a lifetime that was . . . so short!" Tolomeo adds that when Thomas preached and taught and wrote, "it seemed as if a great torrent of truth were pouring into him from God."[137]

Thomas had reflected lovingly on the mystery of the Spirit's outpouring by the crucified and risen Lord. And he had discovered as the most wonderful fruit of this outpouring the Spirit's anointing which inspires our praise and preaching of Christ throughout the world.[138] The Lord had assured him, as he assures each of us, "Ask, and you *shall* receive" (Luke 11:9). The Lord had promised Thomas, as he promises each of us, "If you who are human parents know how to give good things to your children, how much more will your Father give the *Holy Spirit* to those who ask!" (Luke 11:13). Again and again, Thomas had begged for the Spirit's outpouring in all he said and did. He wanted to proclaim Jesus, not in eloquent, empty words, but in the power and anointing of the Spirit of God. As those who love Thomas have discovered, his prayer has not been in vain. During his own lifetime as well as throughout the centuries after him, Thomas has shared with us his preaching, teaching and writing as the generous fruit of his life lived in the anointing of the Spirit of God.

Notes

[1]Alexander Murray notes that in Thomas' thirteenth century a nobleman was usually a knight and therefore a military man; war was a nobleman's "work." When a nobleman was not fighting in a war, his other pursuits were usually duels and tournaments. This is why "open or veiled references to murders by noblemen are not uncommon" in stories of their conversions (*Reason and Society in the Middle Ages* [Oxford: Clarendon, 1978] 379).

[2]In Gal 6, lect. 1.

[3]Gui, c. 3.

[4]Gui, c. 33; Foster, *Life,* 52; Tocco, c. 36; Calo, c. 19.

[5]I Can 83; Foster, *Life,* 113.

[6]I Can 58; 83.

[7]CG IV, 21, 5.

[8]In Jn 3, lect. 6.

[9]ST I, 43, 5, ad 2.

[10]In Jn 3, lect. 6.

[11]ST I, 37, 1, ad 3.

[12]ST III, 32, 1.

[13]ST III, 7, 5.

[14]In Jn 1, lect. 10.

[15]In Jn 6, lect. 8.

[16]ST III, 7, 6.
[17]ST III, 7, 5, ad 2.
[18]In Jn 3, lect. 6.
[19]In Jn 1, lect. 15.
[20]ST III, 66, 12.
[21]In Jn 3, lect. 6.
[22]ST I, 36, 1.
[23]Ibid.
[24]ST I, 37, 1, ad 2.
[25]ST I, 37, 1.
[26]CG IV, 19, 7.
[27]Ibid.
[28]ST I, 36, 2, ad 4.
[29]CG IV, 21, 3.
[30]In Jn 6, lect. 8.
[31]CG IV, 21, 4.
[32]Comp Theo I, 219; cf. ST I, 37, 1, ad 3.
[33]In Rom 5, lect. 1; CG IV, 23, 5; IV, 23, 11.
[34]In Rom 5, lect. 1.
[35]In Eph 3, lect. 5.
[36]CG IV, 21, 3.
[37]CG IV, 21, 1.
[38]CG IV, 22, 1.
[39]ST I-II, 109, 9, ad 2.
[40]ST I-II, 113, 7.
[41]CG IV, 21, 10; ST I-II, 14, 1.
[42]ST II-II, 1, 9, ad 5.
[43]In Eph 2, lect. 5.
[44]In Jn 1, lect. 14.
[45]Ibid.
[46]In Gal 1, lect. 6.
[47]ST I, 38, 2.
[48]ST I, 38, 2, ad 2.
[49]ST I, 43, 5, ad 1.
[50]ST I, 38, 2, ad 3.
[51]Ibid.
[52]ST I, 43, 3.
[53]CG IV, 23, 11.
[54]ST I, 43, 3, ad 1.
[55]ST I, 38, 2.
[56]ST II-II, 24, 3, ad 1.

[57] In Gal 3, lect. 6.

[58] ST III, 32, 1, ad 1.

[59] Ibid.

[60] ST III, 32, 1; In Eph 1, lect. 5.

[61] ST III, 23, 3.

[62] In Jn 8, lect. 7.

[63] ST II-II, 147, 5, ad 3.

[64] In 2 Cor 3, lect. 3.

[65] CG IV, 22, 5.

[66] In Gal 4, lect. 1.

[67] In Gal 5, lect. 7.

[68] In Gal 5, lect. 3.

[69] In Gal 4, lect. 4.

[70] In Jn 14, lect. 2.

[71] In 1 Cor 14, lect. 3.

[72] ST III, 26, 1, ad 3.

[73] In Rom 8, lect. 3.

[74] CG IV, 22, 3.

[75] CG IV, 22, 4.

[76] CG IV, 22, 3.

[77] Ibid.

[78] In Gal 5, lect. 3.

[79] In Jn 15, lect. 7.

[80] In 2 Cor 6, lect. 2.

[81] In Jn 14, lect. 2.

[82] ST I-II, 27, 4.

[83] In Gal 5, lect. 6.

[84] In Jn 4, lect. 2; In 1 Cor 12, lect. 3.

[85] ST I, 43, 5, ad 2.

[86] In Eph 5, lect. 7.

[87] In 1 Cor 12, lect. 3.

[88] In Eph 5, lect. 7.

[89] In Ps 45:3.

[90] Ibid.

[91] In Jn 15, lect. 7.

[92] In Ps 44:5.

[93] In Jn 4, lect. 2.

[94] In Ps 44:5.

[95] In Jn 3, lect. 1; In 2 Cor 3, lect. 2.

[96] In Jn 4, lect. 2.

[97] In Jn 7, lect. 5.

[98]In Jn 4, lect. 2.
[99]In Jn 7, lect. 5.
[100]In Jn 4, lect. 2.
[101]In 1 Cor 12, lect. 3.
[102]In Jn 4, lect. 2.
[103]Ibid.
[104]In Eph 1, lect. 5.
[105]In Eph 4, lect. 7.
[106]ST I-II, 114, 3, ad 3.
[107]In Eph 1, lect. 5.
[108]In Gal 4, lect. 3.
[109]In 2 Cor 5, lect. 2.
[110]In Eph 4, lect. 10.
[111]In Jn 7, lect. 5.
[112]In Eph 6, lect. 5.
[113]In Ps 41:5.
[114]In Ps, Preface.
[115]In Ps 44:1.
[116]In Jn 14, lect. 3.
[117]In 1 Cor 2, lect. 3.
[118]In Jn 15, lect. 7.
[119]Cf. ST I-II, 109, 1, ad 1.
[120]In 1 Th 4:1.
[121]In 1 Cor 2, lect. 3.
[122]In Jn 3, lect. 2.
[123]In Rom 8, lect. 6.
[124]Cf. In Ps 49:4.
[125]In Jn 14, lect. 6.
[126]Ibid.
[127]In 1 Cor 12, lect. 1.
[128]CG IV, 21, 5; In Jn 14, lect. 3.
[129]ST I, 43, 7, ad 6.
[130]In Ps 18:4.
[131]Ibid.
[132]In Ps 21:11.
[133]CG IV, 19, 11.
[134]In Gal 6, lect. 1.
[135]I Can 83; Foster, *Life,* 113-14.
[136]Gui, c. 32; Foster, *Life,* 51.
[137]HE 23:15; Foster, *Life,* 138.
[138]In Ps 21:18.

5

Praying Always

Those who knew Thomas could see for themselves the great paradox of his life. Though his days were hectic—he was always preaching, teaching, writing, traveling, responding to some urgent request for scholarly help—his whole life was nevertheless one continual prayer. Even the most pressing responsibilities could not draw him away from living in God's intimate company, for Thomas' prayer had become the wellspring from which he shared with others the Spirit's anointing in his mind and heart.

Prayer as Desire

Paul himself considered prayer as so central to our lives that he urged his community to "pray always" (1 Thess 5:17). Far from finding Paul's command to be an impossible ideal, Thomas discovered that "praying always" is as natural and easy to us as breathing. Prayer is simply desire, and desiring is what we human beings do best. Whether we are conscious of it or not, we live and grow only because we are always wanting something else, desiring something more. We learn to walk, to talk, to love because we want something. Indeed, we cannot live without desiring —desiring to breathe, to love, to be loved. Every choice we make is an implicit or explicit desire.

Prayer is simply directing the natural impulse of our desires to the God who wants to and can satisfy our every desire for good. "Take delight in the Lord and he will grant you your heart's desire," the psalmist tells us (Ps 37:4). Thomas adds, "In prayer we simply express our desires to God. When I desire something, I ask for it by praying. We pray, therefore, simply by asking suitable things from God."[1] Prayer is our simplest, surest way to the God who is our heart's joy,[2] since we pray simply by turning our mind and heart to God.[3] The Trinity in this way has made it easy and natural for us to pray—just as we breathe—not simply at certain times or at special places, but always and everywhere. "Our desire has the power of prayer, since all that we do results from our desires. And since our good actions flow from our good desires, we are always praying in whatever good we do."[4] Indeed, this is why "our every work ought to begin with prayer."[5]

Thomas knew that the Father delights in all that the Holy Spirit desires. Far from being an annoyance, our requests in fact delight our Abba, because the Spirit of love inspires us to want only what pleases the Father. In asking the Father for blessings like peace and joy and love, therefore, we are simply making explicit the desires that the Holy Spirit has placed in our heart through love (Rom 5:5).[6]

The Father's Nearness

When Thomas situates the heart of prayer in desire, his whole point is that prayer is as easy, natural, and necessary for our life as breathing. But he knows, too, that prayer is desire we direct to the God who is near and dear to us. Prayer in this way is both our desire for and our confidence in the God who is utterly close to our hearts. Thomas develops this insight in a work he wrote as a *Compendium* or handbook of theology for his dear friend and *socius,* Brother Reginald, and his own closeness to Reginald surely forms the context for his tenderness in speaking about prayer. Thomas writes that the Holy Spirit makes us ask for good things in prayer by drawing us to want what is good. Indeed, with the Holy Spirit leading us and goading our heart, we cannot help desiring the truest blessings. Moreover, we pray by directing our heart's desires to the God who is utterly near to us. Why, then, do we find it so hard to pray? Thomas finds the answer in our suspicion that God is far from us and does not care for us personally. "And yet," he tells us, "the Apostle Paul taught the contrary in his sermon to the Athenians, when he said that God is 'not far from every one of us: for in God we live and move and have our being' " (Acts 17:27-28). Indeed, not even the most insignificant occurrences in our life fall outside of God's providence; the Lord himself assures us, "The very hairs of your head are numbered" (Matt 10:30).[7]

"Let us then banish all fear and timidity from our hearts," Thomas urges us; "let us place all of our trust under the covert of God's wings!" (cf. Ps 36:7). For "God is near to all people by a special care for them, but God is *exceptionally* near to those who strive to draw close in faith and love. Indeed, God not only draws near to them but even *dwells* in them through grace." This is why the Lord encourages us, "Fear not; *you* are more important than many sparrows" (Matt 10:32).[8]

Thomas was convinced that the God who lives in us so intimately also wants to be addressed in the most intimate terms possible. Paul reminds us that "the Spirit within us cries out, 'Abba, Father' " (Gal 4:6). It is this intimate name, "Abba," "Daddy," which Jesus has given to us as a share in his own closeness to his Father. The Spirit of love thus fills our heart with the close familiarity which the Father longs to have with us as our "Abba": "since God is our Father, we ought to have a sweet and loving affection for God."[9]

When Thomas reflects on the meaning of prayer in our life, therefore, he turns most of all to the prayer Jesus himself gave us, the "Our Father." We can learn all that we need to know about prayer simply by saying the "Our Father" with faith and confidence, since Jesus himself taught it to us and with his Father hears us when we pray it. Thomas was struck by Augustine's insight: said with love, this one prayer has the power to gain our forgiveness and healing. St. Cyprian had described the "Our Father" as a "friendly, familiar, and devout prayer to ask of the Lord in his own words." "*No one* goes away from this prayer without fruit," Thomas adds.[10] Jesus gave us this prayer not to keep us from using other words, but to inspire in us its sentiments, regardless of the words we use.[11]

As we pray, "Father in *heaven,*" we may be tempted to think that "heaven" means a place far removed and distant from us. No, Thomas assures us; when Jesus tells us to pray to our Father in heaven, he means, as Augustine himself knew, the heaven within us, the heaven of our own hearts where the Holy Spirit makes us holy. To pray to our Father in heaven, therefore, is to direct our prayer not to some distant place where God dwells, but to the depths of our being where God is closer to us than we are to ourselves. By praying in this way to our Father in heaven, our hope and "confidence in praying are increased by God's *nearness.*"[12]

In the sermon on the "Our Father" which he preached to the townspeople of Naples during the last Lent of his life, Thomas speaks again of these same themes. "Some have said that because of God's great distance from us God does not care for us. On the contrary, however, God is nearer to us than we are to ourselves, giving us confidence when we pray." Thomas recalls the Lord's words, "When you pray, enter into your chamber." For Thomas, that chamber is the intimacy of our own heart. Thus, the words, "Father in heaven," far from signifying God's distance from us, instead show how familiar our conversation with God ought to be.[13]

Thomas knew that the "loving affection for our Father" which the Holy Spirit inspires in us is inseparable from the tenderness we need to have "for all who are in trouble." To know God as our gentle Abba is to discover everyone else, especially the most needy of all, as the brothers and sisters to whom we are also bound. Significantly, Thomas—whose own father undoubtedly had been far removed from his life[14]—thinks of his own heart's affection for his family. "We are wont to direct our thoughts to where we have a father," Thomas writes. But our mother's and father's home is also the home of our brothers and sisters. And in thinking of our dear Abba in heaven, we cannot help thinking also of our brothers and sisters whom we love: "Where your treasure is, there also is your heart" (Matt 6:21). We cannot separate the God intimately near to us from the brothers and sisters God has given us as our treasure.[15]

To pray to our Father "in heaven," therefore, means not only loving and honoring God in our own heart, but also in the hearts of others. The words "Who art in heaven" refer to the God who hears us and who is utterly near to us. But God's "heaven," is also those in whom God dwells. In the words of Psalm 19:1, "The heavens show forth the glory of God," Thomas sees the truth that we ourselves are God's "heavens," since God truly dwells in us through faith (Eph 3:17) and love (1 John 4:16).[16]

Thomas also found that we need to pray not simply with words but also with our whole heart's attention. When we truly pray, our lives are changed by our prayer: "What we say with our lips,

let our heart fulfill." Thomas reflects on the power of our request that "God's name may be hallowed." "This name is *wonderful* because it *works wonders* in *us,* " and it is lovable because
"there is no other name under heaven given to us, whereby we
can be saved" (Acts 4:12). When we pray, "Hallowed be thy
name," therefore, we beg God to change us, to convert our hearts,
so that "God's name will be glorified and made known in *us.* "[17]

Chrysostom's words especially touched Thomas: "To offer God
worthy prayer means that we ask for nothing before the Father's
glory; everything else comes after the Father's praise."[18] Because
love inspires us to cling to God by putting God first in our life,
our very first petition is, "Hallowed be thy name!"[19] For love
makes us ready to serve our *friend;* and just as we safeguard and
deepen our friendships by "friendly deeds," so, too, Thomas tells
us, "our charity both causes our devotion and nourishes it as
well."[20] Our very prayer in this way draws us to give ourselves
completely to God.[21] As Thomas reflects on the psalmist's intense
longing to "see" the face of God, he urges us to note how the
psalmist prays not simply with his mouth but also with his whole
heart's attention: "I have cried out with my *whole heart!*" (Ps
119:145). We, too, need to pray with our whole heart's attention,
to "yoke" ourselves to our gentle and loving God, the source of
our wholeness and peace.[22]

Sometimes our prayer can become so intense that, with the
psalmist, we actually "cry out" our heart's desire with our voice.
This kind of prayer is wonderfully pleasing to God, Thomas tells
us. Voicing our prayer strengthens our inner intention and gives
us a sense of freedom in our communion with God. And when
we cry out with our whole heart we are always heard,[23] since Christ
himself prays for us and in us, his members (cf. John 11:42).[24]

The Prayer of Petition as Intimacy

We may be tempted to view the prayer of petition as a "lowly"
form of prayer, one far removed from the truly intimate prayer
of the mystics. Yet, Thomas stresses, even if we do not realize
this at first, our prayer of petition can be a deep form of *intimacy* with the triune God. Thomas thinks of the great difference
between entreating each other and asking a favor of God. When
we beg a kindness of one another, our request *"presupposes* a
certain intimacy" or we would not ask. "But when we pray to

God, our very prayer *makes* us intimate with God.'' In our prayer of petition, we speak with God in spiritual affection, adoring God in spirit and truth. In addition, the familiar affection we experience in prayer inspires us to pray again with even greater confidence.[25]

Thomas thinks, too, of how, in requests of one another, persistence can become irritating: our constant asking for a favor can become a nagging that annoys our friend. But the opposite is true of God: God loves our "nagging." In our prayer of petition, therefore, "perseverance and the repetition of our request are not at all unseemly." Indeed, as Jesus himself tells us, "we ought always to pray and never lose heart" (Luke 18:1), precisely because our very persistence forms us in deeper confidence and intimacy with God.[26] And although we cannot know by ourselves what we ought to pray for, the Spirit helps us in our weakness (Rom 8:26) by inspiring us to desire what God longs to give us.[27]

For Thomas, then, petition—asking things of God—is not the prayer of one far away from God, but the prayer of an intimate friend of God. Because we trust God implicitly as our closest friend, we have the confidence of a dear friend in asking God for what we need. And Thomas views God's granting of our petition as an act of God's intimate friendship with *us*. He recalls the saying of Sallust, the Roman historian: "It is characteristic of friends to will the same thing" (Catiline, 20). Since we want only the good of our loved ones, Thomas assures us, at the very heart of friendship is our wanting to fulfill our friend's desires. This is infinitely more true of the divine persons who are our dearest friends. Thus it is not only "appropriate" to God's providence to fulfill our desires when we present them through prayer. Indeed, because we *are* God's friends, "God *wants* our desires to be satisfied!"[28] This is why, more than anything else, we should ask for intimate, loving union with the triune God.[29]

Thomas himself poured out his heart's desires to God in prayer, and because the Spirit of love inspired his prayer, he seemed always to get what he prayed for. Indeed, as Thomas' death was drawing near, he confided to his close friend, Reginald, who was weeping, "My son, do not be sad. God has given me *everything* I have asked." He went on to tell Reginald that he had prayed especially for three things during his life: first, that his body, mind, and heart would remain virginal and free for God; second, that he would stay a humble and poor friar and never be raised to any high dignity in the Church. Finally, Thomas confessed, "I have prayed to know what has become of the soul of my brother Rinaldo who suffered so cruel a death in defense of the Church. And all three prayers my God has answered and assured me of this in prayer."[30]

In prayer, Thomas discovered how powerful and desirous the triune God is to help us not only in our important needs but in our small wants as well. We have a delightful story, for example, about a difficulty Thomas once had with a troublesome tooth. He awoke one day to find that one of his teeth had grown in such a way as to impede his speech. Since he was scheduled to conduct a public disputation the next day, and the tooth's protrusion prevented him from speaking clearly, he asked Reginald what to do! Reginald told him that his only recourse was to get excused from the disputation, and have the tooth extracted.

But Thomas was afraid his absence would be misinterpreted as a reluctance to defend his own teachings. He told Reginald that he preferred to put himself in *God's* hands. He went to the church and "prayed long and earnestly. Suddenly, the tooth came away in his hand easily and painlessly, and he could speak as well as ever."[31] Tocco adds the charming detail that for a long time Thomas actually carried this tooth with him "as a reminder of God's goodness to him."[32]

On another occasion, his dear friend, Reginald, was suffering from a recurring fever. Thomas "showed his sympathy and gently recommended patience." But someone suggested to Thomas that St. Agnes was a special friend of his, and that she might gain Reginald's healing. Thomas, himself a virgin, had a special devotion to this young saint, and always carried a relic of hers around his neck. He placed her relic on Reginald's chest as he prayed, and Reginald was cured.[33]

On still another occasion, during the Christmas season, Thomas was visiting his friend, Cardinal Richard, at his castle in Molara near Rome. Two wealthy, influential and learned Jewish men also used to stay at the castle every year during the feast. The cardinal asked Thomas to talk with them. Thomas did so, and promised to continue to speak with them the next day. But "in the meantime, he gave himself to prayer on their behalf, begging him who was born for us to come to these visitors on his birthday." Through the power of Thomas' intercession, both men "were clothed with the Lord Christ in baptism the very next morning."[34]

Thomas thus found by experience that we stake our prayer of petition on trust in God's infinitely loving care for us as dearest friends. Even in our weakness and sin, even in our mistakes, God's love can turn everything to our good. And God *wants* to grant our heart's desires which we confidently express in prayer. Thus, while sometimes seeming to refuse what we ask for, the triune God can grant us something far deeper, our heart's truest desires.[35]

We pray, therefore, not to change God's mind, but to ask for what God already intends to fulfill in answer to our heart's desire. Thomas recalls the words of St. Gregory the Great, "By asking, we receive what God from all eternity has desired to give us" (Dial 1.8).[36] We pray, not to remind God of our needs or desires, but so that we ourselves will be reminded of our need for God and turn confidently to God in every situation.[37] In this context, Thomas again thinks of the immense difference between our requesting favors of one another and entreating God. When we ask other people for something, we usually want to change their minds to want what we want. But when we request something of God, we beg that we ourselves might be changed and become receptive to the gifts God wants to give us.[38]

Thomas loved John Damascene's insight that in praying, we simply turn our minds and hearts to God by confidently asking God to grant our heart's desires.[39] But since trust in God is so necessary in this kind of prayer, Jesus himself gave us a prayer that "mightily raises up our hope to God." "We are taught by *God* what we ought to request from God. For God would not urge us to pray unless God were determined to hear us."[40] God uses the prayer of petition, therefore, as the wonderful means of deepening our trust, since we hope only for what we also desire,[41] and God alone inspires us to want what is good. How, then, Thomas asks us, can the triune God not answer the request the Spirit inspires within us?[42]

By his own experience Thomas discovered that one of the greatest effects of our prayer of petition is deepening trust and confidence in the triune God. Indeed, God "bestows many things on us out of the divine largesse, even without our asking for them."[43] God fulfills both the secret, unspoken desires of our heart and the desires we express in words. When we pray wordlessly, with our heart's longing, God hears and answers us even before we ask.[44] Yet for our own good, God often wishes to give us certain things only when we ask for them, so that we will grow in confidence in God, and "recognize *God* as the source of our good."[45]

Yet our trust in the triune God can come only from God's closeness to us. "We must hope in God," Thomas tells us, simply because "we *belong* to God." We are called to have unbounded confidence in God, a trust and hope that will never be disappointed.[46] And since prayer is simply speaking our heart's desires to God,[47] we pray, not so that God's will might be bent to ours, but rather so that our very asking might deepen our confidence in the God who loves us so much. For it is in reflecting on the triune God's incomprehensible love for us that our trust in God most grows.[48]

Our confidence, too, is based not only on God's desire to help us, but most of all on God's infinite *power* to help us and to change any circumstance, even the most hopeless, into good. "When we give up hope, the reason is usually the powerlessness of the one we expected to help us. Our hope's confidence, therefore, is not wholly grounded on the mere willingness to help, but also on real *power* to help us."[49] But God alone has that power which can triumph even in situations which push us to despair. Thomas' commentary on Ephesians rings out with the depth of his trust in God's power even to change people who seem beyond all hope. "We should never give up hope for anyone as long as he or she lives." Even if we despair of those about whom we are worried, we may never despair of God's power to heal them. "People may be despaired of as far as they themselves, in their own helplessness, are concerned. But we must never lose our confidence in *God.*"[50]

Thomas finds in the story of the Lord's raising of Lazarus from the dead a compelling image of the triune God's power to triumph in even the most hopeless of situations. Lazarus' death and burial are a symbol of sin's power to enslave us, and "people rightly despaired of Lazarus, for he had no power to bring himself back to life. But no trust should be lost in the God who raised him up," Thomas assures us. So, too, "those who out of malice are sunk in their many sins can be despaired of from the point of view of their own strength. But we should never despair when it is a question of *God's* power!"[51]

If God's power can conquer in even the most hopelessly sinful persons, how much more can we trust God in our own sufferings. "Regardless of how much we are afflicted, we must always hope in God and trust in God's help. For nothing is as serious as being in 'hell.' And if Christ delivered those in *hell,* how much more will God deliver his *friends* from all their troubles." What infinite confidence, therefore, "the *friends* of God should have that God will rescue them in *all* their troubles."[52] But does God's desire to help us apply also to our sickness and physical ailments? Do not our trials and illnesses prove that God is far away from us, not treating us as dearest friends? For Thomas, the answer is obvious. "Our sufferings are *not* signs that we are not God's friends." On the contrary, Jesus' own dear friend, Lazarus, became sick. But Lazarus' friends had so much confidence in Jesus that they did not even ask Jesus to heal him; they simply told him, "The one you love is sick." In their great confidence, they show us that all we need to do with a close friend is present our need. The sisters of Lazarus so intimately trusted Jesus that they did not even tell him themselves of their brother's sickness. They simply sent word to him. They knew that Jesus, their beloved friend, wills the good of his loved ones as if it were his own good.[53]

Thomas could write these insights with such assurance because from his own experience he had learned how we ourselves protect our dear ones from evil with the same and even greater force than we protect ourselves. This is infinitely more true of the Lord, our beloved friend, who fiercely "guards those who love him" (Ps 145:20),[54] *especially* when we are poor in mind and body, in heart or spirit. Indeed, God's special care is for the poor, and we are, all of us, poor. "The Lord hears the desire of the poor," Thomas assures us, even before they are able to pray: "Before they call I will hear" (Isa 65:24).[55]

Yet what if we persistently beg God for a favor and God seems to be deaf to our prayer? Thomas was convinced that the triune God's loving care for us never fails, regardless of appearances. "We should not be surprised if at times God does not grant the petition even of those he especially loves. For God will provide something even more helpful for them." Thomas drew confidence from Paul's experience. Paul continually begged to be delivered from the "sting of the flesh" that caused him such suffering. But God did not grant his constant petition. In order to understand why, Thomas turns to Romans 8:26: "We do not know how to pray as we ought." He also recalls Augustine's words in his Letter to Paulinus and Therasia: "The Lord is so good; he often re-

fuses to give us what we are asking, only so that we may be given
something else that we desire even more." Precisely in not granting Paul's *request,* therefore, the all-good God granted instead
Paul's deepest *desire,* his longing for a humble spirit, for wholehearted dependence on the Lord (2 Cor 12:7-9).[56]

Our heart's deepest petitions are those Jesus himself has given
us in the "Our Father." When we pray, for example, that God's
kingdom may come upon us, we are begging for the grace to abandon ourselves completely to God. When we pray that God's will
may be done, we are asking for the glorious gift of our own salvation, since God's will *is* our salvation: God "wills all to be
saved" (1 Tim 2:4). Though we may not see our every petition
granted here on earth, in heaven we will find our every desire perfectly fulfilled, and far beyond all that we could have dreamed.[57]

Praying as One Community

Thomas stresses that prayer is our personal and intimate communion with God. But does this mean that our prayer is a *private* matter between us and God? No, quite the contrary, Thomas
assures us. Jesus lovingly commands us to pray, *"Our* Father,"
not "My Father." For "God's love is not reserved to us as individuals but embraces all of us together." Thomas recalls Cyprian's insight that our prayer, though very personal, is also "public," offered for all. "When we pray, we pray not for one person
alone, but for all people, since we are bound to each other as one
people."[58]

The Lord calls us not only to pray *for* but also *with* one another. Thomas' life with his Dominican community made real for
him the truth of Matthew 18:19: "If two of you agree on earth
to ask for anything, it will be done for you by my Father in
heaven." Thomas takes the Lord's promise seriously: "Our hope
rests primarily on God's aid, but we also can help one another
to gain more easily what we pray for." At the same time, he recalls
the beautiful words of Ambrose: "Many insignificant people,
when they are gathered together and are of one mind, become
powerful, and the prayers of many cannot help being heard."[59]

But does God need us to pray together for our requests to be
granted? Again, for Thomas, the answer is obvious. It is not lack
of power that impels God to grant our desires through our prayer

for each other. Rather, God's lavish goodness has created us as persons who can freely pour out our love on others. Having bound us together in a charity that makes it impossible for us to live without one another's help, the triune God loves to grant our petitions through the charity of our prayer for each other.[60] Dominic de Guzman, founder of Thomas' community, had begged his followers to speak always to God and about God with one another. His community learned in this way that speaking about God with each other becomes prayer with each other. Our prayer in turn leads to our deeper sharing of God's love with one another in word and deed, and to deeper gratitude to God for answered prayers.[61] It is not that *God* needs us to pray for one another, then, but rather that *we* need to pray for each other precisely because we need each other's love. *"Charity* requires us to pray for one another," Thomas tells us; we need prayer for and with one another as much as we need the charity that binds us to each other.[62]

This is why we pray also to the saints in heaven. The triune God does not need to help us through the saints' intercession, but *we* need to experience concretely the love that binds us to one another in the communion of saints, a communion that death itself cannot destroy. The bonds of love among us thus reach beyond death into heaven itself. Heaven is peopled with our brothers and sisters who love and support us, and our very turning to them in prayer draws down upon us their special love and help.[63]

The reality of the "communion of saints" binding us to each other shines also in our petition for forgiveness in the Lord's Prayer. This petition fixes our gaze, first of all, not on our sin but rather on God's wonderful mercy, especially as it is given to us through one another. "Even if we are sinners," Thomas assures us, "we must not give up hope, lest our despair drive us into different and greater sins." On the contrary, in the measure that we are sinners, we need always to trust God to forgive us in our sorrow and repentance. It is precisely this hope in God that is strengthened in us when we pray, "Forgive us our trespasses."[64]

Yet it is not always easy for us to add the second part of this petition, "as we forgive one another." Indeed, we can feel absolutely unable to forgive someone who has deeply hurt us. When Thomas preached about this petition to the townspeople of Naples, he showed the depth of his understanding and compassion for our human weakness. "You may think to yourself that you will pray the first petition, 'forgive us,' but not the second part

of the petition, 'as we forgive those who trespass against us.' "
And yet, Thomas gently reminds us, we cannot deceive the Lord
who gave us this prayer! "What we say with our lips, let our hearts
fulfill."[65]
But if we cannot *feel* this forgiveness, should we stop praying
the "Our Father"? No, Thomas responds. Let us pray it, even
when we are not yet able to forgive someone, even when we do
not yet *want* to forgive. "And we do not lie when we say, 'Forgive us as we forgive those who sin against us,' " since we pray
not only in our own name, but also in the name of the whole
Church. We do not pray, "Forgive me my sins as I forgive those
who have hurt me," but rather, "Forgive *us* our sins as *we* forgive those who have hurt us." And if we faithfully pray this
prayer, our hearts will be changed, and gradually we will experience the beatitude "blessed are the merciful" taking root in
our own heart. As we pray the "Our Father," then, God's own
mercy will increasingly fill us with compassion for each other's
weakness, just as we beg for God's compassion in our own weakness.[66]

Praise, Thanksgiving, Worship

The prayer of each of us is meant to encourage and build up
one another not only in our weakness but also in our joy. "In
the midst of the *assembly* I will praise You" (Ps 22:22; 109:30;
111:1). God's wonderful glory, hidden until Jesus' coming, is now
blazing in full splendor among us. If we truly believe this, Thomas
asks, how can we keep from shouting out with our life and heart
and voice the marvelous praises of God?[67]
Thomas thinks of how easily and spontaneously we rejoice in
a close friend's good fortune. We exult in our dear friends' good
qualities and accomplishments, and spontaneously praise them
when they do something kind or good. Since we are one in heart
and affection, what belongs to one of us belongs to both of us.
When our friend is praised, we are praised, and his or her blessings and joy become ours. In praising God, therefore, we are
simply rejoicing aloud in how wonderful the divine persons, our
dearest friends, are. When others praise the triune God we love,
we rejoice as if they were praising us, since the good of our friend
is our good.[68] The prayer of praise is simply letting our heart feel

this joy in seeing God, our dearest and closest friend, worshipped and praised![69]

The Holy Spirit can give us a joy in God that is sometimes quiet and full of peaceful contentment. But this joy also can erupt in our voice and gestures: we begin to exult in God by letting our inner joy well up into cries of praise.[70] Indeed, Thomas tells us, praising God with our mouth and life is a wonderful way to voice our faith aloud.[71] He recalls how the Hebrew children could not restrain their shouts of praise to God as Jesus entered his own city, Jerusalem. Indeed, their "Hosannas" welled up from the Holy Spirit's own instinct within them.[72]

As a Dominican, Thomas sang the psalms with his community every day, and he found in our praise of God together a wonderful way we also build up one another. Because our praise of God stirs others to exalt God as well, we need to let our heart's worship *voice* itself in our words and song.[73] "The praise of *our* lips helps *others* by stirring their affections toward God."[74] Thomas also hints at his own experience when he tells us that singing praise to God is a powerful weapon against temptation, a great source of joy in God that protects us against evil[75] and stirs up our affection for God.[76]

And the most wonderful music in praise of God is not the sound even of lovely instruments, Thomas assures us, but our own voice.[77] Certainly God does not need us to pray with our voice and gestures, but we need to pray in this way, since we are body-persons. "We use words in speaking to God, not to tell our thoughts to God, who already knows our hearts, but to inspire ourselves and others to worship God."[78] When our prayer makes this kind of impact on our lives, we learn the meaning of the psalmist's words, "My heart and my *flesh* rejoice in the living God" (Ps 84:2). And as others hear us exalting God, our praise stirs up not only our own devotion but theirs as well.[79]

Thomas recalls the wonderful words of Scripture, "All you peoples, *clap* your hands! Rejoice in God with *shouts* of exultation!" (Ps 47:1). God has done such wonderful things for us that we sometimes cannot help clapping our hands and shouting our praise as a sign of our heart's exultation. Our cries of praise express aloud the exultation of our heart. For when our heart's joy cannot be contained, our happiness turns into "jubilation." Thomas calls this jubilation an "ineffable joy, a joy which cannot be silenced." But it exceeds understanding and so is expressed in sounds, not words. Like Paul, who urges us to pray and sing in sounds and "tongues" not limited by our human words, Thomas urges us to praise God with our voices even and especially when our joy exceeds what human words could say. We could never adequately praise in words the wonders of God's goodness, which surpass all that our minds could comprehend, and yet we need to use our voices to sound this praise.[80]

The psalmist himself cries out, "God's praise is always in my mouth!" (Ps 34:1). Our praise becomes sterile noise, however, if our lips are saying what is not in our heart.[81] Our vocal praise needs to express the deeper praise of our heart and soul,[82] for we sing to God not only with our mouth but with our heart and mind as well.[83] This is why Thomas urges us to praise God by our life and actions as well as by our words, and to do everything for the glory of God.[84] In good and happy times, especially, we can let our joy in all the gifts God has showered on us well up into praising God with our voice![85]

As a Dominican, Thomas knew the value of words and gestures, of letting our heart's joy and tears become cries of sorrow or joy before God. The founder of his community, Dominic de Guzman, had worshipped and praised God with his body as well as with his mind and heart; he had prayed with bows and gestures, with hand outstretched, and with his body prostrate on the floor. He had prayed often, too, with loud groans, with weeping and tears for the conversion of sinners. This is why Thomas himself reminds us that we adore God in our minds and hearts, with our interior sentiments, but we also need to praise God with our words and gestures and postures.[86] We need to "worship God in *both* the internal actions of our heart and the external actions of our body."[87]

This is one reason we bless ourselves with the sign of the cross so frequently. Because we are a seal on *God's* heart—"Place me as a seal on your heart" (Cant 8:6)—we want to seal *ourselves* with the sign of the God who so loves us.[88] Paul himself urges us, "Do not sadden the Holy Spirit in whom you were signed" (Eph 4:30). Yes, Thomas adds, just as we were signed by the Spirit internally and by the cross of Jesus externally in our baptism, we ought to bless ourselves every day with this sign. In this way, we will begin to walk "in the light of God's face" (Ps 89:15). Others recognize us by our own face now. But the "face" of God is God's truth shining as a light in us, helping us to discern good, and

breaking forth as a light on our countenance.[89]
Paul also tells us, "In *all* things give thanks!" (1 Thess 5:18).[90]
The apostles "went from the presence of the council, rejoicing
that they were accounted worthy to suffer reproach for the name
of Jesus" (Acts 5:41). If we, too, bless God in every situation,
we begin to recognize that all we have comes from the triune God
and that God can turn even our afflictions into blessings (Jas
1:2).[91]

"I will bless the Lord at all times; God's praise shall be always
in my mouth" (Ps 34:1). Thomas explains that to bless another
is simply to "wish good for our *friend*." We bless our loved ones,
therefore, by asking for God's good upon them. But we can also
bless God, Thomas tells us, precisely because God first blesses
us. Our blessing of one another is a wish and prayer, but God's
blessing is effective of itself, because what God says, God does.
The triune God blesses us not just by wishing us good but also
by lavishing good on us, by making us good. And we bless God
by acknowledging God's great goodness to us; God blesses us,
and we bless God! Yet our blessing does not pour out good on
God the way God's blessing pours out good on us. Rather, our
blessing pours out on God our thanks for such great goodness
to us.[92] Thomas pictures us in the joy of heaven, singing and rejoicing, thanking God with our whole heart for all the blessings
showered upon us.[93] Even now, our life can be a taste of heaven.
We can praise the triune God's glory in all that we say and do,
and in this way make our whole life an act of worship and praise.[94]

Contemplation: Being "Free for God"

From his own experience Thomas knew the beauty of Paul's
insight, "a virgin is free for the Lord" (1 Cor 7:32, 34).[95] But
Thomas was also convinced that the Lord speaks these words to
every one of us: "Be still and know that I am God" (Ps 46:10).[96]
For though we do not all need to live a perfect life of contemplation to reach heaven, we all need to share in some way in the gift
of contemplation. Thomas thinks of Paul's beautiful words: "The
temple of God is holy, and *you* are this temple" (1 Cor 3:17).
In the temple of our soul and body each one of us is meant to
be "free for God" by contemplating God's goodness.[97] Thomas
comments that only sin can keep us from this "freedom," but

God's love can heal even our sin, and so give us "sweet leisure for God" ("vacare Deo dulciter") even in our weakness.[98]

Although we may call any kind of thinking "contemplation," Thomas found that our knowing *God* through love is the truest contemplation,[99] uniting us to the God who loves us unconditionally.[100] The contemplation to which Thomas invites us, therefore, is resting in God, thinking about God's goodness, surrendering ourselves to God's love, for contemplation is "our strongest incentive" to love the supremely lovable God.[101] And since the Spirit's own charity is the source of our prayer, even when we have no words, the Holy Spirit will pray within us (Rom 8:26).[102]

Such contemplation is not burdensome but rather wonderfully restful. It is true that the hectic pace of our day can exhaust our mind and body. But Thomas knew from his experience that this is all the more reason why we *need* to "rest" in God each day. Thomas himself found the quiet of the night especially conducive to prayer and meditation. "Night is the time of knowledge," he tells us, again from his experience, for "during the night's quiet, we can learn many things about God."[103]

When we truly pray, our whole life becomes prayer, and our prayer becomes our life. *We* become a living prayer by offering our heart's love in everything we do. "Our charity *itself* is a continual desire for God, and our charity's desire is the root of our prayer."[104] From his own experience of constant pressure and little time to accomplish all that the Spirit inspired him to do, Thomas knew that we cannot spend every moment of the day in explicit, conscious prayer. Although the desire of our heart is with God at every moment, our conscious "prayer itself cannot be continual, because we need to be busy about other works."[105]

Yet precisely because he was so busy about many works, Thomas also experienced the absolute necessity of resting in God in contemplative prayer. "Martha, Martha, you are busy and troubled about many things," we hear the Lord saying, "but only one thing is needed" (Luke 10:42). Reflecting on this passage helped Thomas to understand that even more than we need physical rest when our bodies are exhausted, we need rest for our soul's tiredness. He encourages us to "rest" from sin's turmoil, from the desires of our passions, from the world's hectic busyness. Let us give ourselves instead to the contemplative rest that makes us "taste and see that the Lord is sweet" (Ps 34:8). For it is this repose, this unending life and heavenly joy which "the saints gave up everything to possess."[106]

We do not need to wait until heaven to enjoy this contentment; we can have a deep "freedom for God" within our heart all day long. "We do need to have a certain time for rest in God"; but we can pray also at all times, as those dedicated to contemplation do, by making the sentiments of the psalmist our own: "I will bless the Lord at *all* times; God's praise shall be *ever* in my mouth" (Ps 34:1).[107]

The Sweetness of Contemplation

Thomas loved to reflect on Gregory the Great's insight that "the contemplative life is exceedingly lovable, exceedingly sweet" (Homily 14 on Ezekiel). Thomas himself discovered this sweetness in his daily prayer and study in preparation for sharing God's Word with others. He found that contemplating God is something like seeing with our eyes. Our sight itself is a precious gift. But it is even more delightful for us when we use it to see someone we love. So, too, Thomas tells us, contemplating any truth gives us joy. But contemplating God's lovely truth gives us the greatest delight of all, since love is the source and goal of our contemplation.[108] Spiritual joy is deeper than any passing pleasure, and our delight in knowing God surpasses all other joy.[109] This is why the psalmist says, "O taste and see that the Lord is sweet!" (Ps 34:8). It is love that causes us joy; and charity's love for God surpasses all other love and thus excels all other joys.[110]

Augustine tells us (De Trin 1.8) that contemplating God will be our purpose and delight in heaven. Even now, Thomas adds, heaven begins here on earth through the love that is contemplation's source and goal.[111] But in heaven our contemplation, and therefore our joy, will be *perfect,* full to overflowing, for we shall see God "face to face."[112] It is true that "contemplating God" forever might seem to be a less than exhilarating description of heaven! But anyone who has ever known the ecstasy of being reunited with his or her beloved after a long separation has experienced a small taste of what Augustine and Thomas are trying to say. To no longer have to rely on letters or phone conversations, but finally to see our beloved "face to face"—*this* is ecstasy for one who loves! And our "seeing" is not a passive use of merely our eyesight, but a total engagement of our whole person with our beloved. This kind of "seeing" is intensely sweet to us!

Thomas knew, however, that while it is easy for us to feel this sweetness in the presence of our beloved whom we can actually see, God's sweetness may often be hidden from us now. Our prayer in communion with the God we cannot see may not *feel* very sweet to us.[113] Thomas also knew that our mind cannot remain undistracted very long because of our human frailty. When we pray, therefore, and even when our mind rests in God through contemplation, all of a sudden our thoughts can become distracted.[114] Yet such distractions do not make our prayer fruitless,[115] for the Spirit can and does pray within us, even when our mind unintentionally wanders.[116]

How long should we spend in explicit prayer at any one time? Thomas thinks that our prayer should be long enough to arouse our heart's desire for God. We should stop, however, when we begin to grow weary,[117] for the depth of our prayer lies not so much in its length nor in praying for many things, but in our continual love and desire for God.[118] The time will come when we will "see" God "face to face" (1 Cor 13:12) and *then* our joy in God's sweetness will be perfect.[119]

"Wisdom's conversation has no bitterness nor her company any tediousness, but only joy and gladness!" (Wis 8:16). Thomas loved to reflect on these scriptural words, for he experienced their truth continually in his own life. We know how our own face lights up with joy when we understand something deep or beautiful for the first time. Thomas himself experienced the natural delight we all have in learning and knowing the truth, for he had found the "company of wisdom" in the contemplation so "pleasant in itself" that it entails no sorrow or burden.[120]

He found, therefore, that a wonderful effect of our contemplating God is a joy so deep that it can bring us tears. As Thomas reflected on these insights, he may have thought of experiences like his brother's safe return from captivity. We cry, he tells us, not only when we are sad, but also when we are deeply touched, as, for example, when we "recover our children or dear friends, whom we thought we had lost. And so our tears flow from our love's devotion."[121] This love surely caused Thomas' own tears very often as he celebrated the Eucharist. Indeed, this love itself causes our prayer[122] and detaches us from what is contrary to the Lord. And the more we are free of attachment to earthly things,

the more we taste "how sweet the *Lord* is" (Ps 34:8).[123] Yet how
can we *not* be filled with joy in God's sweetness? Loving God's
beauty is the very heart of the contemplative life, and the more
we spend time in contemplating God's love, the happier we become. As our contentment grows, our love becomes more intense,
in this way deepening our joy still more.[124]

Thomas increasingly tasted love's sweetness in his own life. His
Dominican brothers marveled at how he would suddenly become
rapt out of himself, as though he were no longer where his body
was. But when people would ask him what he experienced at these
times, he would only smile. Occasionally, however, he "did say
a little, to the joy of his hearers."[125] Especially toward the end
of his life, Thomas seemed continually absorbed in God, even
when he talked with others,[126] and several times the brother
sacristan at Naples saw Thomas lifted off the ground as he
prayed.[127]

Intriguing stories are told from this last period of Thomas' life,
when his absorption in God was growing more and more intense.
Once, he had been invited to a dinner in Paris by King Louis of
France. Thomas wanted to decline because of his pressing responsibilities of study and writing, but the prior of his community
made him accept the invitation. When he arrived at the dinner
he was seated in the place of honor right next to the king. In his
studies, Thomas had been trying to articulate a convincing presentation of the truth against the Manichaean heresy. As he sat at
table, a way to formulate the truth he was struggling to express
suddenly became clear to him. Spontaneously he struck the table
and cried out, "And *that* settles the Manichees!"

He then called for Reginald as though he were still in his little
room: "Reginald, get up and write!" The prior touched Thomas'
hand and reminded him that he was not in his own room but rather
at dinner with the king of France. Embarrassed, Thomas quietly
asked pardon. "I thought I was at my desk." But the king was
so moved by Thomas' contemplative spirit that he called for a
secretary to write down what Thomas wanted to dictate.[128] Today, anecdotes such as this can strike us as rather curious, yet
they express in a marked way Thomas' growing absorption in God
as he approached his death.

Another time, a cardinal legate and the archbishop of Capua,
formerly one of Thomas' students, asked to meet with Thomas.
He reluctantly left his studies, and his guests made him sit down

between them. But Thomas' mind was miles away; he spoke hardly a word. The two prominent figures sat there a long time in complete silence, waiting for Thomas to say something to them. Suddenly he cried out, *"Now* I have it!" The legate had been wondering why Thomas had been showing him no honor, and he now began to despise him. The archbishop saw the legate's annoyance and chided Thomas, who then bowed to the cardinal and asked his pardon. "Please forgive me. A beautiful idea has just come to me for the work I am laboring on now—a really wonderful idea, and it gave me such pleasure!"[129]

As Thomas approached his death at the age of forty-eight, his absentmindedness increased. Gui describes the "frequent, almost continuous, absorption" in God which made Thomas unable to look after himself. Reginald then became like a nurse to his child, caring for his needs, protecting him from accidents and even placing his food on the plate before him, "so that he should take only what he required and avoid eating absent-mindedly" what might have harmed him![130]

Thomas himself described the kinds of experiences that increasingly filled his last days. Earlier in his life, he had distinguished between rapture and ecstasy. Rapture, he had said, is the experience of using our senses in order to relate to the people and things about us, while at the same time our entire inner attention is rapt in contemplating and loving God.[131] In contrast to rapture, ecstasy cuts us off from our bodily senses and raises our mind to the vision of God: our understanding and whole attention are concentrated on God.[132] Yet later in his life, Thomas describes rapture as the experience he had earlier called ecstasy. He was touched by Paul's own description of rapture as being "caught up into paradise" (2 Cor 12:3). Yes, Thomas assures us, in the experience of rapture, we are violently carried away by the force of God's love, and the Holy Spirit lifts us to things above us, while simultaneously withdrawing us from our senses (Ezek 8:3).[133] Only love can bring us this joy, and only the most intense love can take us outside ourselves in such ecstasy.[134]

Prayer that Bears Fruit in Sharing the Word

This ecstatic love not only filled Thomas' prayer but also drew him increasingly out of himself in a love zealous to proclaim his

Lord.[135] Thomas had found that love alone is the heart of holiness, and many who lead a purely contemplative life have more charity than others who spend their lives in service of others. But he also knew that willingness to sacrifice some time for contemplation in order to bring others to the Lord shows greater love for God than if we were reluctant. To please God, true contemplatives willingly forego some cherished time in prayer in order to share God's love and Word.[136] Thomas' Dominican vocation thus convinced him that the contemplative life is inseparable from sharing the fruit of our contemplation with others. Augustine encourages us to "choose the *better* part," (Luke 10:42) by living a contemplative life in whatever way possible to us: "Let us be busy with the Word; let us occupy ourselves with saving knowledge and teaching" (Serm 104.1). Filled with the gift of his own Dominican preaching vocation, Thomas adds that we truly live the contemplative life not only when we contemplate and delight in God's truth, but also when we share with others the good news of the God who so delights our heart.[137] "Just as heat is the source for warming, the contemplative life is a source of teaching." Our ministry, therefore, is meant to dispose us for contemplation, while our contemplation is meant to impel us, for the sake of our beloved Lord, to more zealous ministry in proclaiming the Word.[138]

"The Spirit has anointed me to *preach* good news to the poor!" (Isa 61:1). From his youth, Thomas had chosen communion with Jesus in his own mission by vowing himself to Dominic's preaching community. Precisely for this reason he could never view prayer as a selfish hoarding of personal "time with God." Because it is communion with the God we love, prayer of its very nature pushes us out to the streets! We *must* share with others—who in this very sharing become our friends—the good news of the God we contemplate: "They shall pour forth the fame of your abundant goodness" (Ps 145:7). Thomas was struck by how Gregory the Great applies these beautiful words of the psalmist to anyone who truly prays (Homily 5 on Ezekiel). Moreover, he encourages us to do as he himself had done, to *"publish* the memory of God's sweetness" which we taste in prayer. In company with Jesus, Thomas urges us, let us give ourselves to prayer and study, and go forth from our contemplation to share its precious fruit with others![139]

Notes

[1] In 1 Th 5:2.

[2] In Ps 36:4.

[3] In Ps 38:8; 24:2.

[4] In 1 Th 5:2.

[5] In Ps 36:3.

[6] In Rom 8, lect. 5.

[7] Comp Theo II, 6.

[8] Ibid.

[9] Our Father.

[10] Our Father; Collins, 135.

[11] ST II-II, 83, 14, ad 3.

[12] Comp Theo II, 6.

[13] Ibid.

[14] Michel Goodich notes that Thomas' father, "one of the leading noblemen of Naples, is a veritable phantom." During the thirteenth century this phenomenon of the knight-father who is away on military campaigns seems to be "the rule rather than the exception" (*Vita Perfecta: The Ideal of Sainthood in the Thirteenth Century,* 92).

[15] Our Father.

[16] Ibid.

[17] Ibid.

[18] Comp Theo II, 8.

[19] ST II-II, 82, 2, ad 1.

[20] ST II-II, 82, 2, ad 2.

[21] ST II-II, 82, 1.

[22] In Ps 26:8.

[23] In Ps 16:2.

[24] In Ps 19:4.

[25] Comp Theo II, 2.

[26] Ibid.

[27] ST II-II, 83, 5, ad 1.

[28] CG III, 95, 5.

[29] ST II-II, 83, 1, ad 2.

[30] Gui, c. 22.

[31] Gui, c. 17; Foster, *Life,* 40.

[32] I Can 60; Foster, *Life,* 99.

[33] Gui, c. 18; Foster, *Life,* 40.

[34] Gui, c. 14; Foster, *Life,* 36.

[35] CG III, 96, 7.

[36] ST II-II, 83, 2.

[37]ST II–II, 83, 2, ad 1.
[38]Comp Theo II, 2.
[39]In Ps 24:2.
[40]Comp Theo II, 3.
[41]Comp Theo II, 7.
[42]CG III, 96, 3.
[43]ST II–II, 82, 2, ad 3.
[44]In Ps 20:2, 3; ST II–II, 83, 1, ad 1.
[45]ST II–II, 83, 2, ad 3.
[46]Comp Theo II, 4.
[47]ST II–II, 83, 1, ad 1; II–II, 83, 9, ad 2.
[48]ST II–II, 83, 9, ad 5.
[49]Comp Theo II, 6.
[50]In Eph 3, lect. 1.
[51]Ibid.
[52]Ap Creed.
[53]In Jn 11, lect. 2.
[54]Ibid.
[55]ST II–II, 83, 1, ad 1.
[56]CG III, 96, 7.
[57]Our Father.
[58]Comp Theo, II, 5; in *Compendium of Theology,* trans. Cyril Vollert, S.J. (St. Louis: B. Herder Book Co., 1947) 319–20.
[59]Ibid.
[60]ST Supp, 72, 2, ad 1.
[61]ST II–II, 83, 7, ad 3.
[62]ST II–II, 83, 7.
[63]ST Supp, 72, 2, ad 5.
[64]Our Father.
[65]Ibid.
[66]Ibid.
[67]In Ps 21:18.
[68]In Ps 33:2.
[69]Ibid.
[70]In Ps 31:11.
[71]In Ps 15:1.
[72]In Ps 8:2.
[73]In Ps 33:1.
[74]ST II–II, 91, 1.
[75]In Ps 12:5.
[76]In Ps 32:2.

[77]In Ps 32:3.

[78]ST II–II, 91, 1.

[79]Ibid.

[80]In Ps 46:1.

[81]In Ps 9:11.

[82]ST II–II, 91, 1; II–II, 91, 1, ad 2.

[83]In Ps 46:4.

[84]In Ps 9:1.

[85]In Ps 21:3.

[86]ST II–II, 84, 2, ad 2.

[87]ST II–II, 81, 7.

[88]In Ps 4:5.

[89]Ibid.

[90]In Eph 5, lect. 7.

[91]Cf. In Ps 43:1.

[92]In Ps 40:9; 20:3.

[93]In Ps 9:8.

[94]In Ps 9:2.

[95]In Ps 44:10.

[96]Sent III, 36, a 1, ad 5.

[97]In Ps 44:10.

[98]In 2 Cor 7, lect. 3.

[99]In Jn, Prologue.

[100]Com Div Nom ch. 1, lect. 1.

[101]ST II–II, 82, 3, ad 2.

[102]ST II–II, 83, 15; II–II, 83, 1, ad 2.

[103]In Ps 18:2.

[104]ST II–II, 83, 14.

[105]Ibid.

[106]Ten Com.

[107]Ibid.

[108]ST II–II, 180, 7.

[109]ST I–II, 31, 5.

[110]ST II–II, 180, 7.

[111]ST II–II, 180, 8, ad 1.

[112]ST II–II, 180, 4.

[113]In Ps 30:16.

[114]ST II–II, 83, 13, ad 2.

[115]ST II–II, 83, 13, ad 3.

[116]ST II–II, 83, 13, ad 1.

[117]ST II–II, 83, 14.

[118]ST II-II, 83, 14, ad 2.
[119]In Ps 30:16.
[120]ST I-II, 35, 5.
[121]ST II-II, 82, 4, ad 3.
[122]ST II-II, 83, 15.
[123]In Jn 1, lect. 11.
[124]ST II-II, 180, 1.
[125]Gui, c. 25; Foster, *Life,* 44.
[126]Gui, c. 14; Tocco, c. 30; Calo, c. 17.
[127]Gui, c. 23.
[128]Gui, c. 25; Foster, *Life,* 44-45.
[129]Gui, c. 25; Foster, *Life,* 45.
[130]Gui, c. 41; Foster, *Life,* 57.
[131]Truth q. 13, a 2, ad 9.
[132]Truth q. 13, a 3.
[133]ST II-II, 175, 1.
[134]Truth q. 13, a 2, ad 6.
[135]Gui, c. 15; Tocco, c. 29; Calo, c. 16.
[136]Rel St 23.
[137]ST II-II, 181, 3.
[138]Truth q. 11, a 4, ad 4.
[139]ST II-II, 184, 7, ad 3.

6

Bound Together by Charity

Thomas' experience of God made it impossible for him to interpret life's meaning in a grim way. This Italian nobleman and admirer of Aristotle learned that we were made for joy! But he also learned from his experience of prayer that we cannot help wanting enjoyment precisely because we were made to *enjoy God*.[1] Thomas found the root of this joy in the Spirit's charity, an intimate communion with God and one another that heals our aloneness and begins heaven for us here on earth. Charity gives us the presence of the Holy Spirit,[2] that Spirit of love who enables us to enjoy God and one another in God even now.[3]

The charity about which Thomas writes with such depth of insight is the same charity that shone in his own life. To those who knew him, Thomas was, above all, a "wonderfully kindhearted man, gentle in speech and generous in deed."[4] His Dominican brothers saw how he could never believe ill of anyone; if he heard of another's weakness, he "would grieve as if the sin were his own."[5] The Spirit filled Thomas with a "kindliness" that had a "wonderful effect even on his appearance," and his "sweet graciousness" spoke of the Spirit's charity within him.[6] His Dominican brothers tell us, too, of how "consoling" his presence was to them, of how "lively" and "gentle" his expression always was.[7] They saw how generous and gracious he was, how quick to help others.[8]

When, therefore, Thomas wrote toward the end of his life that wisdom spreads charity's sweet fragrance in our heart,[9] those who knew him recognized that he had painted a portrait of his own soul. It was this same charity that filled Thomas and became the

154

source for his sharing the Spirit's love with others in his preaching, teaching, and writing.

Charity: Sharing in the Holy Spirit

"The love of God has been poured into our hearts by the Holy Spirit who has been given to us" (Rom 5:5). When Thomas reflects on this beautiful passage from Paul, he thinks of how love seems to be the ultimate motive of our every action. Love is the hidden cause of everything we do, the root of all we feel. For God has loved us into life as *persons,* able to return love to God and one another through the Holy Spirit of love.[10] But at various times in our life, we experience the meaning of love in different ways; our love is not always the charity poured forth into our hearts by the Spirit.[11] Thus we know how often we can love in grasping, self-centered ways that push us to seek our own advantage and not the good of those we love.

But we also know what it is to love another just because he or she is so good, so worthy of love. At times like these we sense that our love is not only a gift to others; even more, it is a gift to us, a gift *in* us, flowing from a source deeper than ourselves. Whenever we love in a selfless way, a place deep within us knows that such love does not come merely from our own efforts. Self-giving love wells up from a source far deeper than simply our own heart; our unselfish love sings of an infinite font. When Thomas reflects on the times we love generously, therefore, he sees how our very love speaks of a boundless source, the charity given us by the Holy Spirit, the very person of love.[12] Only the Spirit, the Father and Son's intimate love in person,[13] can pour unselfish love into our hearts, urging and "driving" us to love by causing a *habit* of charity in us.[14]

The Spirit alone can give us this kind of love not only for one another, but also for God. Thomas was convinced that we have a natural inclination to love the God who gives us all that we have and are. But our natural love for God is also naturally selfish. Like self-centered children, we are inclined to love God not because of God's great goodness, but because of what we can get from God. Also, by nature, it is easier for us to love those dear to us, whom we can see, than the God of all love whom we cannot see.[15]

Yet the God who gives us everything we have and are deserves all of our heart and soul's devotion, all of our mind and strength's affection (Mark 12:30). This is why we need God's own love in our hearts, to give us a love stronger and dearer than our own, a love that will cherish God with all that we have and are, above all else that exists.[16] The Spirit's charity is that love, enabling us to love God more than anything else,[17] with a familiar affection full of ease and joy.[18]

When Thomas reflects on the Latin word for charity, *caritas,* he is struck by its root meaning of *carus,* "dear to us."[19] Charity draws us to cherish God in an intimate, familiar way, as "dear" to us. Loving with the Spirit's charity, we cherish the triune God as our heart's delight, not to gain anything from God, but simply to rest in the infinite sweetness and goodness that God is.[20] In charity we have a perfect love, holding God and others in God as precious for their own sake.[21]

The triune God lavishes this charity upon us as sheer gift and not because we are worthy of it.[22] We know by our own experience that our love inevitably inspires us to give gifts to our loved ones. But in every gift, it is really our *love* that we give. This beautiful truth of our experience illumines for Thomas how charity is the Spirit's own intimate likeness in us (Rom 5:5).[23] Through charity, he tells us, we share in the very person of love who is the Holy Spirit.[24] But charity's love not only shows us in a special way the Spirit's own personal richness; it also *causes* love for God to flame up in us.[25] The Spirit lives intimately in us through charity[26] in order to make us lovers of God.[27]

Charity's Ease and Joy

Thomas knew that we were made to be happy, and that love alone makes us truly happy.[28] But we find by experience that we are not always able to give and to receive the love for which we hunger. We know how often we long to touch the hearts of those we love and open them to receive our love, but we cannot. We are just as helpless to open our own hearts to God and to one another. Indeed, we cannot even dispose ourselves or anyone else to receive such love. Even more, when our dear ones reject our love or we ourselves turn away from God's love, we learn how helpless we really are. But even if we are incapable of giving our-

selves this love, *God's* love is not helpless before our unwilling-
ness. God's Spirit not only pours God's own love into our heart,
Thomas tells us, but even opens our heart to want this love![29]
God does this in the sweetest way possible. As we have seen,
Thomas was convinced that the triune God draws us to our fulfillment by giving us natural inclinations to what we need. In the
depths of our being, God implants desires and attractions, drawing us from within our freedom to our own fulfillment; for example, we are naturally drawn to eat, to marry, to create new
life, to protect our young. This is also why we enjoy actively doing things ourselves, especially when we have developed good
habits which make our activities easy and pleasant.[30] In this way,
Thomas comments, God orders all things sweetly (Wis 8:1).[31]

But these natural inclinations can only hint at how tenderly and
freely the Spirit's charity draws us to love God. Thomas knew
that if we were to love God not through our own free inclination
but from the Spirit's power acting outside us, we would be only
passive instruments in the hands of another. Charity's generous
love would be foreign to our deepest inclinations, and it would
not be a gift we would feel inclined to want, nor a gift that would
give us any joy.[32] To love in a truly free way, then, *we* need to
be the source of our own loving; we need to give our love of our
own accord, and to do so with ease and pleasure. Yet our own
power cannot cause us to love God above all else, because we are
naturally inclined to love far more those we can see than the God
we cannot see.[33]

Thus the Spirit is given us to be the intimate source of love
within us. As Giver of Life, the Spirit draws us freely to love God
and one another by creating the habit of charity in our hearts.[34]
On the other hand, through this very habit, the Spirit is poured
into our hearts, making our intimate love for God not only possible but also easy and utterly delightful.[35]

The Holy Spirit opens us to this love not because some external power forces us to accept it, but because from within the very
depths of our own freedom we are given in charity itself the gift
freely to want this love.[36] Through charity, therefore, the Spirit
heals our wounds and gives us ease and joy in loving God,[37] in-
clining us from within the depths of our heart to the very goal
which will totally satisfy our heart.[38]

For Thomas, our natural inclinations and the joy they give us
in being satisfied are a small reflection of charity's sweetness,

which attracts us to God's infinite loveliness.[39] Because nothing delights us more than loving and being loved, nothing can make us happier than the Spirit's charity in our heart.[40] Indeed, charity gives us a joy so deep that we cannot help wanting its sweetness all the time.[41] "No virtue has such a strong inclination to its act as charity has, and no other virtue performs its act with such pleasure."[42]

From his own experience Thomas knew that charity gives us delight even in serving one another, and yet at the same time it makes us more and more free.[43] As a member of the nobility, Thomas had been raised not to serve others, but to be served; he saw for himself the profound difference between a slave and one who is free. Slaves serve others not from their own freedom, but because someone else forces them to serve.[44] Free persons, on the other hand, act of their own accord and inclination.[45] Yet Paul himself shows us the inseparability of being truly free and serving one another in love: "You were called to freedom; through the charity of the Holy Spirit serve one another" (Gal 5:13). Thomas discovered that we are truly free when we love, for all that we do through love, we do from our own heart's inclination. This is why a slave's mentality is utterly foreign to us when we love with the Spirit's charity.[46]

Thus the paradox of charity: it draws us to do gladly, and of our own accord, what we would never do without it: freely, joyfully serve one another. Paul even urges us to be slaves of God by serving each other in charity. Christ's own charity makes this possible, enabling us to care for one another not only willingly but also joyfully. And this is charity's second great paradox: the Spirit's love makes us servants of one another, and yet, in that very service, makes us truly free. Charity gives us delight in serving each other and inspires us to care for one another not because we are forced to, but because the Spirit's own love makes it attractive to us to do so![47]

Paul tells us that without charity we gain nothing at all (1 Cor 13:3). He knew that our "freedom" becomes a great slavery if we use it simply to lead a self-centered life. Charity thus inspires us to serve God and one another, putting others' good ahead of our own selfish interests. We stay truly free, therefore, only by generously helping one another in love and, in the joy of the Spirit's love, gladly carrying each other's burdens.[48]

Charity as Friendship

"I no longer call you *servants* but *friends*" (John 15:15). Thomas never tired of contemplating the wonder of our being made God's intimate friends. For it was in the Spirit's charity binding us to God and to one another that Thomas found the most perfect friendship. We have seen his description of friendship as mutual, self-giving love between equals who share their hearts' secrets with one another in an intimate "life together." Furthermore, Scripture itself assures us that we are called into an intimate "life together" with Jesus (1 John 1:3). Thomas was struck by how such "life together" is the heart of all close friendship. We love to share a meal with our friends, to take walks together, to speak about all that is in our hearts. For Thomas, this intimate "life together" can only hint at the close bond of love that is charity.[49] For charity is, above all, intimate *friendship* with God and one another,[50] giving us joy in God's love.[51] And Thomas found by his own experience that nothing can wrest this joy from us, for it is God's own gladness in our hearts.[52]

Thus, the divine Persons truly love us as intimate friends through charity, sharing with us the secrets of their heart, giving us their own joy in a profound friendship based on this communication. For Thomas, the wonder of this insight is especially striking in light of his stress on friendship as reciprocal love between those who are equals and who open their hearts to one another.[53] We have seen how charity bonds us intimately with God through love.[54] But it also unites us so closely to one another that there is no superiority of one of us over the others, only an equality in which God's own friendship makes us one.[55] Thomas had been struck by Aristotle's insight that "what we accomplish through the efforts of our friends we seem to do ourselves" (*Ethics* 3.3). This beautiful truth illumined for Thomas how in the union and love of charity we can even atone for our loved ones' sin and gain their healing as if it were our own.[56]

Thomas thinks, too, of how we would never be friends with our loved ones unless we believed that we can have a true and close familiarity with them. For Thomas, our experience hints at how inseparable charity is from our faith and hope in God. Through faith we believe that close friendship with God is possible to us, and through hope we long to gain this friendship.[57]

Moreover, charity perfects our hope, Thomas tells us, because our deepest hope is in our friends.[58] And our hope in God, if it is suffused with charity, is not selfishness. When we love selfishly, we hope to possess someone for ourselves; the person we "love" is simply a means to our own happiness. But the opposite is true of charity. Here, hope leads us to charity's *friendship-love* in which we seek not our own interests but rather our beloved's good.[59]

Yet though Thomas shows how our charity is inseparable from even faith and hope, he knows that charity unites us more intimately to God than faith does. He contrasts the depth of union we have with God through love to the lesser union we have only through knowing God. We are united with what we *know* only through ideas,[60] and what we know exists in us through these concepts.[61] But in loving someone, we are taken outside the narrow limits of our own self and united to the very reality of the one we love.[62] This is why we are more closely united to God when we love God than when we simply know God,[63] and why charity is greater even than faith.[64] For though we cannot love the God we do not know,[65] our simply knowing God does not of itself join us to God. Our loving God through the Spirit's charity, therefore, not only heals our sin but intimately unites us to God.[66]

"Those joined to the Lord are one spirit with him" (1 Cor 6:17). In these words, Thomas finds the very heart of the Spirit's charity: a union with God in the most intimate affection.[67] Thomas knew that such love for God comes not from us, but from God's own love drawing our heart.[68] And as our union with God deepens, our desire for God and our delight in God grow deeper and deeper.[69] With charity filling our heart, we love to love; loving becomes itself the very good of charity, making us more eager to love even than to be loved.[70] In the beautiful words from John, "What is mine is yours" (John 17:10), Thomas found the "reward" of such intimate friendship with God not only in heaven but also here on earth. We know from our own experience how love is its own recompense. Because we cannot help enjoying someone we truly love, the reward we enjoy in loving another is not an extrinsic addition to our love but the very joy of our loving. The "reward" of love is love itself. Thomas tells us, therefore, that our "merit" or reward in loving God is enjoying God![71]

In this understanding of love's "merit," Thomas contemplates God's infinite love for us as "equals" and dear friends. We have no claim to any of God's gifts, not even to our very life, and yet charity makes us God's intimate friends.[72] Furthermore, since friends share everything in common, what belongs to the triune God in a wonderful way becomes ours. Without this love at the heart of all we do, even our most heroic actions give us no claim to receive anything from God.[73] Our joy is greater in heaven, therefore, not in the measure that we have done more arduous deeds, but in the measure that greater love has filled our hearts in all we have done. Thus the reward of our love is enjoying forever the God we love.[74] Thomas in this way considers charity as our pledge even now of heaven's joy-filled "life together."[75] For through charity we live in the intimate communion of the Holy Spirit as a foretaste of our eternal gladness.[76] And because we share even now in the friendship-love that is the heart of heaven, charity is both our goal and our way to that goal.[77]

Charity thus makes us true friends of one another even now so that we consider others as part of ourselves, and want for them the same good we want for ourselves.[78] For Thomas, however, only the Spirit of love can give us this kind of loving unity, joining us intimately to those we love. Furthermore, the Spirit's charity joins us not only to our loved ones, but also to the Church throughout the whole world: "One body, one Spirit" (Eph 4:4), "the pledge of our everlasting inheritance" (Eph 1:14).[79] Thomas assures us that the universal Church speaks the languages of all nations because the Holy Spirit pours charity into our hearts, giving us all, regardless of our nation or race, the one language of *love.*[80]

Charity Giving Life to All the Virtues

Thomas knew the truth of Paul's words, "Without charity, I gain nothing at all" (1 Cor 13:3), for he had discovered from his own experience that charity is our very life.[81] In charity Thomas found the "form," the lifeblood of every other virtue, living at their heart, infusing them with life, and directing them all to the one goal of loving God and other people in God.[82] Indeed, charity is the exceedingly fruitful "mother" who conceives all the other virtues in us. When we love with the Spirit's charity, our love gives birth to a host of other virtues—patience, courage, kindness, gentleness, honor, faithfulness, as well as many other beautiful habits.[83] On the other hand, our supposed virtues are only pretenses if they are not filled with the Spirit's charity. So, for example, our faith is real only when it is filled with our heart's love; we truly *believe* God only when we *love* the God we believe.[84]

Thomas saw how every other virtue, even faith and hope, by their very nature entail a certain distance from God. By faith, for example, we believe the God we do not *yet* see, and by hope we strain through our desire toward the God we do not *yet* completely possess. But the Spirit's charity unites us to God, so that the God we love lives intimately within us: "Those who dwell in charity, dwell in God, and God in them" (1 John 4:16). Of all the virtues, then, charity is the greatest, for it alone unites us to God.[85]

This is why charity alone infuses its life into all of our other virtues, and in this way permeates our entire life. Thomas was continually drawn to the depth of insight in Paul's cry, "God's charity is *poured* into our hearts" (Rom 5:5)! The words "poured out" struck Thomas with special force. He thought of how rain gushing from the heavens literally can flood and inundate the earth with its torrents. This is how God's charity is poured out into our heart; it is meant to flood our every action and thought,[86] to permeate and inundate every other virtue as its very heart and root: "*Charity* is patient and kind," Paul assures us (1 Cor 13:4). The Spirit's charity, therefore, is the content of the Christian life and it alone joins us intimately to God; every other virtue simply leads us to her.[87]

Thomas thought, too, of how our body lives only when our life-breath flows within us. Without this breath, our body is only a corpse. But the Spirit's charity is more powerful still; for just as our body lives only by our soul's breath, *we* truly live only through charity.[88] The Spirit's charity is meant to flow in us as the root of all we do, conceiving all the other virtues in us and turning them all to love.[89] Charity's love surpasses even mercy because it unites us to God as the very source of all mercy. For we imitate God's actions by our mercy toward one another, Thomas tells us, but charity makes not only our external actions but even our inmost heart like God's.[90] This is why it is not the "*quantity* of our offering" but the loving affection of our heart that draws God's mercy upon our loved ones.[91]

Love for Ourselves and for Those Dear to Us

Thomas had experienced how our love for God draws us to love one another in God.[92] But his experience convinced him, too, of an even more profound truth: when we love with the Spirit's charity, the love we have for God is the very same love we have for one another.[93] Charity inspires us to love God because God is so wonderful, and *because* of God, we love all others in God. On the other hand, in some profound way, through charity we truly love God in everyone we love. Thomas knew that we certainly can love our dear ones for their own sake and not for God's sake. In this case, however, our love for them is not *charity's* love.

But if we love our dear ones with the Spirit's charity, all the other wonderful reasons we have for loving them become permeated with this one great life-breath of the Holy Spirit, and we love them most of all because of their closeness to God or so that they might become close to God.[94] And since charity for one another is a created sharing in God's own love for us,[95] Thomas urges us to love most in our dear ones what is of God in them, so that they may grow closer and closer to God.[96]

Yet the Spirit's charity is meant to permeate not only our love for one another, but also and especially our love for ourselves. Indeed, we are meant to love ourselves with the very same love that the triune God has for us. In a profound way, Thomas himself experienced the truth that we can and must be our own closest friend by loving ourselves with the Spirit's own charity. Only this charity is *true* self-love, enabling us to love in ourselves what already belongs to God and to love ourselves so that we may belong even more completely to God. Even our love for others must not take precedence over this true self-love, Thomas tells us, because we can love others only in the measure that we truly love ourselves. Our friendship with others simply extends to others the love we have for ourselves.[97]

In some deep way, the Spirit's charity inspires us to love ourselves more than even those dearest to us. It would be no charity at all, for example, if we sinned in order to help a dear one to draw closer to God.[98] This is why Thomas was convinced that our charity for ourselves inspires us to preserve the wonderful gift of our life and to fight against all that would destroy it. Taking our own life, for example, would devastate the very charity we are meant to have for ourselves, whom we should love, with God's own love, even more than those dearest to us.[99] Thomas' profound sense of our interdependence made him see how taking our own life would gravely wound our loved ones as well. As members of one body, he tells us, we belong not to ourselves but to each other, and all that we do affects one another. Thus, the Spirit's own charity obliges us to love and care tenderly for one another.[100]

Thomas knew that the Spirit's charity inspires us also to love ourselves in our very bodiliness; our charity for ourselves, he tells us, means that we are obliged to love our own body,[101] for even the angels love us in the humanness of our bodies.[102] Thomas himself was not known for ascetical practices common to so many of the saints, practices in which they beat or tortured their bodies in order to bring them into subjection to their love for God. Thomas' profound sense of the Spirit's charity shows us why he did not feel called to "hate his body." It is not ascetical practices, he tells us, but love alone that truly unites us to the triune God, the giver of all good. This charity obliges us to love and care not only for our body, but also for our possessions. Thomas was convinced that it is not wrong to love and care for what we have, but only wrong to be attached to our possessions so that we grow less close to God.[103] He knew that real charity inspires us not to hatred, even of our own body, but to love and care— for ourselves, for others, and for all that we have in God.[104]

Indeed, God gives us all good things, but especially the joys of love and friendship, so that we will be drawn all the more to heaven's joy.[105] The tenderness of Thomas' heart shines in his reflections on how charity itself draws us to love some people more deeply than others. He found by experience that not only are we permitted to love some people more than others; the Spirit's charity *obliges* us to do so! It is true that we wish God's good for all the people we love, but we do not love everyone with the same depth of affection. From his own experience Thomas knew that the intensity of our love is greater for those to whom we are united more deeply. We love some people more than others not only because we wish a greater good for them, but also because we want their good with more intense affection.[106]

For Thomas, this greater closeness we feel to some people rather than others is appropriate in God's loving plan, for the Spirit's charity simply deepens the natural inclinations God has placed in us.[107] Thomas thinks of how fire heats most intensely what is nearest to it. Our love is like this fire; we cannot help loving most tenderly and generously those who are nearest and dearest to us.[108] Our affection for our dear ones is more intense than for others who are not so close to us, simply because we have many more reasons for loving them.[109] Yet, charity inspires us to love most of all not simply those who are closest to *us* but also to our beloved God.[110] For though we love our dear ones for many reasons, our deepest reason should be that they belong to God.[111] If we love those close to us with the Spirit's charity, we love them most deeply because they are God's dear ones, and not simply because they are our friends and relatives![112] In this wonderful way, all of our relationships, especially with those dearest to us, are enfolded by the Holy Spirit's charity.[113]

Even the divine Persons show special tenderness for those close to them. The triune God does not love those who are already good, as we do. But the Trinity's love for us *makes* us good, and shines with special intensity in those whom God has showered with the most wonderful goodness.[114] Thomas recalls a lovely story Cassiadorus tells about young storks caring for their beloved parents. When their parents have lost their feathers because of old age and can no longer find food for themselves, young storks make their parents comfortable with their own feathers. They, who themselves once received their parents' tender care, now go out and bring back food for their parents' "worn-out bodies." By this affectionate care, the young ones gratefully repay their parents for all of their love and care.[115]

In this story Thomas finds a hint of how charity itself obliges us to love God above all, and to love ourselves and others in God; but "we ought to love and help *most* those who are related to us and who are closest to us."[116] Thomas himself was so trusted by his family that his brother-in-law made him the executor of his will and asked that, after his death, Thomas make sure that any injustices he might have done would be made right.[117] Thomas gladly accepted this charge for the sake of the love he bore his sister and brother-in-law—who, we surmise from the account, had transacted some less than honest business dealings.

Thomas could be so kind toward his family in matters like these precisely because he had learned that our heart's charity must shine outwardly in this "sweet" graciousness in deed toward others, especially toward those dear to us. Above all, Thomas urges us, let us be kind and truthful to our loved ones, and allow the Spirit's charity to shine in our integrity, simplicity, and honesty with each other. If we live in this charity, we never have to tell lies or pretend with each other, since we can freely show in our lives and actions the loving truth in our hearts.[118] This is why Thomas himself was not embarrassed or reticent to seek out help for his family when they were in need. Indeed, the time came when his relatives were in serious financial difficulties because of changing their allegiance from the emperor to the pope. Thomas—who himself had renounced even the wealth of the ecclesiastical honors Pope Clement IV had tried to bestow on him—went so far as to gain the Pope's permission to help out his relatives with church funds.[119]

Thomas knew from experience how some bonds of friendship based on family relationships take precedence over and are more lasting than other bonds. We ourselves know that other friendships can die as our common interests fade away, but our friendships with relatives more often endure. It is true, Thomas points out, that our friendships with people not related to us can be stronger for other reasons, but we cannot help having a deeper attachment to our own relatives and even fellow citizens than to those unrelated to us or from another country.[120]

Indeeed, Thomas comments, though hatred is always an immense evil, we sin more greatly in hating those who love us than in hating those who have chosen to be our enemies. It is not necessarily more meritorious for us to love our enemy than our friend. One who is closer to God deserves greater love from us, and surely our friend who loves us is better than the enemy who hates us![121]

Love for Those Who Hate Us

As all those who surrender themselves to God's love discover, Thomas found that when we truly love God, we begin to love everyone who belongs to God. We love our dear ones for their own sake, because their very good draws our heart to them. But we love others for the sake of our dear ones, and because they belong to the ones we love. From his own experience of family love, Thomas knew that in loving those who belong to our beloved, we are in some way loving our beloved in them. It is probable that Thomas helped to right his brother-in-law's wrongs not so much for his brother-in-law's sake as for his beloved sister's sake. This tender, common experience hints at how we are meant by the Spirit's charity to love *all* people of the world in God and for God's sake, because they belong to God. In loving them, we are truly loving our beloved God in them.[122] Thomas shows his strong family ties when he spontaneously alludes to all the people of the world as our beloved God's "entire family, relatives and friends!"[123] Thomas knew what it was to love some members of his large, extended Italian family not because he was close to them or naturally drawn to them but simply because they belonged to the ones he *was* close to. His experience made him see how the Spirit's charity draws us to love not only our dear God, but all the people of the world, simply because they are "relatives" of our beloved God! With the one same love of charity, our arms embrace God and one another, since the charity we have for God is the very same charity we have for one another.[124]

This is charity's way: because it shares in the Spirit's limitless love, it cannot help reaching to the very ends of the earth.[125] It is true that charity opens our heart most directly to God, but in this very charity we begin to love even our enemies for our beloved God's sake, and simply because they are "related to," indeed, *belong* to our dear God. When we love our friends, "for their sake we love all who belong to them, even if they hurt or hate us."[126] And since charity is the most perfect friendship with God, we begin to extend our love to everyone who belongs to God, even to our enemies, to those who hate us and have wronged us.[127] The Spirit's charity thus inspires us to love the triune God with all of our heart and our dear ones in God, but it also opens us to love *all* people in our beloved God, simply because they belong to God.[128]

Thomas found that it is not only our love for God that opens our heart to all people of the world. Our love for our dear ones also inspires us to be generous and good even to our enemies.[129] We begin to love even those who hate us, and to hate only their sin, as we keep hoping and praying that we will gain their love and be reconciled with them.[130] The more we grow in true love for God, therefore, the more we begin to love everyone without exception.[131]

The Spirit's charity can grow so intense that it fills us not only with the same depth of love but also with the same depth of felt affection for our enemies as for our dearest friends. Thomas knew

that we love those dear to us for many reasons besides our love
for God, even though charity's love includes all these reasons.[132]
But while we have many reasons to love our friends, nothing but
the Spirit's own charity can fill us with love for our enemies! We
can love those who hate us only as a direct overflow of our intense love for God.[133]

Thomas thought of how a lovely fire burning in the fireplace
warms all that is near it. The fire, however, warms most what
is closest to it. Our charity is like this fire. We cannot help feeling far more intense affection for our loved ones than for our
enemies. But Thomas also pictures the powerful furnace which
proves itself to be all the stronger in radiating its heat to what
is distant from it. The stronger and deeper our love for God, the
more our love and affections extend to what is furthest from us
and even from God, to our enemy, to those who dislike and even
hate us. Though we naturally feel a deeper affection in loving our
dear ones, in fact, our love for those not dear to us shows a
stronger, more intense charity.[134]

The same charity that inspires us to love God above all else thus
inspires us also to love our enemies for God's sake. God's own
love in our heart outweighs any reason we might have for hating
another person, even one who has deeply hurt us.[135] "We find
it difficult, even impossible to love our enemies precisely as our
enemies," Thomas tells us. "But if we love them for God's sake,
God's own love makes *easy* for us what seems impossible in itself."[136] The more we love God, therefore, the more willingly we
love our enemies.[137] Just as the divine Persons love all that belongs to them, the Spirit's love inspires us to love in others, even
our enemies, what is of God.[138]

We can begin to love even our enemies with tender affection
precisely because they are God's dear ones, precisely because they
belong to God. But the ability to do so can come only from God's
special love for us, from God's counsel of perfection in us.[139]
When, for God's sake, we show our enemies the same "special
affection and deeds of love which we give to those close to us,"
this is a special gift of God and, indeed, "perfect charity."[140]

Growing in Charity

"This is my commandment, that you love one another, even
as *I* have loved you" (John 15:12). As Thomas reflects on this

profound text from John, he sees how it is love alone, not ascetical practices or even any other virtue, which flowers as the very
heart of our spiritual life. As John tells us, "We know that we
have passed from death to life, because we love our brothers and
sisters" (1 John 3:14).[141] John assures us, too, that if we live in
charity, we dwell in God, and God dwells in us (1 John 4:16).
Yes, Thomas exclaims, if we truly love God and one another, we
are living a perfect life.[142] For we practice other virtues only some
of the time; when we are asleep, for example, we do not need
to be patient. But "the love of God is *never* idle," since our whole
purpose in loving is to give ourselves completely to God.[143] Thomas views all the other virtues as simply a means to the end of
our living in perfect charity;[144] since love alone unites us to God,
"our Christian life in its perfection consists radically in *charity*."[145]

This is why Paul begs us to make greater and greater progress
in charity, indeed, to devote our entire lives to charity (1 Cor
14:1),[146] since the more we grow in charity, the more God dwells
in and among us.[147] Thomas was especially touched by Paul's insights about charity in his Letter to the Philippians. In commenting on this beautiful epistle, Thomas notes how Paul tells us that
he longs for us with the affection of Christ Jesus. Even more,
Paul wants us to love Christ and to live in his heart, to let his
love abound in us and become our very life. Since God alone can
deepen our charity, Thomas adds, let us seek and pray for this
gift from God. Let us beg for the gift of a continual deepening
of charity in our life.[148] For there is no limit to the heights and
depths to which our charity can grow, since it shares in the unbounded love who is the Holy Spirit.[149] And as our charity
deepens, our capacity to love will become greater and greater (2
Cor 6:11-13),[150] until our life becomes one great act of love.[151]

Thomas chose to make his own life of preaching, teaching, and
writing not a project of self-aggrandisement but an act of selfless
love. In particular, Martin Grabmann[152] calls attention to Thomas'
great charity in answering quickly, and in the midst of many other
pressing responsibilities, the (sometimes impertinent!) requests for
scholarly help which he regularly received. Those who know from
their own experience the burden of demanding responsibilities and
a corresponding schedule in which they need to guard jealously
every precious minute will recognize in the following excerpts from
Thomas' letters the immense charity of his heart: "To my dearest
brother in Christ, Gerard Bisuntinus . . . I, Brother Thomas

Aquinas of the same Order, send my greetings in fraternal charity. I have received your letters containing some articles, to which you ask me to reply. And although I have been busy with many things, nevertheless, lest I should fail the request of your charity, I took care to answer you as soon as the opportunity permitted . . . For this work, if it pleases you, remember me in your prayers."[153]

On another occasion, the Dominican Lector at Venice, knowing Thomas' reputation for charity, had written to him with thirty-six questions to which he demanded an *immediate* reply! Thomas' gracious charity shines in his response: "Having read your letters, I found in them a great number of articles which your charity requested me to answer within four days. And, although I have been very busy, I have set aside for a time the things that I should do and have decided to answer individually the questions which you proposed, so as not to be lacking to the request of your charity. . . . May your charity endure, and for this work, please remember me in your prayers."[154]

In his response to Marguerite of Constantinople (Countess of Flanders and daughter of Louis IX of France), who had asked for Thomas' advice on how to rule justly the Jews in her land, Thomas manifests both his charity and his humility. After graciously acknowledging the "devout love" and generosity which Marguerite has shown for the brothers of his Order,[155] Thomas writes: "It has been difficult for me to answer the articles which you requested in your letter, both because of the labors which the duty of lecturing requires, and because I would be pleased if you would seek the advice of others more learned in these affairs."[156]

On still another occasion, a nobleman asked Thomas for some answers to his questions about games of chance. In the midst of his pressing responsibilities Thomas wrote that he willingly interrupted his labors even during the major vacation because "it is not proper that the requests, which charity faithfully offers, be refused by a friend."[157] In letters like these Thomas shines as the living illustration of what he taught about charity.

Thomas once wrote that as charity takes hold of us, it is so strong a habit in our heart that it dies only with extreme difficulty. In this consoling insight, he develops a truth of immense hopefulness for us. He knew that we can weaken or even destroy our friendships by hurting our friends or failing to communicate with them. But the Spirit's charity is the deepest possible friendship with the triune God. Though we *can* destroy our bond of charity through mortal sin, charity itself makes us not easily inclined to sin.[158] Even our faults and venial sins cannot lessen our charity, since the all-powerful God is its cause. Thomas comments that when we sin venially, we are not rejecting the triune God as our one goal, but only choosing a disordered means to God; and because charity is love for God, not a means to God, even our weaknesses cannot of themselves lessen our charity.[159]

Our venial sins, therefore, are not more powerful than the Spirit's charity in us. Indeed, charity itself lessens the hold of venial sin on us.[160] When we are attached to worldly things, our charity is weak, and so we are less easily and quickly healed of our venial sins. But when we give ourselves completely to God, even though we cannot help sinning venially sometimes, our charity itself quickly heals our sins and we immediately repent of them.[161] Our best help against sin, therefore, is to enter into our heart and there to let ourselves be loved more and more deeply by the triune God.[162] In the meantime, we await and long for heaven, where we will love God perfectly, and our every thought and affection will be turned explicitly to God. We will always be enjoying God, seeing God's loveliness everywhere, loving God with our whole heart, and loving everyone and everything in God.[163]

Even now, we can grow more and more deeply in this charity;[164] we can love more and more each day, consciously giving our whole heart to God, and devoting time to God and the things of God.[165] We can love the triune God with our whole heart and soul and strength, at least by our *desire,* by wanting to love everyone and everything in God, and by surrendering everything in our life to God's love.[166]

Toward Perfect Charity

"One thing I have asked of the Lord" (Ps 27:4). When Thomas reflects on this prayer of the psalmist he sees how truly our having only one great desire gives us an undivided heart. In wanting some one thing very much, we allow that desire to unify and subordinate to itself all our other desires. This is precisely what happens when we love God with all of our heart. The Spirit's charity gathers all of our powers into one strength of love and focuses all of our energy on our beloved God. Charity makes us

truly lovers—"lovers of *God.*"[167] Thomas thinks of how we daily experience the limits of other virtues; we can be too patient, for example, and endure evil that God wants us to resist. But faith, hope and love have no limit: "We can *never* love God as much as God ought to be loved, nor believe and hope in God as much as we should. Much less can there be excess in our love for God."[168]

Our experience of taking care of our health gives us a hint of how unlimited charity is meant to be in our lives. Thomas thinks of how physicians never put a "limit" on our health; they never say to us, "You are *too* healthy!" On the contrary, they want us to be as healthy as possible, and they limit only the medicine we take to gain that good health. Thomas finds in this example an analogy for understanding how every other virtue is only a means to love, and therefore has its limits. But love is not a means to our goal, the way medicine is a *means* of gaining our good health. On the contrary, love itself, just as good health itself, is our goal. Just as we can never be "too healthy" we can never love God too much![169]

St. Bernard had written that "God is the cause of our loving God; the measure of love, therefore, is to love God without measure."[170] The Spirit's charity, therefore, has no measure: we can never love God or others in God too much; indeed, "the measure of charity is this, that it has no measure."[171] Because God's unbounded wisdom is the measure of charity's love, charity transcends even the boundaries that our human reason would set to love.[172]

Furthermore, the deeper our charity grows, the more intense our zeal becomes, until the words of the psalmist become our own: "Zeal for your house *consumes* me" (Ps 69:9; John 2:17). Thomas reflects on our own experience of love: the more we love someone, the more we feel any hurt to our loved one as a wound in our own heart. Our love makes us tolerate not even the slightest affront to our beloved. Yet if this is true of our love for one another, it is infinitely more true of our love for God. Since the least degree of charity surpasses any other kind of love, no hurt equals the pain that sin causes the friends of God. The deeper our charity grows, the more sins of any kind grieve us, and we begin to feel these wounds against God's heart as if they were inflicted on us.[173] Zeal for our beloved God makes us defend God's honor as if it were our own. This is why Thomas urges us, "If we see people sinning, let us try to stop them, regardless of how dear they might be to us. And let us not fear any grief we might have to endure as a result."[174]

From his own experience Thomas knew that the Spirit's charity makes us zealous not only in loving and honoring God but also in helping one another. He saw how the Spirit's charity is expressed concretely in our communion with one another, a communion that makes us members of the same body. We profess our belief in this "communion of saints" every time we proclaim the creed. But we are meant actually to *experience* how real and deep this communion is in us and among us. Close-knit to each other in charity, we share in other's good works even now, just as in heaven we will all rejoice in each other's good.[175] And because of our communion in charity, our prayer for each other truly *helps* those we love.[176]

Indeed, because charity binds us together as one body, the good of each of us in some way belongs to all.[177] This is why our own charity can gain healing for the sins and weakness of those we love. Thomas recalls with tenderness a story in the *Lives of the Fathers*. For love of his brother, a person did penance for a sin which his brother in fact had not committed. But because of this person's great charity, his brother was healed and released from a sin which he had in fact committed.[178]

"As members of one body we belong to one another" (Rom 12:5). Thomas was convinced that we belong to one another even in what we own. God gives us all that is ours not simply for our own benefit but also for the good of one another. What *we* have belongs to our brothers and sisters as well! Thomas urges us to give to our needy brothers and sisters what is superfluous only to what we truly need, not simply what is left over after we have satisfied our every want.[179] "This commandment we have from God, that those who love God should love also their brothers and sisters" (1 John 4:21). Thomas was struck by the poignant words of the First Letter of John: "If we have the world's goods and see our brothers and sisters in need and yet close our heart against them, how does God's love abide in us? Little children, let us love not in word or speech but in deed and in truth" (1 John 3:17-18). The triune God of love commands us to love others, not just by wishing them well, but by actually doing good for them. Helping our brothers and sisters in their need is no option for us, Thomas says, but a *command* of God's love.[180]

Thomas pictures the depths of a perfect charity as the same kind of love that filled Jesus in sacrificing his life for us. If we refuse to deprive ourselves of any luxury or to be inconvenienced by others in their need, our charity is meager and shallow (1 John 3:17).[181] But the stronger our love becomes, the deeper our charity grows, and the more willingly we sacrifice all else for our beloved's sake. Jesus has loved us to the limit of death itself; Thomas urges us to ask the Spirit for this same depth of love. The more we freely sacrifice ourselves for love of our brothers and sisters, the more perfect our love becomes.[182]

Paul assures us that this charity does not come to an end (1 Cor 13:8), since it is "poured forth in our hearts by the Holy Spirit given to us" (Rom 5:5). As we have seen, Thomas finds in the words "poured out" the lavish gift of the Spirit's charity permeating our entire life and filling our every action: "Charity is patient and kind" (1 Cor 13:4). Yet the Spirit's charity not only pervades our every action but pierces through and permeates time itself, giving our every action an everlasting value. Our every thought and deed has enduring significance and remains as an act of love whose joy will be eternal.[183]

This charity inundates our whole life even now and pushes us more and more, not only to care for one another, but also to spend time with our beloved God. Thomas knew how the triune God deserves our time and love, just because God is so good. He knew also, from his experience, that if we readily excuse ourselves from the "leisure of divine contemplation" and are glad to concern ourselves with worldly matters and business, we show how meager our charity is. On the other hand, he knew that we may be so happy to spend time in prayer and study that we selfishly hold ourselves back from our brothers and sisters in need. We have the zeal of true charity, therefore, only when our delight in contemplation overflows into true charity for one another, into generously giving ourselves to our brothers and sisters.[184]

Poured into our hearts by the Spirit of love (Rom 5:5), charity's friendship makes us share with God and one another even now a foretaste of the intimate life together which is heaven.[185] In its "breadth," therefore, God's charity fills us with love even for our enemies. Since it "never falls away" (1 Cor 13:8), in its "length" the Spirit's charity endures into eternity. In its "height" it reaches to the very heavens, filling us not with weak or selfish love, but with an enduring love for God simply because God is so worthy of being loved. And in its "depths" God's charity springs not from ourselves, but from the very person of the Spirit given to our hearts (Rom 5:5).[186]

Chesterton once described Thomas' wonderful charity in these words: Thomas "unconsciously inhabited a large heart and a large head, like one inhabiting a large house, and exercised there an equally generous if rather more absent-minded hospitality."[187] This marvelous "hospitality" of Thomas' heart inspired him to pray with Paul that each one of us may comprehend even now the infinite dimensions of the Spirit's charity within us. It was this charity that permeated Thomas' own life and became the gift that he lavished on others in all that he preached, taught, and wrote.

Notes

[1] ST I-II, 23, 7.
[2] ST I-II, 70, 3.
[3] ST II-II, 23, 2.
[4] Gui, c. 33; Foster, *Life*, 51.
[5] Gui, c. 33; Foster, *Life*, 52; Tocco, c. 36; Calo, c. 19.
[6] Gui, c. 33; Foster, *Life*, 51.
[7] I Can 77; Foster, *Life*, 107.
[8] Gui, c 33.
[9] ST I-II, 70, 3, ad 4.
[10] CG IV, 21, 4.
[11] ST I-II, 62, 2, ad 3.
[12] Char a 1, ad 7.
[13] ST I, 37, 1, ad 3.
[14] Char a 1, ad 2.
[15] ST II-II, 24, 2, ad 2.
[16] Ibid.
[17] Char a 10, ad 4.
[18] ST I-II, 109, 3, ad 1.
[19] ST I-II, 26 3.
[20] ST II-II, 23, 6.
[21] ST II-II, 23, 1; II-II, 23, 1, ad 2.
[22] ST II-II, 24, 3.
[23] ST I-II, 70, 3.
[24] ST II-II, 24, 7; I-II, 24, 2.

[25]CG IV, 21, 4.

[26]ST II-II, 24, 11; I, 43, 5, ad 2.

[27]In Rom 5, lect. 1; CG IV, 23, 11.

[28]ST II-II, 23, 3, ad 2.

[29]ST II-I, 24, 3, ad 1.

[30]Char a 1.

[31]ST II-II, 23, 2.

[32]Char a 1.

[33]ST II-II, 23, 2.

[34]Char a 1, ad 2.

[35]ST II-II, 23, 2.

[36]Ibid.

[37]Char a 1; ST II-II, 23, 2.

[38]Char a 1.

[39]Char a 9.

[40]In Ps 50:6.

[41]Char a 1.

[42]ST II-II, 23, 2.

[43]In Gal 5, lect. 3.

[44]In Jn 15, lect. 2; ST II-II, 19, 4.

[45]ST I-II, 108, 1, ad 2.

[46]ST II-II, 19, 4.

[47]In Gal 5, lect. 3.

[48]Ibid.

[49]ST II-II, 25, 3.

[50]ST II-II, 23, 1.

[51]ST II-II, 28, 1.

[52]ST II-II, 26, 3.

[53]ST II-II, 23, 1.

[54]ST II-II, 27, 2.

[55]Char a 9, ad 3.

[56]CG III, 158, 7.

[57]ST I-II, 65, 5.

[58]ST II-II, 17, 8.

[59]ST I-II, 66, 6, ad 2.

[60]ST I-II, 28, 1, ad 3; I-II, 66, 6, ad 1.

[61]ST II-II, 23, 6, ad 1.

[62]ST I-II, 28, 1, ad 3; I-II, 66, 6, ad 1.

[63]ST I-II, 28, 1, ad 3; Truth q. 22, a 11.

[64]ST II-II, 23, 6, ad 1.

[65]ST II-II, 27, 4, ad 1; II-II, 27, 4, ad 2.

[66]ST II-I, 27, 4, ad 3; cf. ST III, 79, 5.
[67]Char a 1, ad 3.
[68]ST I-II, 26, 3, ad 4.
[69]Char a 2, ad 6.
[70]ST II-II, 27, 1.
[71]ST II-II, 27, 8.
[72]ST Supp, 14, 4.
[73]ST Supp, 14, 4, ad 1.
[74]ST II-II, 27, 8.
[75]ST II-II, 25, 3, ad 2.
[76]ST I-II, 65, 5; II-II, 24, 2.
[77]ST II-II, 25, 2, ad 2.
[78]Char a 2, ad 6.
[79]In Jn 6, lect. 7.
[80]In Jn 7, lect. 5.
[81]ST II-II, 23, 2, ad 2.
[82]ST II-II, 23, 8.
[83]Char a 3; ST II-II, 23, 8, ad 3.
[84]In Jn 6, lect. 6.
[85]ST I-II, 66, 6.
[86]In Rom 5, lect. 1.
[87]ST II-II, 184, 1, ad 2.
[88]ST II-II, 23, 3, ad 2.
[89]ST II-II, 23, 8, ad 2; III, 85, 2, ad 1; In 2 Cor 12, lect. 3; ST I-II, 65, 3.
[90]ST II-II, 30, 4, ad 3.
[91]ST III, 79, 5.
[92]ST II-II, 25, 1.
[93]ST II-II, 81, 4, ad 3; Char a 4.
[94]Char a 4.
[95]ST II-II, 23, 2, ad 1.
[96]ST II-II, 25, 1.
[97]Char a 7, ad 11; ST II-II, 35, 4.
[98]ST II-II, 26, 4.
[99]ST II-II, 64, 5, ad 3.
[100]ST II-II, 64, 5.
[101]Char a 7, ad 14.
[102]Truth q. 8, a 11.
[103]Char a 7, ad 14.
[104]Char a 7, ad 15.
[105]Char a 7.
[106]Char a 9, ad 10.

[107]ST II–II, 26, 7.

[108]ST II–II, 31, 3.

[109]ST II–II, 26, 8.

[110]ST II–II, 26, 7.

[111]Char a 7.

[112]ST II–II, 27, 7, ad 1.

[113]ST II–II, 26, 7; Char a 7.

[114]Comp Theo I, 143.

[115]Ten Com.

[116]Char a 9.

[117]Count Roger of Aquila, the husband of Thomas' sister Adelesia, died on August 26, 1272. He had asked that Thomas serve as executor of his estate and provide for the restitution of funds for certain goods that he had "incorrectly appropriated" (Weisheipl, *Friar,* 298–99).

[118]In 2 Cor 6, lect. 2.

[119]Gui, c. 29; see also Synan, "Aquinas and His Age," 15.

[120]ST II–II, 26, 8.

[121]ST II–II, 27, 7.

[122]Char a 4.

[123]Ibid.

[124]ST II–II, 25, 1; II–II, 81, 4, ad 3; Char a 4.

[125]Cf. ST II–II, 24, 7.

[126]ST II–II, 23, 1, ad 2.

[127]Char a 4, ad 11.

[128]Char a 8, ad 6; a 8, ad 12.

[129]Char a 8, ad 17.

[130]Char a 8, ad 6; cf. ST II–II, 83, 8.

[131]Char a 4, ad 11.

[132]Char a 8.

[133]Rel St 14.

[134]ST II–II, 27, 7.

[135]Rel St 14.

[136]Char a 8, ad 13.

[137]Rel St 14.

[138]Char a 8, ad 8.

[139]Rel St 14.

[140]Char a 8.

[141]Rel St 1.

[142]Ten Com.

[143]Char a 12, ad 9.

[144]ST II–II, 184, 1, ad 2.

[145]ST II-II, 184, 1.

[146]In 1 Th 4:1.

[147]In Eph 2, lect. 6.

[148]In Phil 1:2.

[149]ST II-II, 24, 7.

[150]ST II-II, 24, 7, ad 2; II-II, 24, 5, ad 3.

[151]Cf. ST II-II, 24, 5.

[152]Martin Grabmann, *The Interior Life of St. Thomas Aquinas: Presented from His Works and the Acts of His Canonization Process* (Milwaukee: Bruce Publishing Company, 1951).

[153]*Responsio de VI articulis ad lectorum Bisuntinus;* Grabmann, *Interior Life,* 7.

[154]*Responsio de articulis XXXVI ad lectorem Venetum;* Grabmann, *Interior Life,* 8.

[155]For many years, Marguerite was a very great benefactress of the Dominicans.

[156]*De Regimine Judaeorum;* Grabmann, *Interior Life,* 9. Weisheipl (*Friar,* 486) gives helpful information about this letter, whose proper title is "Epistola ad commitissam Flandriae." An English translation is available in "On the Government of the Jews in Aquinas," *Selected Political Writings,* trans. J. G. Dawson (Oxford: Basil Blackwell, 1948) 84-95.

[157]*De Sortibus;* Grabmann, *Interior Life,* 9.

[158]Char a 1, ad 8.

[159]ST II-II, 24, 10.

[160]ST II-II, 24, 10, ad 2.

[161]ST I-II, 89, 2, ad 3.

[162]Char a 12, ad 19.

[163]Rel St 4; ST II-II, 24, 8.

[164]Char a 10, ad 3.

[165]ST II-II, 24, 8.

[166]Rel St 5.

[167]In Ps 26:3.

[168]ST I-II, 64, 4.

[169]ST II-II, 27, 6.

[170]Ibid.

[171]Char a 2, ad 13.

[172]ST II-II, 24, 1, ad 2.

[173]In Ps 38:1.

[174]In Jn 2, lect. 2.

[175]Ap Creed.

[176]ST II-II, 83, 7.

[177]Ap Creed; ST Supp, 25, 2, ad 5.

[178]ST Supp, 13, 2.

[179]ST II-II, 32, 5, ad 2.

[180]ST II–II, 32, 5.

[181]Rel St 14.

[182]Ibid.

[183]In Rom 5, lect. 1.

[184]Cf. Char a 11, ad 6.

[185]ST II–II, 24, 2.

[186]In Eph 3, lect. 5.

[187]Chesterton, *Aquinas,* 22–23.

7

Bearers of Good News

Of its very nature God's love fills us with joy,[1] Thomas once wrote, and the Spirit's joy within us eventually *must* overflow to our lips! Having found that charity's love is the very heart of our Christian faith,[2] Thomas chose to make his preaching an act of unrestrained love. It was in Dionysius' writings that he found the words to explain why, when he was seventeen, he had made the radical decision to join Dominic's preaching community. For it is the very nature of love that "lovers belong, not to themselves, but to the beloved" (cf. 2 Cor 5:14). "God's love, therefore, causes us to go out of ourselves so that we belong no longer to ourselves but to God."[3] In perfect love we surrender to our beloved Lord "not only our exterior possessions but also, in a sense, our very selves."[4] Thomas thus found how the infinitely good God allures us: the more we know, the more we love; and the more we love, the more we have to *speak* about the God we love. The same Spirit who fills the earth, therefore, also fills us,[5] and the Spirit's love within us cannot help erupting into exultant preaching about God's goodness![6]

Those who knew Thomas spoke of how he was always "reading, writing, dictating, praying, or *preaching.*"[7] Ordinary people became so attached to him that nearly "the entire city" came to hear his sermons at Naples during the Lent before he died.[8] For he spoke with a "sweet graciousness"[9] and a "singular grace and power"[10] that expressed a heart surrendered to the Holy Spirit. When Thomas preached, it was not only his ideas but also the Spirit's love within him that touched others' hearts.

As a preacher, Thomas did not try to impress his listeners with his own erudition—"subtleties he kept for the Schools!"[11] He simply shared with others the depth and beauty of God's Word. Those who heard him preach tell of how his words were filled with a warmth that lifted their hearts and inspired them to love God more deeply. Once, at Rome during Holy Week, he preached so tenderly about the passion of Jesus that the congregation wept openly. The next day, he preached on the resurrection of Jesus with such jubilation that the people were stirred to great joy in the Lord.[12]

The Content of Our Preaching: The Spirit's Joy-Filled Wisdom

In his preaching, teaching, and writing, Thomas thus shared the joy of his faith with others. But he knew by experience the difference between preaching that mouths empty words, and preaching that feeds others with the deep things of God's heart. Very early in his life, he learned that his words would be life-giving to others only in the measure that they were filled with the depths of the Spirit's joyful wisdom.

Thomas turned instinctively to our experience of intimate friendship in order to understand more deeply the meaning of this wisdom at the heart of preaching and sharing our faith with others. He reflects on our precious experience of love: the more deeply we love another person, the more we want to "know intimately everything about our loved one, so as to penetrate our loved one's very soul." Indeed, Thomas continues, this is why the Holy Spirit, the Father's and Son's love in person, "is said to 'search all things, yes, the deep things of God' " (1 Cor 2:10).[13] As our relationship with our loved one deepens, we begin to discover that the very heart of intimate friendship is this mutual self-revelation in which we unveil our heart and soul to one another. We become intimate friends precisely by entrusting our hearts' secrets to one another. As Thomas reflected on this experience, he began to see that the Holy Spirit reveals the secrets of God's heart to us through the gift of an intimate wisdom that "makes us *friends* of God" (Wis 7:27).[14]

It was as a university student at Naples that Thomas had begun to love this wisdom at the heart of all preaching. At the imperial school of Naples, professors had openly rejected the papal ban on teaching Aristotle's philosophy. The young Thomas learned at the pagan Aristotle's feet to delight in contemplating the mysteries of the created world. Yet also from Aristotle, whom he called for the rest of his life *"the* Philosopher,"* Thomas learned that "the most slender knowledge of spiritual realities is more desirable than the most certain knowledge of lesser things."[15] What Thomas tasted of the world's beauty served to awaken him even more to the beauty of its creator. Regardless of how much our reason can know of the created world, he tells us, "it is not enough to satisfy completely our immense desire for wisdom."[16]

Thomas became convinced that since "grace does not destroy nature but perfects it," what our reason knows about creation's truth and beauty does not take us away from God, but is meant to lead us to God.[17] In admiring the wonders of God's world, therefore, we cannot help admiring the wisdom and goodness of its creator.[18] Thomas' pleasure in learning about the created world in this way opened him to the delight of feasting on God, its source. "If the goodness, beauty, and delightfulness of creatures are so alluring to our minds, how much more will the fountain of *God's* own goodness, compared with the rivulets of goodness found in creatures, draw our enkindled minds."[19] Thomas recalls the beautiful words of Psalm 36: "They shall be inebriated with the plenty of your house, and You shall make them drink of the torrent of your pleasure!" (Ps 36:8).

For Thomas, the "plenty" of God's house is the entire universe in all of its splendor. But this plenty inevitably leads us to drink of the torrent of God's own delight.[20] Aristotle himself had spoken of the "intense joy" we can experience in learning even merely plausible theories about the vast heavens.[21] How much more intense, then, Thomas assures us, is the gladness of knowing *God.*[22] Even "in the midst of tribulations we find joy in contemplating God and our future bliss;" indeed, contemplating the truth is the greatest pleasure of all.[23] Thomas turned to our own experience of sadness and joy to understand how contemplating truth, but especially God's beautiful truth, makes us happy. Even as little children we learn by experience that *any* kind of pleasure—a piece of candy, a lovely flower, a good hug—can help us feel better when we are sad.[24] Even crying helps, since "a pain hurts more if we keep it shut up. But our grief is lessened if we let it escape, so to speak, through tears." So, Thomas notes, "when we are burdened with sorrow, if we express it by tears or groans or words, our heartache is soothed."[25]

However, although any pleasure lessens our pain when we are sad, contemplating God's goodness comforts us most of all. Our learning about anything more deeply, but most especially about God, cannot help filling us with a natural "high." We realize this truth especially when we see a child's face light up as she or he begins to *understand* something. Thomas, too, discovered that contemplating truth fills us with a joy that no merely physical pleasure can give.

Refusing to seek the wealth and pleasures that his brothers valued so much, Thomas chose to pursue instead a life of enjoying God's sweet wisdom. He began to picture wisdom as a wonderful companion who joins us when we give ourselves to prayer and study. Unlike physical pleasures which after a while turn to pain, contemplating truth is delightful, extremely "pleasant in itself."[26] Thomas began to experience what so many people before and after him have found, that giving ourselves to the contemplation of God, far from making us solitary, greatly assuages loneliness. Delighting in the wonders of God's goodness, we find our mind and heart and soul filled with a contentment that dispels isolation. This is perhaps one reason why Thomas did not feel the need for daily recreation more complicated than a pleasant walk in the priory garden! He had found that contemplating the things of God brings with it no bitterness; unlike physical pleasures, "spiritual joys never exhaust or weary us," he writes,[27] for wisdom, especially, fills us with only delight and peace (Wis 8:16).[28]

Having spent his life sharing with others the wisdom he treasured through contemplation, Thomas once described the joy of his own call: "Of its very nature, contemplating truth is beautiful. We read of wisdom, 'I became a lover of her beauty' " (Wis 8:2).[29] Precisely through falling in love with wisdom, Thomas had found the joy of Jesus. Since "we are drawn by our own pleasure," he writes, "how much more strongly ought we to be drawn to Christ if we find our pleasure in truth, happiness, justice, eternal life: for Christ is all of these! If we would be drawn by him, let us be drawn through love of the *truth.* "[30] For wisdom is Jesus himself, God's "truth in person."[31] And, Thomas tells us from his own experience, "among all human pursuits, the pursuit of wisdom is more perfect, more noble, more useful, more full of joy."[32] For wisdom is the Spirit's gift to *enjoy* intimately knowing God.[33] And because wisdom is the virtue by which we put things in order[34] and see everything in the light of God's love, it flowers into a profound peace in our life.[35]

Thomas knew that the gifts of the Spirit's wisdom and eloquence are bestowed not merely on highly intelligent or educated people. He had seen how the Spirit's wisdom makes even simple, unlearned people a more compelling witness to the Holy Spirit's power than corpses rising from the dead! "There are wonderful cures of illnesses, the raising of the dead. But even more wonderfully, the Holy Spirit inspires even simple, unschooled persons, and fills them instantaneously with the deepest wisdom and the most ready eloquence."[36]

While this is true, however, Thomas also knew that the pursuit of wisdom at the heart of all preaching also demands much prayer and study in preparation for our preaching. We are told that Thomas would read from the Homilies of the Fathers to refresh his heart after intense study.[37] Indeed, he assures us, our search for this wisdom through contemplative prayer and study will be difficult, especially at first, and will demand great sacrifices. Our words about God are meant to pour out the wisdom for which we have sacrificed much, and which we have pursued through the hard times of disciplined study, writing, and faithful prayer. This wisdom is the "precious pearl" for which we sell everything (Matt 13:45-46), generously sharing it with others precisely because we have made the hard sacrifices to treasure and lovingly contemplate it in our own mind and heart.[38]

Thomas knew that the path of contemplative prayer and study is difficult for us at first, but with time it does become sweet. "Christ does not serve the *good* wine *first!* But the more we progress in Christ's teaching, the more pleasant and sweet it becomes."[39] Likewise, the more willingly we pour out our heart's wisdom, giving to others what we ourselves lovingly contemplate, the more precious and fruitful our ministry of preaching becomes.

Preaching from the Abundance of Our Contemplation

It was thus from the depth of his own experience that Thomas discovered how "very great" this ministry of bearing witness to

Christ is.[40] He found that we alone, of all creation, can herald God's love with our voice and words. Unlike other creatures, which can only give silent glory to God by their existence, we are meant to *proclaim* God's goodness, not simply by our passive existence, but also by our life and words. Jesus himself urges us, "Let *your* light so shine before others, that they may see your good works, and glorify your Father who is in heaven!" (Matt 5:16).[41] Thomas could not help thinking of how the best sources of light do not simply shine but also *give* light to others.[42] The sun itself, for example, floods other heavenly bodies with light, so that they, too, can shine and illumine still others. We are most like God, Thomas tells us, when we enlighten others so that they in turn can share their own light.[43]

But we give to others only what we ourselves have.[44] This is why, for Thomas, we truly preach not simply by saying words, but by sharing with others what is rich within us, what we treasure in our minds and hearts.[45] We know what it is to hear the preaching of empty words—words that are hollow because they come only from the preachers' mouths, not from their intimate study, prayer and experience of God. Thomas loved to emphasize that "we can testify about something only in the manner in which we have *shared* in it."[46] Indeed, when Thomas comments on Psalm 19:8 he tells us, "We can bear witness only to what we have experienced. I can *say,* for example, that 'your precepts are sweet' only because I love them and have *experienced* them."[47]

We are true preachers, therefore, only when we proclaim the God we intimately experience. This sense of the preacher as one who is *intimate* with Jesus inspired Thomas to interpret the Song of Songs as a description of Jesus' intimacy with all those who share God's Word with others. "Let us dwell together," (Cant 7:11) the lover tells the beloved in this Canticle; for Thomas, Christ is the lover, and the beloved is the one who shares God's Word with others. Christ invites the preacher to dwell *intimately* with him, to live in his company and simultaneously to "go out" with him: " 'Let us go out together' I, by inspiring you, and you, by preaching." We are never alone in our preaching: Jesus dwells intimately with us in our contemplation and hearing of the Word, and he also goes forth with us as our beloved companion, inspiring us in our preaching, and inspiring, too, those who hear the Word we preach.[48]

Thomas loved to think of how we find in John the Baptist the call held out to each of us as preachers of the Word. John was simply the *"friend* of the bridegroom,'' who wanted the bridegroom's glory and not his own. If, like the Baptist, we keep grasping Christ through knowledge and love, Thomas tells us, the more we decrease, and the more Jesus is glorified in us. We preachers of the Word are simply beloved *"friends* of the truth'' who is Jesus. As preachers, we are called to care for the "bride" entrusted to us, the Church community, not for our own advantage and glory—this would be "adultery"—but for *God's* glory.[49]

John the Baptist, friend and preacher of Jesus par excellence, once had cried out, "I am not worthy to unfasten the strap of his sandal" (John 1:27). For Thomas, John the Baptist is the symbol of every preacher who in the very act of preaching "unfastens the strap of Christ's sandal." Every preacher knows from experience how utterly unworthy, how completely inadequate he or she is to the great mission of unveiling to others the mystery of Jesus. Yet we must try to do this, Thomas tells us, by sharing with others the good news of Jesus, our beloved friend and theirs.[50]

In his maturity, when Thomas had to defend the very right of the Dominicans to exist, he broke forth into praise of our Christian mission to proclaim the good news of Jesus. "The life that comes from the fullness of contemplation, such as teaching and preaching, is more excellent than simply contemplating God,'' he writes. "Just as it is better to enlighten others than merely to shine, it is better to give the fruits of our contemplation to others than merely to contemplate."[51] As we have seen, Thomas loved to reflect on the grandeur of our call to share in Jesus' own mission of proclaiming the good news to others: "The life of preaching and teaching, in which we give to others the fruits of our contemplation, is more perfect than the life that stops at contemplation. For such a life flows from an *abundance* of contemplation, and such was the life Christ chose."[52]

Preaching is a wonderful way of pouring out on others what we lovingly contemplate: Thomas gained this key insight from his intuition into the largesse of a God who is the fullness of being itself. Each of us springs from the triune God whose very nature is to give existence to what is not.[53] And God lavishes life on us not only to make us rich and full, but to make us a source of life to others.[54] This immense goodness of God is the pattern and archetype for each of us as preachers.

Thomas had recognized in his own family the vices of nobility, including the violent greed that lays up material treasures for itself. He would have none of this kind of wealth. He chose to embrace instead the most noble virtue of his noble station, a generous heart, the wonderful largesse that lavishly gives to others from its own great abundance. He chose communion with God's own generosity in pouring out on others, not an abundance of the material goods he had renounced, but rather the riches of mind and heart which no earthly force can wrest from us. Thomas found that in giving this kind of wealth to others he could most deeply imitate God's own self-giving. And he found the truth of a wonderful paradox: in giving to others as God does, freely, lavishly, selflessly, we attain our own truest identity.[55] From his own experience Thomas discovered that our most noble way of sharing in God's goodness and of becoming "co-creators" with God is sharing God's Word with others.[56]

But Thomas stresses that we who proclaim the Word need always to be loving *hearers* of the Word. All of God's words are in some way like Jesus, *the* Word. We who preach God's Word are called, therefore, to love the Word who is Jesus with all of our soul, and to listen to and believe God's Word with love and joy (cf. John 5:38). Ours is the wonderful task of pondering the Word (Ps 119:11) as Mary did, treasuring it in our heart (Luke 2:19). The beautiful exhortation of Colossians thus speaks our own call: "Let the word of Christ dwell in you *abundantly* in all wisdom, teaching and admonishing one another" (Col 3:16). From the fullness of our heart's treasure, then, we cannot help proclaiming the good news of Jesus so that others' hearts, too, will be filled with love.

Ask and You Shall Receive

Anyone who has ever tried to share God's Word with others only to see it fall on deaf ears knows that we are *called* preachers and teachers, but we cannot truly teach others. We can only speak the word of truth exteriorly, to the ears of others. God alone can teach them *interiorly,* by speaking to their hearts. As Thomas himself knew from experience, only when the Spirit inspires our words and anoints our listeners' hearts do they truly hear the Word we proclaim.[57]

It was through a particularly difficult experience early in his teaching career that Thomas learned this profound truth. He was only thirty when he became a master in theology at Paris in 1256; the required age was thirty-five. In assuming this position, he had to face the hostility of jealous teachers. Even more, he himself felt so unprepared and inadequate to the task assigned him that he could not even decide upon a topic for his inaugural address. In his anxiety, Thomas could only beg God to inspire him. During one restless night he seems to have had a dream which calmed his fears and filled him with trust that God would bear the burden for him. Thomas woke from his dream with the inspiration to take as his inaugural text verse 13 of Psalm 104: "You water the hills from your upper rooms; the earth shall be filled with the fruit of your works."[58]

Psalm 104 pictures the skies raining down water, filling the rivers and finally spilling over to water the earth and make it rich and fruitful. The true source of the earth's plenty is not the rivers but the sky which waters them. So, too, Thomas tells us in his inaugural address, we who preach and teach are simply the overflowing "rivers" pouring out on others a wisdom that comes not from ourselves but from the heavens, the Spirit's own wisdom (1 Cor 2:13). Without this outpouring in our own heart and in the hearts of our hearers, we preachers are only dry river beds. This is why we who preach and share God's Word with others need always to be praying for the outpouring of the Spirit's "rain" upon our own parched minds and hearts, and those of our hearers. In our very helplessness, Thomas continues, we who of ourselves lack the anointing of God's wisdom must ask it again and again of God (Jas 1:5). "May Christ grant this [wisdom] to *us*"!"[59]

From his very first days as a master of theology, then, faced with a lifework which he knew exceeded his ability, Thomas did what he would not stop doing until his death. With tears he knocked and pounded at the door of God's heart, begging from God what he knew he could not produce from his own resources. He had learned from his own experience that when we begin truly to feast on the banquet of Scripture, to hear and live God's Word with "perfect knowledge," we also realize that all we give to others in our preaching "is above us."[60] The depths of our heart calls others' hearts to Christ not through any power of our own but only through the Holy Spirit, who alone gives power to the preacher's tongue.[61]

In his Commentary on the Gospel of John, written near the end of his life, Thomas found special poignancy in the story of Jesus and the woman at the well (John 4:1-42). The well from which not only the woman, but also each one of us, longs to drink is the depths of the Spirit's wisdom. Yet even though the water is plentiful, if we have no bucket with which to draw up the water, we will go away thirsty. The only "bucket" which can draw forth the richness of the Spirit's wisdom for us is our tears and prayer: "If any of you lack wisdom, ask it of God" (Jas 1:5).[62]

For his entire life as a preacher in Dominic's community, Thomas did precisely this. In joining the Dominicans, Thomas the nobleman had become brother Thomas the beggar. But after his entrance into the Dominicans, Thomas became a beggar in an even deeper sense: everything he said and wrote he literally begged from God. At night "he would rise, after a short sleep, and pray, lying prostrate on the ground." "It was in those nights of prayer," Gui continues, that Thomas "learned what he would write or dictate in the daytime."[63] We who read Thomas' writings today can be misled by their depth and brilliance into thinking that Thomas' natural genius was the source of their profundity. But Reginald of Piperno, the theologian-friar who was Thomas' intimate friend, secretary, and *socius,* knew otherwise.

Once, for example, when Thomas was at Paris and commenting on Paul's epistles, he was struggling to understand a particularly difficult passage. "Dismissing his secretaries, he fell to the ground and prayed with tears; then what he desired was given him and it all became clear."[64]

At another time, Thomas was grappling with an enigmatic text of Isaiah. Unable to explain its meaning, he gave himself to intense prayer and fasting, begging for the Spirit's light. Reginald heard him praying throughout the night, and was astounded to hear him talking with other persons, even though no one else was in Thomas' room. Suddenly, Thomas called to Reginald to come with a light and to bring the commentary on Isaiah which he had been composing. Reginald quickly wrote down all that Thomas dictated to him. But before he would leave, Reginald insisted that Thomas tell him who was speaking with him. With tears running down his face, Thomas answered, "You have seen the distress I have suffered lately because of that text which I have only now finished explaining. I could not understand it, and I begged our Lord to help me. And tonight he sent his blessed Apostles to me,

Peter and Paul, whose intercession I had also begged for. And they have spoken with me and told me all I desired to know."[65] Reginald knew that Thomas prayed constantly to receive from the Holy Spirit what he would then teach or preach to others. When Thomas would find himself struggling for the words he needed for a sermon or class or writing, he would go "to the altar and stay there a while weeping and sobbing," and only after he received from God what he would say would he return to his cell and his writing.[66] Preachers who know from experience what it is literally to weep and sob for a life-giving Word to well up from their poverty and emptiness recognize the truth in this description of Thomas the begging preacher. Thomas could be the nobleman of God, rich and lavish in pouring out the treasure of God's Word on others, only because at every moment and in every sense he had become literally Thomas the beggar.

At the end of his four years as master at Paris, Thomas had begun his great *Summa Contra Gentiles* by acknowledging his own inadequacy and his complete dependence on God. "In the name of the divine mercy, I have the confidence to embark upon the work of a wise person, even though this may surpass my powers," he had written.[67] And indeed, Thomas' lifework *did* surpass his own powers. Those who knew him recognized the true source of his brilliance. For Thomas "never set himself to study or argue a point, or lecture or write or dictate without first having recourse inwardly—but with tears—to prayer for the understanding and the words" he needed. Thomas himself assured Reginald that prayer had assisted him in the search for truth far more than his own intelligence and study.[68]

In his counsel to preachers and teachers, Thomas stresses that every one of us has a natural desire not only to know what is true, but also to know *why* it is true. If we give no satisfying reasons for the truth we speak, our hearers gain no real understanding and go away from us empty-handed.[69] But where can we find these "reasons for the truth" that will touch our hearers and lead them to God? Thomas sought them not only in his study but also in his prayer. After Thomas' death, Reginald wept as he told his Dominican brothers of the "secret" Thomas had asked him to keep while he lived: his "amazing knowledge was not an effect of human intelligence but of *prayer.*"[70]

Always, before Thomas "studied or disputed or lectured or wrote or dictated, he would pray from the heart, begging with tears to be shown the truth" about what he was studying. In every difficulty which arose he "had recourse to prayer, whereupon the matter would become wonderfully clear to him."[71] Reginald recounts how Thomas would then dictate to three and even four secretaries on different topics at the same time, "as if a great torrent of truth were pouring into him from God."[72]

Yet Thomas knew that it is not only our prayer but also our *life* that is inseparable from the words we preach. We truly preach not only what we contemplate through prayer and study, but also what we actually *live*. In a sermon Thomas himself preached on the parable of the sower and the seed, he tells us, "Preachers ought not preach to others what they themselves do not *do*.*"*[73] For he knew by experience that truly to preach is to be continually converted. If we faithfully give ourselves to our preaching task, the Word we preach will transform us. We will begin to live what we are preaching, or we will stop truly preaching. Tocco writes of Thomas himself: "What he said with his mouth he was always carrying out in his actions. He did not dare to say anything except what God had given him as a gift of actually living in his own life."[74]

The Love of Christ Impels Us

It is significant at this point to consider Thomas' insights about the contemplative-preaching call of bishops, for his reflections are relevant for all who are called to proclaim Jesus by sharing the fruits of their contemplation with others. Dominic had founded his community of preachers for a bold mission: to claim as their own the work that had been reserved only to bishops, namely, preaching the Word of God. Bishops of Dominic's time too often occupied themselves with the task of increasing their own wealth and power rather than with their apostolic vocation of "proclaiming the Good News to all the world." Dominic received the extraordinary papal permission to dedicate his mendicant community to the apostolic, and hitherto episcopal, task of "preaching Jesus Christ."

In joining Dominic's community—at first called simply "the Preaching of Jesus Christ"—Thomas was in some way sharing in the mission proper to bishops. His description of the contemplative vocation of bishops has significance for all who are called to share their faith with others. Thomas recalls the words of Gregory the Great: bishops should surpass others in the holiness of their life and in the depth of their contemplation (Pastor 2.1). But Thomas also explains the reason why this is so: bishops must contemplate not only for their own sake, but for the sake of all their people. Their contemplation must be the wellspring from which they preach and teach the people entrusted to their care.[75] By their very call, bishops bind themselves to seek the holiness which means laying down their lives for their people (cf. John 10:15).[76]

Surely from his dear friend Albert's stressful days ministering as a bishop Thomas knew the hectic pace of bishops' lives. But their activity must be dedicated to seeking not their own wealth and power but their people's good. Their busy days must flow from "their abundant love of God" and sacrificial love for their people.[77] Thomas knew that "we are often led to the busyness of exterior works more from the tedium we experience in contemplation than from desiring the fullness of God's love." On the other hand, God's own love inspires us to "lay aside for a time the delight of our contemplation" in order to bring others to the Lord.[78] This is why the Lord asks Peter first of all if he loves him, and then entrusts the care of his people to him. Thomas adds that it is a sign of far greater love if we devote ourselves to others, for our beloved friend's sake, than if we are willing to serve only our friend.[79]

It was precisely this love that inspired Thomas to give himself radically to Jesus in his own preaching mission. Although he lived with a peaceful heart, his life was nonetheless full of pressing responsibilities which the force of love impelled him to undertake. While his writings give forth the aroma of tranquility, Thomas nevertheless "lived very hard and was capable of exertions that would seem prodigious today."[80] After three years at Paris, Thomas left in 1259 and embarked on a lifelong wandering, never staying in the same city or retaining the same assignment for more than three years.

These constant changes made him a true *itinerant* preacher and teacher, as Dominic himself had been. Like other thirteenth-century preaching friars, Thomas walked across Europe, unprotected from the elements and brigands, for weeks and months at a time. In 1245 he traveled on foot most of the way from Naples to Paris; in 1248 and again in 1252, he walked from Paris to Cologne and back. In 1259–60, he walked from Paris back to Italy. In the following years, he made frequent moves from city to city, especially on assignments connected with the organization of studies for young Dominicans. In 1268–69 he made the treacherous winter journey, also by foot, from Viterbo to Paris; in 1272, he walked all the way back from Paris to Naples.[81]

Members of the nobility rode horses; mendicant friars walked, even when they had to journey hundreds of miles. These begging preachers were an easy prey for thieves. Nor was there protection for them from fierce thunder and lightning storms, storms that we know terrified Thomas himself.[82] Yet Thomas crossed Europe four times—from Italy to Paris and back—on foot. He had begun the journey a fifth time on foot, this time on his way to the Second Council of Lyons. But he was so ill that he had to be carried by horse to the Cistercian monastery at Fossanova. It was a very grave fault for a Dominican to ride a horse except in extreme necessity. When he rode from Maenza to Fossanova, therefore,[83] Thomas was a "very sick man indeed."[84] Within a short time of his being taken to Fossanova, he died.

What drove Thomas to traverse these countless miles by foot, enduring sickness, anxiety, and terror on the way? Even more, what pushed him, in his final years, to writing, teaching, preaching tasks that in the end robbed him of his health, and finally of his life? Surely, there is only one answer Thomas would offer us, the very reason Paul himself gave for enduring his trials in the preaching of the gospel: "The love of Christ impels us!" (2 Cor 5:14).

A story is told about Thomas as a child, a story which those who loved him treasured as a premonition of his call to give to others the riches of the God whom he contemplated. Once, when Thomas was still small, his mother had been getting ready to bathe him. He picked up a piece of paper from the floor, refused to give it to his mother and kept the paper clenched in his small fist during the entire time of his bath. When Theodora later retrieved the paper from the child's hands, she found the Ave Maria written on it.[85] Whether this story is true or not, we do not know. But it does point to what those close to Thomas intuitively knew: since his childhood, he had been consumed by an ache to know God with his mind, and in this very knowing, to hold God with his hands and heart. Long after his death, his biographer, Bernard Gui, found in Thomas the figure of that other Thomas, the apostle. For just as the apostle had done, Thomas himself had entered into the "'abyss of the side of Christ as one invited there, with the finger of his intellect pointing to what his hands had lovingly touched and held.''[86]

Because he had "entered into the abyss" of Christ's heart, Thomas, lover of Jesus, inevitably had become also Thomas, lover of those who belong to Jesus. Thomas learned by experience that true preaching flows only from a heart full of love, since "no other virtue has such a strong inclination to its act as charity has, and no other virtue performs its act with such great pleasure.''[87] Again and again he learned the truth which he himself taught, that the measure of charity is that it has no measure,[88] and that perfect love for God inspires us to care for our brothers' and sisters' needs,[89] even to the point of sacrificing our life for them (John 15:13). Indeed, the more intense our love for God, the more willingly we give ourselves, not only to our beloved Lord, but also to our brothers and sisters.[90]

Thus Thomas himself preached, taught, and wrote as immense acts of love not only for Jesus, but also for others. His own experience had convinced him that we care for our brothers and sisters most deeply by sharing the fruit of our contemplation as an act of the most profound friendship with them.[91] In proclaiming the wonders of God's love which we treasure in our mind and heart, Thomas tells us, we give our friends something far more than material goods which will pass away; we share with them blessings that will endure into eternity.[92] For the good news truly saves us, and if we center our whole life on it, the Word we preach and share will become the best possible gift we give to others.[93]

At the beginning of his great work, the *Summa Contra Gentiles,* Thomas used these words of Hilary to voice the radical meaning of his own call: "I owe this to God as the chief duty of my life, that my every word and sense may speak of God.''[94] This Thomas did with his whole life, and with his every breath. He had learned from his own experience "how beautiful upon the mountains are the feet of those who bring *good news* to others!'' (Isa 52:7; cf. Isa 40:9).

But Thomas also became convinced that the inner content of this preaching call is available to every one of us, in every way of life. He recalls how the Lord invited Abraham, "who was married and rich": "Walk before me and be perfect" (Gen 17:1). The "perfect" are all those who, "whether religious or secular, cleric or lay people joined in marriage," allow their minds and hearts to be "affected interiorly," so that for God's sake, their hearts cling to God.[95] Thomas saw that each one of us, regardless of our vocation or state in life, is called to this same path of holiness: "You shall love the Lord your God with *all* your heart" (Luke 10:27). Every one of us, he says, can become a saint by living our call in love, by yielding our whole heart to God's tenderness[96] and sharing it with others.

As we have seen, love like this cannot be kept pent up within us. The wonderful gift of sharing our faith with others is the triune God's call to every one of us, in every way of life. Whatever our vocation, we can find a means of sharing our faith as an act of profound friendship-love, and of becoming in our own person, as Thomas himself was, a "bearer of *good* news to others."

Notes

[1]ST II-II, 28, 1; cf. I-II, 26, 2; I-II, 26, 3.

[2]ST II-II, 184, 1.

[3]Com Div Nom 4.

[4]Rel St 10.

[5]In Ps 38:1.

[6]In Ps 34:18.

[7]I Can 6; Foster, *Life,* 83.

[8]I Can 87; Foster, *Life,* 116.

[9]Gui, c. 33; Foster, *Life,* 51.

[10]Gui, c. 29; Foster, *Life,* 47.

[11]Ibid. Though Thomas preached in Latin in university settings, he also preached to the townspeople in his native Neapolitan tongue, and his sermons, copied in the form of notes by someone else, often show us his heart in a way that his written works do not. Many sermons have been attributed to Thomas; unfortunately, however, few of his authentic sermons have been preserved. Louis J. Bataillon, who is preparing the critical Leonine edition of Thomas' sermons, gives a tentative list of those sermons in his study, "Les sermons attribués a Saint Thomas: questions d'authenticité," (in Albert Zimmerman, ed. *Thomas von Aquin: Werk und Wirkung im Licht neuerer Forschungen,* Miscellanea Mediaevalia, 19 [Berlin, New York: Walter de Gruyter, 1988] 325–41). Bataillon also indicates (p. 340) where these sermons can be found in various editions of Thomas' works, including, most recently, the study by J. B. Schneyer, *Repertorium der lateinischen Sermones des Mittelalters für die Zeit von 1150–1350* (Münster: 1969–80): "Abiciamus," (Schneyer, n. 18; the following numbers refer to the number of each sermon in Schneyer); "Attendite" (6–7); "Ave Maria" (transmitted with the *opuscules);* "Beata gens" (22–23); "Beati qui habitant" (37); "Beatus vir" (26); "Celum et terra" (17); "Ecce ego mitto" (19); "Ecce rex tuus" (14–15); "Emitte Spiri-

tum (33-34); "Exiit qui seminat" (31-32); "Germinat terra" (20-21); "Homo quidam fecit" (35-36); "Lauda et letare" (29); "Lux orta est" (9-10); "Osanna filio Dauid" (30); "Puer Iesus" (4-5); "Seraphim stabant" (27); "Veniet desideratus" (28).

[12]Foster, *Life,* 47-48.

[13]ST I-II, 28, 2.

[14]In Jn 15, lect. 3; cf. ST II-II, 45, 5; II-II, 45, 2.

[15]Thomas quotes Aristotle (*De Animalibus* II) in ST I, 1, 5, ad 1.

[16]In Jn 6, lect. 1.

[17]ST I, 1, 8, ad 2.

[18]CG II, 2, 2; II, 2, 4.

[19]CG II, 2, 4.

[20]Ibid.

[21]Aristotle, *De caelo et mundo;* CG I, 5, 5.

[22]ST I-II, 31, 3.

[23]ST I-II, 38, 4.

[24]ST I-II, 38, 1.

[25]ST I-II, 38, 2.

[26]ST I-II, 35, 5; cf. CG III, 37, 8.

[27]ST I-II, 33, 2.

[28]ST I-II, 35, 5; CG I, 2, 1.

[29]ST II-II, 180, 2, ad 3.

[30]In Jn 6, lect. 5.

[31]Ibid.

[32]CG I, 2, 1.

[33]In Eph 1, lect. 6.

[34]ST II-II, 45, 6.

[35]ST II-II, 45, 6, ad 1.

[36]CG I, 6, 1.

[37]Gui, c. 15.

[38]In Ps 44:1.

[39]In Jn 2, lect. 1.

[40]In Jn 1, lect. 4.

[41]Ibid.

[42]CG III, 21, 6.

[43]Truth q. 5, a 8.

[44]Cf. CG III, 21, 8.

[45]In Ps 36:21.

[46]In Jn 1, lect. 4.

[47]In Ps 18:7.

[48]Exiit.

[49]In Jn 3, lect. 5.

[50]In Jn 1, lect. 13.

[51]ST II–II, 188, 6.

[52]ST III, 40, 1, ad 2.

[53]ST I, 19, 2.

[54]Truth q. 9, a 2; CG III, 21, 8; III, 70, 7.

[55]CG III, 24, 9; ST I, 22, 3.

[56]Truth q. 9, a 2; CG III, 21, 8.

[57]Truth q. 11, a 1, ad 7.

[58]Gui, c. 12.

[59]Rigans Montes.

[60]Rel St 14.

[61]In Ps 41:5.

[62]In Jn 4, lect. 2.

[63]Gui, c. 15; Foster, *Life,* 37.

[64]Gui, c. 16; Foster, *Life,* 38.

[65]Gui, c. 16; Foster, *Life,* 39; cf. I Can 58; Foster, *Life,* 98.

[66]I Can 81; Foster, *Life,* 111.

[67]CG I, 2, 2.

[68]Gui, c. 15; Foster, *Life,* 37.

[69]Quaest lib q. 9, a 3.

[70]Tocco, c. 30; Foster, *Life,* 70, n. 44.

[71]Ibid.

[72]Gui, c. 32; Foster, *Life,* 51.

[73]Exiit.

[74]Tocco, c. 48.

[75]ST II–II, 184, 7, ad 3.

[76]ST II–II, 184, 5.

[77]ST II–II, 184, 7, ad 2.

[78]Rel St 23.

[79]ST II–II, 184, 7, ad 2.

[80]Foster, *Life,* 76, n. 83.

[81]Ibid.

[82]Gui, c. 35.

[83]I Can 49.

[84]Foster, *Life,* 76, n. 83.

[85]I Can 90.

[86]Gui, c. 13.

[87]ST II–II, 23, 2.

[88]Char a 2, ad 13.

[89]ST II–II, 27, 8.

[90]Rel St 14.

[91]CG III, 134, 4.
[92]Rel St 14.
[93]In Eph 1, lect. 5.
[94]CG I, 2, 2.
[95]Quaest lib, q. 6, a 3.
[96]Rel St 13.

8

Spreading God's Peace in the World

Thomas once wrote that charity flowers in the sweet fruit of a peaceful heart—a truth he had learned not from books but from his own experience. In contemplating the things of God, in reflecting constantly on the love which upheld and sustained him, Thomas gained a humble peace that set him apart from many of his contemporaries, known as arrogant seekers of wisdom.

Yet Thomas did not gain this peace through freedom from outer conflict and inner anguish. On the contrary, the tranquil spirit of his writings masks the painful circumstances under which he often taught, wrote, and preached. With Paul, he learned that no one who preaches the good news of Jesus can have an easy peace. The trials in which Paul had begged comfort from "the God of all consolation" were the same trials which Thomas himself came to know by experience: "We are fools for Christ's sake. When reviled, we bless; when persecuted we endure; when slandered, we try to conciliate" (1 Cor 4:10, 12, 13).

In the very midst of these hardships, however, Thomas found the peace which the Lord has promised us: "My peace I leave you, my own peace I give to you" (John 14:27). Augustine had described God's peace as the "tranquility of order," the contentment that fills us when everything is "right" within us (De Civ Dei 19.13). Thomas found this peace within his heart as he gave himself to study and prayer. He himself had written that wisdom puts everything in its right place, in God's tender order within us, flooding our heart with charity, joy,[1] and peace.[2] It was this peace that Thomas drank in through his study and prayer, and shared generously with others in his preaching, teaching, and writing.

Thomas' Hard-Won Peace

We can understand more fully the hard-won nature of Thomas' peace if we reflect first on the extremely troubling circumstances he faced in becoming a master of theology at Paris. The distress Thomas endured at the very beginning of his life as a Dominican preacher foreshadowed similar trials which he would undergo with serenity for the rest of his life.

The first Dominicans had come to Paris in September of 1217, scarcely a year after Dominic had founded his mendicant community dedicated to the "preaching of Jesus Christ." A year later, Jean de Barrastre, a professor of theology at Paris, handed over to the Dominicans the hospice of St. Jacques which he had built. As the Dominican community of St. Jacques became a kind of student corporation within the university, its influence began to spread with tremendous vitality. One year after its founding, there were thirty friars at St. Jacques; five short years later the Dominican community at Paris numbered one hundred and twenty, all of them masters and scholars of the university.[3]

During the next few years the community continued to flourish. But in the early 1230s the Dominican friars at Paris came upon difficult times. From 1229–31, teachers and students at the university went on strike and left Paris in protest of poor treatment. But the Dominicans did not join them. Later, when the striking professors did return to Paris, they found that the Dominicans had gained two of the twelve chairs of theology. In 1229 Roland of Cremona, one of the most distinguished professors of philosophy at the university, had joined the Dominicans. Called in as a "strike-breaker," he gained the first Dominican chair of theology. Two years later the Dominicans acquired a second chair through the secular cleric, professor John of St. Giles. John had been preaching a sermon on evangelical poverty at St. Jacques when his heart became so moved by the call to renounce everything in order to follow Jesus that in the midst of his sermon he suddenly stopped and asked to be accepted into the Dominican community.[4]

Unlike the Benedictines, who supported themselves by their own labor, the preaching friars begged for their food. But though the Dominicans lived in a radically different way from the contemplative monks familiar to the professors, students, and townspeople, they nevertheless "forced their way into public ministries with enormous dynamism.''⁵ People flocked to their sermons, sought their help in confession and on their deathbeds, and began to turn their revenues toward them. The regular clergy were hard hit; the money that used to come to their churches now went to the Dominicans. Parish priests began a war of slander against the Dominicans, accusing them of living as leeches on society by their mendicant way of life.

Yet while many people turned against the Dominicans, still others grew even more loyal to them. The Dominican convent of St. Jacques was located near the parish church of St. Benoit and the cathedral chapter of Notre Dame. The friars' preaching became so popular that they were commanded not to preach at St. Jacques when the bishop was preaching at Notre Dame. On special holy days, townspeople were forbidden to attend the Dominican services and were ordered to attend their own parish church instead. Under pain of excommunication, the Dominicans themselves were forced to announce this ruling publicly. And if people did make contributions to them on these days, the friars were commanded to turn over all that money to the Church of St. Benoit. Finally, to call even their own brothers to prayer, they could ring only one small bell not weighing more than three hundred pounds.⁶

Such was the hostility from university professors and townspeople alike that greeted Thomas when he arrived at Paris in 1252. But his arrival proved difficult for him for still other reasons. Thomas had been ordained probably in Cologne in 1251, when he was about twenty-five. A year later, the Master General had asked Albert to recommend someone to prepare as master in theology at Paris. Albert pressured the Dominican Cardinal Hugh of Saint-Cher, a former master at the University of Paris, to suggest Thomas. But Thomas was at least three years younger than the minimal age required to prepare as a master and he felt his youth and inadequacy for the task keenly. His attempts to have himself removed from the assignment fell on deaf ears. In 1252, at the age of twenty-six, Thomas was sent from Cologne to lecture at St. Jacques on Peter Lombard's *Sentences.*⁷

In the very year that Thomas came to Paris, the clergy who were university professors held a secret meeting and decided to accept into their ranks only one professor from the Franciscans and one from the Dominicans. In this way they completely eliminated the chair for non-French Dominicans—precisely the position intended for Thomas. Under these circumstances Thomas became even more reluctant to begin his studies. Nevertheless, he was commanded by his Dominican superiors to undertake his preparation as master. In sheer obedience, Thomas began his lectures on Lombard's *Sentences* in 1252, a task he would continue until 1256. But though Thomas lived constantly under this stress, Bernard Gui tells us how excited his students were with the freshness of his approach. In his creativity, depth of insight and new ordering of the material, Thomas far surpassed the other professors who simply repeated past formulas. Indeed, Gui remarks, he taught his students with a brilliance that displayed how truly "his mind was full of a *new* light from God."[8]

Thomas' four years of preparation as master in theology passed quickly. But in the winter of 1255–56, as he neared the time when he would begin his duties as master, violence again erupted against the Dominicans. In March, 1256, a month before Thomas was to give his inaugural lecture as master, another university professor, William of Saint-Amour, published a vicious attack on the Dominicans. Writing his polemic, "On the Dangers of the Last Days," on commission from the university and with the encouragement of the French episcopate, William chastised the friars for not living the command, "Those do not work should not eat" (2 Thess 3:10). People who want to live for God, he wrote, should enter a monastery, not beg. These Dominican "pseudo-apostles," whose parasitical life signaled the coming of the last days, must be forbidden to teach and preach.[9]

William's slander incited such animosity against the friars that the mere appearance of Dominicans on the street was enough to provoke a riot. People threw objects at them from their windows and shot at them with arrows. The situation became so dangerous for the Dominicans that King Louis IX ordered royal troops to guard St. Jacques day and night. Special prayers every day for the brothers' safety were mandated in the priory.[10] The Dominicans themselves sometimes fought fire with fire, and several Dominican scholars assaulted the rector of the university, a clergyman. Dominican superiors were ordered to ensure that their friars treated Church officials with respect.

In the middle of this controversy the newly elected Franciscan Pope Alexander IV demanded that the university accept Thomas as master in theology. Wishing to spare Thomas the pain of violent demonstrations and rioting at his inauguration as a master,

Alexander IV ordered the bishop of Paris to excommunicate publicly all masters who refused to accept Thomas and other new masters. Professors who prevented students from attending their lectures would also be excommunicated. The situation was extremely upsetting to Thomas. He was already disturbed by the weight of a theological assignment for which he felt himself unready, and the violence of the reaction against him compounded his anguish. We have already seen the depth of Thomas' commitment to obedience, and yet the strength of his distress pushed him to try to refuse the charge. He attempted to withdraw his candidacy by pleading his lack of learning and young age, but his Dominican superiors would not remove him.[11]

Thomas' anxiety deepened as he learned that his teaching position had been eliminated, and that he had been rejected by the other theologians from the association of teaching masters. The theology professors refused to grant Thomas the license to teach theology; his only accreditation was the teaching license the university chancellor gave him. In addition, the faculty forbade students to attend Thomas' lectures, even his inaugural lecture as master of theology.[12] For one year Thomas taught his students without any official recognition of his master's status from his colleagues. And the university professors' rejection was only one of the attacks he had to endure. His duties as a master of theology included preaching regularly at the university, and even in this task he was often assaulted. Once, for example, as he was preaching, a member of William of St. Amour's circle stood up and shouted a verse lampoon against the mendicant friars.[13]

In Thomas' reflections on the psalms, which he undertook near the end of his life, he hints at how much it had cost him to keep his peace during those days at Paris. Commenting on Psalm 50:19-20, Thomas notes that we can tolerate someone lashing out against us, if our own evil deeds and words have provoked the attack. But when someone speaks evil to us or against us without provocation, "this," Thomas writes, "is *detestable.*"[14] And, indeed, the Dominicans at Paris *had* endured detestable treatment. Matters had become so intolerable that in September–October of 1256, Thomas felt impelled to write his work, *Contra Inpugnantes* —"Against those Hostile to Religion and the Honor of God"— defending the Dominicans' very right to exist.[15]

In his other writings Thomas regularly shows regard even for those who disagree with him. This respect shines especially in words like the following: "We must love them both, those whose opinions we share and those whose opinions we reject. Both have labored in the search for truth and both have helped us in the finding of it."[16] In his *Summa Contra Gentiles,* Thomas explains the ideas of Averroes and Aristotle on our ultimate happiness, yet he shows how, in spite of the right starting point, they arrived at the wrong conclusion. Then, "with sovereign charity," one commentator notes, Thomas draws attention to "how much these illustrious minds must have suffered from such confinement."[17]

In his work defending the Dominican way of life, on the other hand, we find a very different Thomas! We feel the force of his anger over the unjust treatment of his Dominican brothers when he writes that the arguments of those who slander the Dominicans, accusing them of living as parasites on society, are simply "frivolous," "absurd," "erroneous." Indeed, these arguments are "worthless," "utterly inconsistent," "untrue," and "too foolish to need an answer"![18]

Thomas' Choice for Peace

Thomas' harsh words against those who attacked the Dominicans are all the more striking when we learn how gentle he almost always was when *he* was under attack, which often happened verbally at Paris. As master of theology, he had to conduct regular public disputations. Although every theology professor at Paris had this same duty, Thomas' disputations were different. He chose not simply to repeat past formulas as the other professors did but to approach theological and philosophical questions with his own "new," fresh insight. He used many of Aristotle's ideas, even though Church officials and many professors had condemned some of Aristotle's insights as too pagan, too inimical to the Christian faith.

For this reason, Thomas' public disputations often attracted people who were anxious to see him humiliated. He could have answered his opponents with the same abuse they meted out to him, but he chose, instead, to respond with humility and peace. Indeed, he gained a reputation for his wise, gentle responses to those who tried to abuse him verbally. Though Thomas "outshone others in his wisdom," Gui comments, "he was never found guilty of despising his companions or of using any arrrogant language or of giving himself airs."[19]

Once, for example, when Thomas was conducting a disputation at Paris, the Franciscan John Pecham, later archbishop of Canterbury, began to lash out at him. Thomas chose to respond with a peaceful heart, and the brilliance of his answers was matched by his humility in presenting them.[20] On another occasion, Thomas was representing the university chancellor in examining a young candidate for the licentiate in theology. The man was a theological neophyte, yet he presented himself as Thomas' superior, and challenged many of Thomas' own ideas. Gui comments that Thomas said nothing, thinking it of no importance that someone young and inexperienced would try to embarrass him publicly. Thomas' humility allowed him to "overlook any slight to himself"; after the public presentation, he went home in peace. But his Dominican brothers were angered by the candidate's attempts to humiliate him. Thomas replied quietly, "It seemed to me kinder to say nothing; I don't like to put a new master to shame on his first public appearance." But the brothers insisted that Thomas comment publicly on the candidate's opinions.[21]

On the following day, Thomas gently pointed out to the man the contradictions involved in his approach. The young candidate pretended to alter his position, but simply changed his words. Thomas continued to point out gently how the man's position contradicted the Christian faith. Thomas' humility eventually softened the candidate's heart; asking Thomas' help, he restated his response. Thomas' final remark to this arrogant young man who had tried to embarrass him evidences the peace and charity in his own heart. Instead of humiliating him—which Thomas was more than capable of doing—he complimented him: "You've said that very well."[22] Gui adds, "All the masters and others present were amazed at the calmness of mind and speech which Thomas displayed; at his manner of addressing an opponent as though he were teaching a pupil" and at his ability to meet, at one and the same time, "the claims both of charity and truth."[23] This humble peace was Thomas' usual way in disputations, even when his opponents ridiculed him.[24]

Yet, as we have seen, Thomas' peace came from a heart filled with the Spirit's charity, not from a tongue incapable of a sharp retort. The noble, kindly Thomas had, in addition to a sharp mind, a keen tongue and an iron will. He was unafraid to lash out against those who attacked the very way of life he was convinced Jesus had inspired in the Dominican community of preachers. He could be sarcastic when provoked. "This argument rather deserves to be laughed at than to be answered," he writes of those who attack the Dominicans. "If anyone wants to contest this, let him not babble about the matter in front of boys, but let him rather publicly present a pamphlet on it, so that those who have insight will be able to judge what is true and to refute what is false with the authority of truth."[25]

Thomas' potential for speaking with a sharp tongue shows itself perhaps even more forcefully when he writes against a false philosophical stance damaging to the truth of the Christian faith. He concludes his philosophical work defending the "Unity of the Intellect," with these words, "If anyone who boastfully claims the deceptive name of science for himself has anything to say against what we have written here, let him not do so in privacy and before boys, who have no judgment on such difficult matters, but let him write against this work, if he dares."

Thomas knew the difference between a just anger that strengthens our resolve to work for what is right and a bitter anger that destroys us. Unjust anger pushes us to avenge an injury, he writes, and this is the kind of anger that Christ forbade us to nurture in our heart. The Lord commands us to refrain not only from murder but also from that anger which is a form of murder. Jesus, our good physician, in this way wants to heal not only the symptoms of our wound but also the anger at its very root.[26] Thomas knew that when we are angry and bitter, we lose the peace of heart we need to contemplate God's love: "We possess truth's certitude more surely when we abandon a spirit of controversy," he tells us.[27] This is why the Lord urges us to be humble and gentle of heart, for it is kindliness that softens arguments and preserves God's peace in and among us.[28]

God's Charity Fills Us with Peace

Thomas knew, as we all know, how helpless we are to give ourselves this peace. We experience the torment of sleepless nights, the disturbance of noise within and around us, the pain of anxieties that destroy our peace. We struggle with desires that divide us from ourselves and conflicts that separate us from one another.[29] When we try to quiet this turmoil, when we try to heal these divisions, we find ourselves helpless.[30] Soon enough, we learn that only *God's* peace can quiet our soul, reconciling us with one another and with our own deepest self.[31] Thomas described this peace as both a concord joining us to each other and an inner harmony uniting us to our own self.[32] He knew that we experience peace only when we no longer have conflicting desires and our one great desire is fulfilled. But true peace is ours only when we both desire and possess what is good.[33]

It is sin, the enemy of what is good, that robs us of peace and makes war within us. "How wise we are, then," Thomas writes, "if we convert our many conflicting desires for passing goods into one desire for *God.*"[34] In this way we will learn that only the Spirit's charity can heal our opposing desires, uniting us to ourselves and to one another in the one desire for God. Charity alone causes peace in and among us because it draws us to love one another as ourselves, and to desire each other's true good as if it were our own.[35]

This is why, even without knowing it, we cannot help longing for the peace of God in our heart.[36] Thomas was struck by Augustine's insight that we all crave peace (De Civ Dei 19.13). In everything we want we are really seeking the peace to enjoy our blessings undisturbed, for peace is the "tranquility of order,"[37] the calm that fills us when our desires are satisfied.[38] Yet we learn from experience that the world's "peace"—the promised "satisfaction" of our desires for power, or wealth, or pleasure—is a sham peace that can never satisfy us.[39] God's peace, however, is true, lasting peace that not only satisfies our desires,[40] but contents our heart[41] and fills us with joy.[42] This is the very peace the Lord himself has promised: "My peace I give you . . . not as the world gives" (John 14:27).

There is only one source of this peace: the Spirit's own charity. For of its very nature, charity unites all our desires into one great desire for God. Indeed, wherever charity's love flourishes, peace also reigns.[43] As love of God and one another, charity alone flowers not only in peace but in joy.[44] Thomas knew how happy it makes us to be with someone we love.[45] But since we naturally love ourselves more than others, the nearer our loved one is to us, the more we love him or her; and the deeper our love, the greater our joy.[46] As Thomas tells us, when we *possess* the one we love, joy and peace cannot help flooding our heart.⁴⁷ Yet perfect joy is ours only in possessing God, who is joy itself! Since God, the dearest of all loves, lives intimately in us through charity, charity always overflows into joy and peace in our heart. Because we have *God's* presence within us and therefore have in God all that we could ever want or need, our charity and joy fill us with a peace which nothing can take from us.

With God's love enfolding us, therefore, nothing at all—trials, misunderstandings, heartache, rejection, disappointments—can rob us of the joy of being truly loved. This is why the Spirit's charity always flowers in a joy deeper even than our pain. And since the Spirit's charity is the wellspring of joy and peace, when charity fills us, peace anoints our heart and permeates our relationships with others.⁴⁸ Since charity makes us want God most of all, we are not divided by conflicting desires, and a profound contentment fills us at a level deeper than any trial we might be suffering.⁴⁹ As God's own love within us, therefore, charity cannot help filling us with the lovely fruit of joy and peace (Gal 5:22; Rom 14:17).⁵⁰

Humility as the Path to Peace

Thomas had let the Holy Spirit fill him with peace by turning all the desires he could have satisfied as a nobleman into one great desire for God. As God became all that he wanted, he let go of conflicting desires—for riches, power, prestige—that would have divided his energies and thus destroyed his peace of heart. This singleness of heart in turn gave him a humility that fostered even more deeply his peace of soul.

In his commentary on the Gospel of John, Thomas quotes these words of Cicero: "Let us beware of that glory that robs us of all freedom, for which a person of great spirit should risk everything."⁵¹ Thomas unwittingly reveals here the conscious choice he himself had made to live with a humble heart as the only path to true peace. The freedom of which Cicero had spoken was the freedom that Thomas himself wanted, the freedom for which his own great soul risked everything.

Thomas quotes also the Gloss on Cicero's text: "It is a great vice to boast and to strive for human praise, to desire what others think you have but you really do not have." Thomas reflects on how, at the time of Christ, those "whose proud minds were craving their own glory and praise could not believe in Christ. They considered themselves superior to others in glory, and thought it a disgrace to believe in Christ, who seemed common and poor." In contrast, however, the people "who are humble, who seek only God's glory, *these* believe in Jesus."[52] Thomas the nobleman had himself become a poor and humble beggar for the sake of Jesus. In company with this Lord who humbled himself for us, Thomas found not only his call, but also the peace which the Lord promised us, the "peace which the world cannot give" (John 14:27).

This humble peace was the outstanding virtue that distinguished Thomas as a scholar and preacher, setting him apart from many of his proud and vain contemporaries. As Gui remarks, Thomas learned well the lesson from Jesus that wisdom "dwells only with humility."[53] Literature of Thomas' time shows how other scholars took pride in their learning, using it to advance their own glory. But Thomas repudiated the vices of his noble station—arrogance, pride, vain-glory—and gave himself to fostering its virtues— liberality, generosity, great-heartedness.[54] Central to this greatheartedness was his humility, an uncommon virtue among the learned of his day.[55] Thomas in this way lived a radically different life from his arrogant contemporaries in the scholarly world; he was always "courteous in speech, gentle, and approachable." Gui comments that even his outward bearing "came from an inward humility; it expressed what he really *was.*"[56]

Those who knew Thomas described how peaceful and humble he was, how unconcerned about his clothes and food. In contrast to other members of the nobility who had become friars, Thomas "never asked for anything special."[57] And though he could easily have done so in response to his enemies, he never used "haughty or aggressive speech against anyone."[58]

This humility which nurtured Thomas' peace was not simply the virtue of his more mature years. People who knew him told of the time when he was a young student studying under Albert and intently following his course on Dionysius' *The Divine Names*. Mistaking Thomas' reserve for stupidity, one of the other students had offered to help Thomas with his studies. Thomas humbly, "cheerfully" accepted the student's kindness. But when the student began to founder, Thomas himself gently began to explain Albert's lecture with great clarity and brilliance, especially in adding his own insights. Amazed, the young man reported to

the student master that Thomas had explained the lecture to him
with more acuity than Albert himself had done.[59]
Drawn by both Thomas' humility and by his brilliance, Albert
began to choose Thomas for the key role in the difficult disputations he sponsored. Thomas proved himself again and again to
be the most outstanding student. Yet what people found in him
was far more than an intelligent mind: they saw the Spirit's own
wisdom and humble peace. Albert himself knew that those who
flaunt their learning have no true wisdom because they have no
humility. Thomas possessed both. "The Holy Spirit was in him.
Indeed, while he outshone the others in knowledge and understanding, he never despised his companions nor used arrogant language nor gave himself airs."[60]
Thomas the nobleman and scholar chose this humble way for
his entire life. He would have nothing of the world's wealth, honor
or power. While he was at Cologne—sometime between 1248-50,
and several years after he had become a Dominican—Pope Innocent IV tried to make him abbot of Monte Cassino while still
permitting him to remain a Dominican. This offer, surely insti-
gated by his family, Thomas absolutely refused. Later in his life,
Pope Clement IV wanted to appoint Thomas as archbishop of
Naples and abbot of St. Peter *ad aram,* with rich revenues from
both the abbacy and the archbishopric. Again, Thomas utterly
refused both offers.[61]
Thomas had learned early in his life what Albert himself discovered by experience. Albert had been made bishop of Ratis-
bon; yet, as one contemporary historian comments, the office of
bishop at that time included "excessively military occupations,"
and no bishop was consecrated there without a sword. "Amid
those swords and lances," Albert's time for prayer and study dis-
appeared. Unable to live his true vocation to teach and write in
the Church, Albert begged the Pope for permission to resign. His
request became so insistent that the Pope eventually was forced
to acquiesce.[62]
Thomas surely remembered Albert's experience as he himself
was traveling to the Second Council of Lyons at Pope Gregory
X's behest. Reginald had heard rumors that Thomas and the great
Franciscan theologian, Bonaventure, would be made cardinals at
this council. When Reginald suggested that it would be an immense honor for the Dominicans if Thomas were made a cardinal, Thomas would not hear of it. He assured his friend that he

would remain a poor, humble friar until death. Thomas' words proved true. He never arrived at the council; already sick and weary before he had begun the journey, Thomas became even more ill on the way. Within a few weeks he was dead.[63]

Thomas remained a "poor, humble friar," however, not by accident but by his own choice. His experience had taught him that seeking possessions and power, even those entailed in ecclesiastical positions and honors, destroys our peace of heart.[64] In his homily on the Ten Commandments, Thomas describes how we all desire so many things, and yet continually find that nothing completely satisfies us. At the same time, preserving and maintaining what we do gain requires immense energy. We grow tired of something we have saved for a long time to buy, and start looking for something better. Soon enough, we find that the time and energy we spend on gaining prestige and possessions erode the peace of heart that we most want.[65]

Yet it is not only greed but also envy that destroys our peace. If we spend much time and energy in gaining honors or wealth, we envy those who gain the same thing with only a little effort. Likewise, we grieve if we lose what we have spent so much energy obtaining, at the same time that we envy those who possess what we do not have.[66] Thomas comments, too, that although we are not usually tempted to try to excel in matters where we have no talent, it is easy for us to envy those who have great gifts in an area in which we have only some small talent. We feel that we can do as well and better than they, and so we strive to surpass them. But we become sad and envious if our efforts fail and someone else gains a reputation greater than ours in that area. Yet Thomas remarks that, while all of us can fall prey to envy, the cowardly and those who love power and prestige are most envious of all. *Everything* seems great to them! If others gain something good, envious people think that they have been bested in something wonderful, even when the matter is very small.[67]

Thomas assures us, however, that even though we ought to honor the good of others, we should not do so in a way that disparages our own gifts. Others' good fortune would then sadden us rather than prompt us to share their joy. Instead of proving our humility, despising the gifts *we* have from God only shows our ingratitude. On the other hand, it is a sign of true humility if we do not dwell excessively on our *faults*.[68] A truly humble person accepts humiliations without hesitation—but only when necessary, Thomas adds quickly! As a virtue, humility needs to be practiced with discretion. To accept *every* kind of humiliation is "not humility, but stupidity."[69] Thomas himself more than once submitted to humiliations out of love for Christ. On one occasion, while at the Dominican convent at Bologna, he was walking and meditating in the cloister garden as he often did. A brother from another priory who did not know who Thomas was accosted him in the garden and told him to accompany him into the city for some business he had there. (The prior had directed this friar to take as his companion the first brother he met.) Thomas, the renowned theologian who was weighed down with pressing responsibilities, followed at once. But he could not keep up with his companion's fast pace, and the friar began deriding him for being so slow. Each time he was berated, Thomas would beg the brother's pardon.

The friar did not know who Thomas was, but the townspeople did. They recognized him as the "great teacher who was hurrying after that undistinguished friar!" Stopping the friar, they chided him for not recognizing who Thomas was and for treating him so badly. Embarrassed and confused, the brother apologized and begged Thomas to forgive his ignorance. But when Thomas saw how much honor the townspeople were giving him, and how indignant they were at his being treated so badly, he said gently, "If God . . . has [so] humbled himself for our sake, should not we submit to one another for God's sake?"[70]

Peace in Misunderstandings

Maritain comments that Thomas could be so humble because he "drank from a certain secret spring far superior to the intellectual life itself." He abounded in riches of the mind and heart and spirit, but "he was truly poor in spirit."[71] Thomas found his peace not in the accomplishments of an inflated ego, but in the heart of his Lord who said, "Learn from me, for I am gentle and humble of heart, and you will find rest for your souls" (Matt 11:29). Thomas knew that his beloved Paul had found this peace even in the midst of trials. He was struck by how the sufferings Paul endured for the gospel did not make him anxious or destroy his inner peace. Indeed, Thomas seemed to hear Paul saying, "I am upset by what goes on around me, but I am not disturbed by what is *within* me."[72]

Thomas himself endured with humble serenity misunderstandings and severe trials even to the end of his life. The worst trial of all was to find that his teaching was suspect in the Church. Could any ordeal be more difficult for Thomas, master in theology and lover not only of Jesus but also of his Church? Yet, as Maritain points out, the "four years of heroic struggle which occupied his last sojourn in Paris were darkened by the shadow of such an ordeal."[73] Because his theological approach relied far more on the "worldly" Aristotle than on the "mystical" Plato, many of Thomas' own Dominican brothers criticized his theology, argued against him, and refused to stand by him. Theology professors at Paris and even the bishop there rejoiced to see him dishonored.[74]

Nearly all the masters in theology at the University of Paris, including the Franciscans, opposed him. The Averroists idolized the mind and Aristotle's teachings, while the Augustinian theologians disparaged the mind. Even the bishop of Paris supported the Augustinians against Thomas, because Thomas' theology seemed too pagan, too worldly, too influenced by Aristotle.[75] After his death, the Franciscans forbade any of their friars except the most intelligent teachers to study Thomas' writings,[76] and at the 1282 General Chapter of Friars Minor held at Strasburg, the reading of Thomas' *Summa* was prohibited in Franciscan schools.[77] When the Franciscan John Pecham succeeded Edward Kilwardby as the bishop of Canterbury, he reinforced the condemnations of 1284 and 1286 of various teachings viewed as inimical to the Christian faith. He published his own condemnations, explicitly including some of Thomas' supposed teachings. Referring to Thomas, Pecham wrote that he wanted to apply the "medicine" of his pastoral charge "to this cancerous itch"![78]

Yet even though Thomas was considered a "cancerous itch" whose downfall others labored hard to bring about, "every attempt failed against his mildness."[79] Gerald Vann calls attention to two very different portraits depicting the "Triumph of St. Thomas." One, by Benozzo Gozzoli, shows Thomas crushing under his foot a "vanquished" Averroes. The other portrait, by his brother Dominican, Fra Angelico, depicts Averroes being treated with respect by Thomas, and Averroes himself sitting peacefully at his feet, as his students at Paris had done.[80]

Thomas "had nothing to lose, no vanity to be wounded."[81] He "was attached to absolutely none of the riches of his mind; he was perfectly poor and simple, ingenuous, innocent."[82] Indeed, Thomas had both an "almost reckless intellectual audacity" and a "perfect intellectual modesty."[83] He was "by birth a gentleman of a great house," Chesterton writes, and Thomas' "effortless courtesy and patience" manifest how truly he preserved the peaceful repose characteristic of "those who work when they need not work,"[84]—and, we might add, who serve when they need not serve.

A Life and Death in the Sweet Fragrance of God's Peace

Thomas had begun to foster the gift of God's peace in his life even as a young student at Cologne. There he had eagerly followed Albert's class on Dionysius' *The Divine Names*. Serving as Albert's student assistant, Thomas had been responsible for recording the master's class notes. Thomas' later writings show how deeply the insights of Dionysius, the anonymous fifth-century mystic, had struck a chord in his heart, for he found described in them the peace which enfolded his own life.

Dionysius had reflected on the alluring peace that God is, the peace that we all long to possess in our hearts.[85] Indeed, our hunger for this contentment mirrors the longing of the whole universe for God's peace, a peace that unites the entire cosmos in a "kindly order," an inner harmony and "friendship."[86] Every creature in some way longs for this peace of God and mirrors it in the harmony and friendship it has with itself, with others, and with God.[87] Yes, Thomas comments, even the smallest creatures share in God's peace by a natural "friendship" with other creatures, a "friendship" that reflects God's own peace secretly enfolding the entire universe.[88] Yet though all of God's creatures long for this peace and seek it in their lives, we long for it most of all, and we are meant to have it through enjoying *God*.[89]

It is precisely by giving ourselves to contemplating and proclaiming God that we *enjoy* God and show this joy and peace in our lives. Thomas was known as a gentle, "sweet-tempered" man[90] who never spoke "haughty or aggressive" words against others;[91] because his heart was always "enjoying God," he learned to let the peace of God's joy enfold him in every situation, regardless of how volatile. Toward the end of his life Thomas wrote that there will be times when, in the midst of those who hurt and attack us, we have no place to turn but to God. And yet, he tells us from his own experience, in God's arms, we have everything we need to console us.[92]

Thomas' trust in God's care kept him calm and peaceful even in his fears. In his lectures on the Gospel of Matthew, for example, he reflects on how the grandeur of a bolt of lightning and its accompanying thunder both delights us with its splendor and terrifies us with its violence.[93] In this insight, charming in its simplicity, Thomas alludes to his own fear in thunderstorms, a terror which surely stemmed from a tragic experience in his childhood. When he was only a boy, his little sister had been killed by a lightning bolt, while he and his nurse had been spared in a nearby section of the same castle.[94] Friends tell of how Thomas never outgrew his child's fear of storms; during them, he would bless himself and pray the psalmist's cry for God's protection.[95] Surely past experiences like these lie at the heart of Thomas' assurance to us that while friends can assuage our pain in some ways, only God comforts us perfectly and in all of our sufferings. Even when our anguish comes from our own weakness and sin, God consoles us by the most tender mercy and delivers us from our afflictions.[96]

Thomas urges us, therefore, to nurture Christ's peace in our heart.[97] For like a gentle doctor, the triune God never prescribes harsh medicines in our weakness but always protects us from trials too heavy. If we do ask for Christ's peace, Thomas assures us, we need never fear what life will bring us. Our trials and even our sin will not destroy us, and in difficult times we will find a profound peace and contentment.[98] In this way the Holy Spirit will fill us with peace, delight,[99] and even joy in suffering for love for Christ (1 Thess 1:6). Indeed, God will tenderly care for us and console us in our every anguish, all the while ensuring that our trials will last only a "little while."[100]

This peace of God enfolds us not only in our difficult times, but also in our times of joy, especially the joy of our love for one another. For though the Spirit's charity joins us to one another, it is "the bond of peace" that *keeps* us united to each other. Thomas thinks of how material objects stay fused only if held together by a sturdy bond. We ourselves stay united to those we love only if an unbreakable bond holds us together; and this bond is Christ's peace.[101] The Holy Spirit, the fire of charity and the living bond of perfection poured out on us by Christ, *makes* us one and *keeps* us one, enabling us to dwell with one heart and soul, as one family, in one home of love. The triune God's peace, therefore, is a bond that is unbreakable, for Christ himself is that bond.[102]

In order to nurture this peace among us, Paul tells us to greet each other with a "holy kiss." A kiss, Thomas comments, is a sign of peace; and to kiss one another is a way we unite our spirits in peace. Yet if we speak words of peace while harboring resentment against each other in our hearts, our peace is a sham and our kiss is fraudulent. If, however, we kiss one another as a sign of our charity and true union with each other, our kiss actually brings about the peace of God that unites us in the Holy Spirit. Through the "holy kiss" we give each other at the Eucharist, therefore, God's peace is poured out on us and shared among us in our churches.[103]

We need to treasure this truth that Christ is our healing peace, and that in Christ the Father's overflowing compassion pours out peace in our world. For since we approach securely one with whom we are at peace, Thomas assures us that we can come close with absolute confidence to Christ.[104] Even our daily prayer, the "Our Father," is a means of our growing in this peace. Thomas was convinced that the Holy Spirit gives us the "Our Father" precisely as a way of increasing the trust that both fosters our peace and helps us to arrive at heaven's joy, the reward of peace. But we gain this peace here on earth, Thomas tells us, by patience in both the good times and the bad.[105] Love itself makes us happy in what is good, and a key sign of a peaceful, happy heart is our seeing the good far more than the evil in every situation.[106]

Thomas himself had begged God to enfold him with peace in his anxieties and in the stress he faced each day. In the end, Thomas' humble, peaceful heart prevailed over those who had sought his downfall. At their General Chapter in 1278, his Dominican brothers finally defended his teaching publicly and made it the official teaching of the Order. In 1346 Pope Clement VI even charged the Dominicans with the task of guarding and promoting Thomas' doctrine so that future generations could be fed with its riches.[107]

The victory of Thomas' peace, therefore, did not come until after his death. He himself had written that our peace is imperfect here on earth, since we can never be completely free from worry and anxiety within and conflicts around us.[108] Disagreements are inevitable, and even when we are united in charity and desire for God, we can have very different opinions from our close friends on various issues. But in heaven, Thomas tells us, we will have not even the slightest dissension or even disagreement.[109] Perfect peace will fill our hearts, because our every desire will be satisfied in our perfectly enjoying God.[110]

In a profound way Thomas tasted more and more of this peace as he approached his death. In his adolescence he had left Benedict's community where he had learned the twelve degrees of humility as the path of true peace. At the end, it was from a Cistercian community that Thomas asked hospitality, and in which he humbly yielded himself in death to God's peace.[111] In these final days, the monks of Fossanova tell us, Thomas was "always gentle and no trouble to anyone";[112] he was without fail "kindly and patient, never upset or annoyed."[113]

Near the end of his life, Thomas had reflected on the words of the psalmist, "Be still and know that I am God" (Ps 46:10; RSV). In his commentary on this beautiful passage, Thomas stresses that God fills us with peace so that our heart will be free for prayer and contemplation.[114] Thomas had learned this from his own experience: when we are good and choose the good, true peace fills our heart.[115] Even more, when we cling to God in love,[116] our peace is real and lasting, for contemplation gives us the peace of God's forgiveness and love.[117] It was this peace in Thomas' own heart that impelled him to share its fragrance with others, and this same peace that he encourages us to pour out upon the world in our preaching and sharing of our faith. Indeed, Thomas urges us, let us proclaim the good news of Jesus precisely in order that the whole world might be suffused with the fragrance of Christ's peace.[118]

Notes

[1]ST I-II, 70, 3, ad 4.
[2]ST II-II, 45, 6, ad 1.
[3]Pieper, *Guide,* 66–67.
[4]Ibid., 71.
[5]Ibid., 67.
[6]Ibid., 68–69.

[7]Ibid., 71.

[8]Gui, c. 11.

[9]Weisheipl, *Friar,* 88-90.

[10]Ibid., 93, 94.

[11]Gui, c. 12; Weisheipl, *Friar,* 96.

[12]Pieper, *Guide,* 64, 72.

[13]Ibid., 73-74.

[14]In Ps 49:10.

[15]Weisheipl, *Friar,* 88.

[16]In Met 12, 9.

[17]Pieper, *Guide,* 85.

[18]Rel St 23, 26; *Disputed Questions: Truth,* trans. Milligan and others (Chicago: Regnery, 1952-54) 137, 159.

[19]Gui, c. 10; Foster, *Life,* 33.

[20]I Can 76.

[21]Gui, c. 31; Foster, *Life,* 50.

[22]Foster, *Life,* 74, n. 73.

[23]Gui, c. 31; Foster, *Life,* 50.

[24]I Can 76.

[25]Contra Retrah, 16.

[26]Ten Com.

[27]In Jn 7, lect. 2.

[28]In Eph 4, lect. 1.

[29]Com Div Nom ch. 11, lect. 2; cf. ST II-II, 29, 1.

[30]Com Div Nom ch. 11, lect. 3.

[31]Ibid., lect. 1.

[32]ST II-II, 29, 1.

[33]ST II-II, 29, 2, ad 3; II-II, 29, 2, ad 4.

[34]Com Div Nom ch. 11, lect. 3.

[35]ST II-II, 29, 3.

[36]Com Div Nom ch. 11, lect. 3.

[37]ST II-II, 29, 2.

[38]ST II-II, 29, 1, ad 1.

[39]In Jn 14, lect. 7.

[40]ST II-II, 29, 2, ad 4.

[41]In Jn 14, lect. 7.

[42]In Ps 36:3.

[43]ST II-II, 29, 3, ad 3.

[44]ST II-II, 29, 3; II-II, 29, 4.

[45]ST I-II, 48, 2.

[46]CG I, 102, 3.

[47]In Gal 5, lect. 6.

[48]ST II-II, 29, 3, ad 3.

[49]ST I-II, 70, 3.

[50]ST II-II, 28, 1; II-II, 28, 4; II-II, 28, 4, ad 1.

[51]In Jn 5, lect. 7.

[52]Ibid.

[53]Gui, c. 30; Foster, *Life,* 48.

[54]See Murray, *Reason and Society in the Middle Ages,* 353–81.

[55]Ibid., 232.

[56]Gui, c. 30; Foster, *Life,* 48.

[57]I Can 47; Foster, *Life,* 93. Jacques Le Gof notes that it was ostentatious eating that gave the higher classes a great opportunity of flaunting their "superiority" (*Medieval Civilization 400–1500,* 358).

[58]I Can 45; Foster, *Life,* 93.

[59]Gui, c. 9.

[60]Gui, c. 10; Foster, *Life,* 33.

[61]HE 22:39.

[62]HE 22:19.

[63]I Can 78; Foster, *Life,* 108.

[64]Ten Com.

[65]Ibid.

[66]ST II-II, 36, 1, ad 4.

[67]ST II-II, 36, 1, ad 3.

[68]Ibid.

[69]CG II, 135, 23.

[70]Gui, c. 31; Foster, *Life,* 49.

[71]Maritain, *Aquinas,* 36.

[72]In Eph 6, lect. 5.

[73]Maritain, *Aquinas,* 49.

[74]Maritain, *Aquinas,* 50.

[75]Ibid.

[76]Vann, *Aquinas,* 65.

[77]Maritain, *Aquinas,* 54.

[78]Vann, *Aquinas,* 66.

[79]Maritain, *Aquinas,* 50.

[80]Vann, *Aquinas,* 75.

[81]Ibid., 49.

[82]Maritain, *Aquinas,* 116.

[83]Etienne Gilson, *Reason and Revelation in the Middle Ages* (New York: Charles Scribner's Sons, 1954) 71; Vann, *Aquinas,* 49.

[84]Chesteron, *Aquinas,* 22.

[85]Com Div Nom ch. 11, lect. 3.

86Ibid., lect. 2.
87Ibid., lect. 1, lect. 2.
88Ibid., lect. 1.
89Ibid., lect. 2.
90I Can 58; Foster, *Life,* 97.
91I Can 45; Foster, *Life,* 93.
92In Ps 31:19.
93In Mt 24, lect. 3.
94Tocco, c. 2; FVST, 67.
95Gui, c. 35.
96In 2 Cor 1, lect. 2.
97In Jn 16, lect. 3.
98Ibid.
99Com Div Nom ch. 11, lect. 3.
100Our Father.
101In Eph 4, lect. 2.
102In Heb 13, lect. 13.
103In 2 Cor 13, lect. 3.
104In Eph 2, lect. 5.
105Our Father.
106ST II–II, 106, 3, ad 2.
107Maritain, *Aquinas,* 55.
108ST II–II, 29, 2, ad 4.
109ST II–II, 29, 3, ad 3.
110ST II–II, 29, 2, ad 4.
111Maritain, *Aquinas,* 100.
112I Can 15; Foster, *Life,* 87.
113I Can 19; Foster, *Life,* 88.
114In Ps 45:8.
115ST II–II, 29, 2, ad 3.
116In Ps 37:3.
117Cf. ST I–II, 113, 2.
118In Jn 16, lect. 3; cf. Ps 118:165.

9

Aglow with the Spirit

The peace that comes from the Spirit of wisdom set Thomas apart from his arrogant contemporaries. Yet, aside from this remarkable peace, those who knew Thomas found little that was extraordinary in him. Unlike saints whom popular imagination pictures as emaciated from fasting, Thomas was no ascetic. He was, in fact, rather overweight. He enjoyed no fame as a miracle worker. When his cause for canonization was investigated nearly fifty years after his death, the pope demanded a second inquiry because the first had produced too few accounts of miracles. The inquiries themselves yielded only simple tales told by ordinary folk about a very ordinary friend they loved. One person, for example, relates the "miracle" that happened when he needed to find a particular passage from Thomas' writings. After asking for Thomas' help, he immediately opened to the exact text. "And so it was, he had found, in all his needs; brother Thomas never failed to help him!"[1]

Thomas' life and holiness were modest, unassuming. But there was one extraordinary dimension of his life: the profound depth and prodigious output of his writings. Thomas knew that this "one great miracle" of his life did not come from his own efforts or genius but from the Holy Spirit's gifts within him. He had discovered that the "spiritual" life is simply our day-to-day life filled with the Holy Spirit's extraordinary love and anointing. Holiness means performing the ordinary tasks of our call by a power not our own: the person and gifts of the Spirit given to us at our baptism.

Paul had urged the Galatian community to "live by the Spirit" (Gal 5:16), to be "led by the Spirit" in everything they did (Gal 5:18). Thomas agrees: let us be *"full* of the Holy Spirit," "availing ourselves of the Spirit in *all* we do!"[2] And it was by preaching the gospel "in season and out," by sharing his faith with others, that Thomas learned what "living in the Spirit" and "availing" ourselves of the Spirit mean. He found that "in the flesh" we "quench" the Spirit by drawing only from our own empty resources (1 Thess 5:19). Failing to share our faith with others, we close up the Spirit's presence in our hearts.[3] But "aglow with the Spirit" (Rom 12:11) we live from a vastly different source, the wellspring of the Holy Spirit, "Giver of Life," whose love will not allow us to keep our faith pent up inside us. Thomas became a saint, therefore, not by undertaking a life of rigorous mortifications nor by working great miracles, but by surrendering himself to the Holy Spirit in his life's task of proclaiming the good news of Jesus.

Living from God's Spirit

Thomas learned that we truly share with others only what we actually experience in our own lives, and that only the Spirit of love enables us both to experience and to share the fruit of our contemplation with others.[4] This is why he urges us to do as he did, to live a "spiritual" life[5] at the heart of the Church and world by drawing our every breath from the Spirit of love.[6] For it is this Spirit whose presence and gifts in us inspire us to share with others the fruit of the Spirit's joy in our heart.

Thomas thinks of how the air we breathe hints at the far deeper life-breath of the Spirit within us. We live only because at every second we draw into ourselves the air that makes us live; if we stop breathing from this life-breath, we literally die. Yet it is not simply by breathing air that we have real life.[7] Only by "breathing in" the Spirit of life at every second of the day do we "live and move and have our being" (Acts 17:28),[8] since only the Spirit of life makes us truly *live* and not merely exist (cf. Ps 104:30).

If we have suffered the pain of watching a loved one die, we know that, as his or her life ebbs away, we see the once warm body become cold and lifeless. After death, the corpse before us is no more like the inmost heart of our loved one than stone is like the flesh of a new-born child. Yet Thomas was convinced that more life surges in this corpse than in one who lives without the Spirit of God. Devoid of God's Spirit, the only Giver of Life, our inmost being is more dead than any corpse. It is true that our soul breathes the warmth of life into our body; but without the Holy Spirit, the "life" in us is only a pale existence, a mere shadow and imitation of true life. This is why Thomas urges us to hand over our entire life to the Spirit's anointing, availing ourselves of the Spirit not only in our bigger problems but also in our smaller needs, and indeed, in all that we do. Let us draw our every breath from the Holy Spirit, Thomas urges us, for "only the *Spirit* gives *life*" (John 6:63).[9] Thomas thinks of coals he has watched burning in the fireplace. Aglow with fire, the coals themselves become like fire. But even more than red-hot fire inflames burning coals, the Holy Spirit warms and transforms our hearts.[10]

Yet we are far more than simply "burning coals": "You are God's *temple* and God's Spirit dwells in you" (1 Cor 3:16). A house without love is simply a building. But when our dear ones live within, light and warmth fill it and the house becomes a home. Indeed, wherever our loved ones live becomes home for us. And *we* are God's loved ones; only in us does God live not simply as in a house, but as in the warmth of a "familiar home."[11] Even more, Paul tells us that our very *body* is the temple and home of the Spirit (1 Cor 6:19). Thomas finds in this wonderful truth the deepest reason for our unique loveliness as persons. Just as we love to make our own home warm and beautiful, the Spirit of love makes our heart and flesh the Spirit's gracious home.[12] God's loving presence fills the whole universe, Thomas reminds us, but only we who are persons, whose minds and hearts are "capable of God," can know and love God in return. And precisely in knowing and loving the triune God, we become God's *home*.[13]

Yet we are able to love God in return, as intimate friends and equals, only because the Spirit of love dwells in us (1 John 4:13). Indeed, the more we love Jesus, the more we also "receive the Holy Spirit in greater and greater fullness" and the more the Spirit deepens our love for God and one another.[14] We begin to "walk in the Spirit" (Gal 5:16), knowing the divine persons as our beloved friends and desiring to serve and care for each other.[15] Our surrender to the Spirit in this way becomes an endless circle, deepening without limit.

The Spirit's "Instinct" within Us

"Those *led* by the Spirit are God's children" (Rom 8:14). In these beautiful words, Thomas hears Paul urging us to abandon ourselves more and more to the Holy Spirit's leading in our life.[16] Thomas knew that even when we want to yield ourselves to the Holy Spirit, we can fear that our self-surrender will rob us of who we are. But he also learned from his own experience that being led by the Holy Spirit means *gaining* who we are. It is true that we are slaves when anyone else "leads" us. But when the Spirit of God guides us, we gain our fulfillment as unique persons whose life and gifts are unrepeatable in the world.

To develop the wonderful insight that our being led by the Spirit frees us and makes us fully who we are, Thomas uses the engaging image of following the Spirit's "instinct." In urging us to obey not simply our own weak will but rather the gentle leading of the Spirit of love, Thomas compares the Spirit's leading to an "instinct" within us. As we have seen, God has given us natural instincts for what is good for us—instincts to eat, to love, to protect ourselves and our dear ones, to have children, to nurture and care for our family. These very instincts make it easy and in fact delightful for us to do the very things we need to do to gain the wonderful fulfillment God has planned for us.[17]

The Holy Spirit's leading within us is like these natural instincts. If we are in good health, no one has to force us to eat; we naturally want to eat, and we enjoy eating. Eating good food is easy, natural, delightful for us. But our natural inclinations are not instincts we are meant to act upon as animals do. As human persons, we have the power to guide our instincts by our reason, and so to live a higher, deeper life than mere animals have. And when we do direct our natural instincts by the light of our reason, we find not simply pleasure but true joy. There are times, for example, when we who are married might be tempted to enjoy this "natural instinct" for sexual union with someone who is not our spouse. But if with the Holy Spirit's love we remain faithful to our spouse, we experience not simply pleasure but even more the profound joy and contentment of the Holy Spirit in our heart.

From his own experience, Thomas knew that it truly is delightful for us to direct our natural instincts by our reason to the loving purpose God has intended for us. But we are also meant to be led by a far higher power than our own reason, the "instinct" of the Spirit of love within us.[18] In letting ourselves be led by *this* Spirit, we follow the Holy Spirit's inclination in our heart, an inclination so "natural" to all that is good for us that it seems like "instinct."

Laws can be only external guides, telling us from outside ourselves what we should do, without giving us the power to do it. But the Holy Spirit dwells in our hearts, enlightening us, drawing us to want and to do the good that is our freedom and wholeness: "I will write my law in their *hearts*" (Jer 31:33). Deeper even than our reason, Thomas tells us, the very person of the Spirit desires to lead us in all that we do. If we give ourselves to the Holy Spirit's leading, we increasingly make our decisions based, not simply on what our intellect tells us to do, but even more on what the Spirit of God inspires us to do. Unlike our "natural" instincts, the Spirit's "instinct" within us draws us to want what the Holy Spirit wants for us. We are meant to flourish according to the *Spirit's* generous, loving purposes, not our own narrow plans.[19]

Thomas recalls the apostles before Pentecost. Without the Holy Spirit they made their decisions based simply on their own reasoning. Thus, for example, they felt they had to cast lots to fill Judas' place. But after Pentecost, Thomas reminds us, the apostles did not need to "resort to lots!" They relied completely on the Spirit's leading in choosing the seven deacons.[20] Thomas recalls, too, the marvels that happened when Peter preached at Pentecost. The Holy Spirit gathered different peoples and made them one family as God's own children (Acts 2:7-11). Peter preached with such power precisely because he followed the *Spirit's* leading, not simply his own will and plan. He listened to his inmost heart and followed the Spirit's "instinct" within him. People were converted to the Lord because the Holy Spirit anointed his preaching.[21]

The apostles experienced the leading of the Spirit in other matters as well. Thomas thinks of how they were led by the Spirit to proclaim truths that were later written down. But they also handed on other teachings which they felt no need to put into writing. After Pentecost, they followed the Spirit's inspiration and not simply their own will and plans.[22] In all they did, they let the Spirit's "instinct" guide them.[23]

Thomas urges us also to lead "spiritual" lives at the heart of the world, lives full of the Spirit's truth and love.[24] For love alone makes us free, and the Spirit of love causes our freedom.[25] This is why Thomas urges us to draw our life not simply from our own plans and desires but even more deeply from the Holy Spirit's inclination and "instinct" within us.[26]

The Gifts of the Spirit

Thomas learned by experience how wonderful our life becomes when we "avail ourselves of the Spirit in all that we do."[27] He found also in his own life the way we can actually "avail ourselves" of the Holy Spirit's power. He knew that the Holy Spirit dwells in us through sanctifying grace,[28] which flowers into faith, hope and love. These precious virtues join us intimately to God, but they are powerful in us only according to our limited ways of knowing and loving. Thomas in this way became convinced that we need more than even the theological virtues to enable us to surrender ourselves to the Holy Spirit.[29] He saw how at baptism the Spirit also fills us with the gifts of wisdom, understanding, counsel, fortitude, knowledge, piety, and fear of the Lord.[30] These gifts dispose us to follow the Holy Spirit's leadings promptly, easily, gladly, for through them the very person of the Holy Spirit moves and leads us.[31]

Thomas knew that it is Jesus, our risen Lord, who pours out the Spirit's gifts upon us. Jesus himself was *"full* of the Holy Spirit" when he returned from the Jordan, Luke tells us, and it was the Spirit who led Jesus into the desert (Luke 4:1). Indeed, Thomas assures us, Jesus was filled to overflowing both with the Holy Spirit and with the Spirit's gifts.[32] He received them in his humanity, but, after his resurrection, in his divinity Jesus has poured them out on *us,*[33] enabling us to live God's own way of living, in a manner that seems "natural" to us, full of ease and joy.[34]

Our own experience hints at the depth of Thomas' insight. If we appreciate good music, we love to hear great artists play. Yet unless we are great artists ourselves, we can never enjoy the music with the *very same joy* that exquisite musicians experience in playing it. After many years of practice we may learn to play the same music that they do, but we never do so with the same ease and pleasure. Even if we could play a great work, it is literally impossible for us to share these artists' *own* intimate experience of the music, playing and enjoying it with *their own* skill and joy.

It would be the greatest intimacy, impossible to imagine, if we *could* share literally the very joy that a great musician experiences in playing. Famous artists, for example, might long to share their inner joy and skill with their beloved children who may not be so gifted. Such a grace would be one of great intimacy, of actually sharing the inner experience of one we love and admire. But if such an experience were possible to us, we would have only a small hint of what Thomas means when he says that the Spirit's gifts enable us to live, in a created way, God's own unbounded way of living, with God's own ease and joy.[35] This is why Thomas stresses that through the virtues of faith, hope and love, we love *what* God loves, but through the Spirit's gifts we love the very *way* God loves.

The martyrs show us in a striking way what the Spirit can and longs to do in us through these gifts. When Maximilian Kolbe, for example, stepped forward and offered himself as a victim in place of a prisoner the Nazis had singled out, Kolbe was loving not only *what* God loves, the young prisoner, but also the very *way* God does, to the limit of death itself. Kolbe's self-offering came not simply from the virtue of courage, since it far surpassed the dictates simply of human valor. His love and herosim came from the Spirit's gift of fortitude within him, inspiring and enabling him to love in the way Jesus loves us, by handing over his life. This gift not only inspired him but actually gave him the Spirit's power to carry out the Spirit's inspiration, with ease and joy, as if by second nature. Kolbe did not simply offer his life to the Nazis in place of another prisoner, and then go to his death with the natural fear that takes hold of us in the face of death. No, like myriads of martyrs before and after him, he went to his death with the joy of a person anticipating his or her own wedding.

It is true that when we read of the saints' heroic love, as well as of the martyrs' peace and joy, we cannot help feeling ourselves incapable of such courage. And we are right: of ourselves, we *are* incapable of such heroism! But Thomas assures us that the saints, too, are incapable by their own power of such love. It is not *our* wisdom or courage but rather the Spirit's gifts within each of us that enable us to live with the joy and love of the saints. The martyrs themselves would tell us that it was not *they* who suffered with fortitude and joy, but rather the Holy Spirit who gave them the gift of courage to do so.

The gifts which filled the saints are the very same gifts the Holy Spirit pours out upon us at our baptism. This is why the Lord assures us that in difficult times the very person of the Spirit will speak in and through us. We do not need to worry about mustering our own small courage or patience or love in the time of trial, or in the tasks of our daily life. By these gifts, the person of the Holy Spirit will be love and wisdom and courage in us, if only we ask for this.

The Spirit's gifts thus bring the virtues of faith, hope and love to full flowering in our life.[36] Thomas compares us without these gifts to damp wood unable to burn. The wood has to be made able to bear the fire. In a similar way, the Spirit's gifts make us able to bear the fire of God's own inner joy and love. This is why, for Thomas, the gifts are absolutely necessary for us. Without them we remain so foreign to the fire of God's love that we literally cannot live heaven's life.[37]

In heaven, our ecstasy will not only be enjoying God, but doing so with God's own joy. Faith, hope, and love unite us to God, but they cannot make it "natural" for us to live God's own life, since they have power in us only according to our human measure and reason. Here on earth we know God through faith's *created* concepts, and our love now cannot be as great as in heaven where our way of knowing God will make us love God more.[38] Thus we need more than our own reason to reach heaven's joy; the Holy Spirit needs to draw and lead us there through the Spirit's "instinct" and gifts within us.[39]

The gifts of the Holy Spirit in this way differ even from the virtues of faith, hope and love, since they empower us to live and act, not simply according to our own reason and measure, but according to *God's*.[40] These gifts thus perfect the virtues by raising us above our limited, human way of deciding and acting, so that God's unlimited love is the measure not only of *what* we do but also of *how* we do it.[41]

The Spirit's gifts thus enflesh God's desire for the most intense intimacy with us, even to the point of sharing with us not only God's own life, but also God's own *joy* in experiencing the divine life. This intimacy is itself the sheer gift of God's love. Paul knew our human weakness by experience; but he also knew the great gift of God to us: "The weak things of the world God has chosen, to confound the strong" (1 Cor 1:27). Thomas, too, realized that of ourselves we can do nothing, not even prepare ourselves to receive the Holy Spirit and the Spirit's gifts in our heart.[42] But he also knew that the Spirit's gifts are lavished on each of us at our baptism. The Holy Spirit longs to release the power of these gifts in our lives, just as in the saints' lives, if only we would desire and ask for the grace to surrender ourselves to the Spirit's leadings.

Thomas found that when the Holy Spirit does lead us we begin to live our life more from the Spirit than from ourselves.[43] Yet we are not simply passive instruments of the Spirit; on the contrary, the more receptive we are to the Holy Spirit, the more actualized we become in our own freedom and identity,[44] and the more our actions are truly our own.[45]

Thomas discovered that the Spirit acts in our inmost depths as the very *creator* of our freedom; the more we yield ourselves to the Holy Spirit, the more truly free and active we become.[46] And the more receptive we are to the Holy Spirit, the more we become not only creative and self-directive but also true leaders and inspirers of others.[47]

The Spirit's Anointing Teaches Us

Those who knew Thomas could see the Spirit's gifts radiate in him, especially the gifts of wisdom, understanding, and knowledge. They saw how each year he became more and more productive, until, toward the end of his brief life, he was creating scriptural, theological, and philosophical works with astounding energy. His friends knew that the sheer depth and prodigious output of his writings were impossible to any person's unaided efforts. They realized that only the Holy Spirit could fill Thomas with such a remarkable outpouring of wisdom.

Indeed, it was this gift of wisdom that marked Thomas' entire life with special radiance. Perhaps this is why he loved to reflect on the words of 1 John 2:27: "The *Spirit's* anointing teaches you everything." Thomas had seen for himself how the Spirit's anointing teaches us to avoid what is not of God and to believe and cling to the things of God, even if we are unlearned or lacking great intelligence. Unschooled, simple people who are close to God, Thomas observes, have a wisdom from the Holy Spirit that is far more remarkable than the natural "wisdom" of highly intelligent people.[48]

Thomas had found from his own experience that love makes

us know things our reason alone could never teach us about our dear one. Thus, for example, we can know someone with our mind, as we know that two and two are four. Or we can know someone through love, as we know our dearest friend. This latter is how we know God through the gift of wisdom.[49] *Love* is ultimately the source of all we know, since we truly learn only what we *want* to know in some way.[50] The more intense our love, the more it helps us to know our beloved by freeing us from preoccupations and concentrating our attention on our dear one.[51] It is true that charity gives us this kind of intimate knowing of God. But at our baptism the Spirit gives us also the gift of wisdom to perfect even our charity, so that we know God and the things of God by an intimate loving union with them.[52]

Parents who love their children need no prompting to embrace them; they spontaneously reach out to hold their little ones just because they cherish them. For Thomas, the Spirit's gift of wisdom is like this. Without effort and strain we have a certain "familiarity" with the things of God,[53] and charity's love gives us this wisdom.[54] We seem to recognize instinctively what is of God and what is not, for "this manner of discerning the things of God belongs to the Spirit's gift of wisdom in us."[55]

Through this gift we participate in God's own wisdom and know God in a way that far excels what we could know by our own reasoning. This is how Thomas himself learned all that he wrote, taught and preached about God—not simply by his study but even more by the Spirit's wisdom within him. Yet it was not only the gift of wisdom but also that of understanding which shone with special radiance in Thomas. From his own experience he gives his beautiful reflections on what this gift means in our lives. Our usual way of knowing reality is through our senses opening us to the *external* qualities of what we know. When we are young, our eyes may see a lovely flower; but we are not yet able to understand clearly what a flower is. When we reach that wonderful point of truly *understanding* the difference between a flower and a rock, we do not merely see external qualities with our senses, but we also "see" clearly with our mind. Even if we are not able to articulate our understanding, we penetrate to the very heart and essence of a flower to realize what a flower is, and why a flower is not a rock.[56]

Thomas tells us that to "understand" ("intelligere") in this way is to have an "intimate" knowing whereby we "read *inwardly*" ("intus legere") what we understand.[57] We are blessed by God with a "keen" mind when we can penetrate to the very heart of things.[58] Though there are myriads of dimensions "hidden within" every reality which we need to penetrate in order truly to understand its meaning,[59] when we do understand something, we seem to grasp in some intuitive way its very essence.[60] Thomas finds in this experience common to all of us a hint of what the Spirit's gift of "understanding" means in our life, for it is an *intimate knowing*,[61] making us pierce to the very heart of what we hear or read about God.[62]

This understanding is like having a brilliant light turned on in a dark room. What we could not see suddenly becomes wonderfully clear! Thomas thinks of how our human knowing begins with the "outside" of things; the stronger the "light" of our understanding, the further it can "see" into the heart of things. Yet the natural light of our understanding is limited, and so can reach only to a certain point. We need a light in our minds which allows us to see further still, to know what we cannot know simply by the small light of our reason. This great light is the gift of the Spirit's understanding,[63] incomparably stronger than our reason's dim light.[64]

Thomas contrasts this gift of understanding in us with the virtue of faith. Through faith we simply say "yes" to what is proclaimed to us. We do not necessarily understand anything at all about the depths of what we believe about the Trinity, or Jesus, or the Eucharist. But through the gift of understanding, we see the depth meaning of what we believe.[65] The Spirit's gift of understanding makes us penetrate to the very heart and essence of what we believe.[66] Through this gift, the Holy Spirit enlightens us so that we know the depths of God and the things of God in a way that far exceeds what we could know by our own limited minds.[67]

These insights of Thomas about the gifts of wisdom and understanding are especially profound since he knew their meaning from his own experience. But he writes also of the other gifts of the Spirit, gifts which likewise can shine with special force in us. Thomas describes the gift of knowledge, for example, as a sure judgment about God's truth in creation. We know truth about the world through the Spirit's simple, deep intuition rather than by a long process of reasoning. Sharing in God's own knowing of the world,[68] we have a gentle certainty about what we should believe about created reality, an intuitive, sure judgment in discerning the truth from error.[69] This is why even unschooled people who love Jesus seem to have an intuitive feel for the truth about created reality. Thomas reflects also on the other four gifts of the Spirit in our lives. By the Spirit's gift of counsel we know intuitively what we should do in certain situations, but in a way that far exceeds and perfects what our prudence alone could advise us to do. When we are prudent, our own good common sense leads us. But when we are inspired by the gift of counsel, the person of the Spirit guides us in what we should do.[70] And from his own experience Thomas knew that the more we submit ourselves to the Spirit's counsel, the more able we are to direct and guide others.[71] He also reflects on the gift of fortitude as the inner confidence the Spirit gives us to conquer our fear and empower us to face difficult situations with God's own strength and courage.[72] The gift of piety gives us an affection and familiarity with the Father, intensifying our desire to give God glory with our life and to do good to all people.[73] Finally, the gift of fear of the Lord tempers our lust for pleasure and draws us to revere God and to avoid everything that could separate us from God.[74]

Contemplation, Wisdom's Gift

Thomas was convinced that each one of us is meant to experience the power of all the Spirit's gifts in our lives. But God wants at least one of the gifts to shine in each of us in a special way. In Thomas himself, the gift of wisdom shone with special radiance and enabled him to write with particular depth about the paradox of the Spirit's wisdom which will not stay pent up within us. As a mendicant preacher in Dominic's community, Thomas could not imagine keeping what we know of God locked in our mind and heart. He knew that we *must* generously share the fruits of our contemplation with others; thus Thomas' beautiful phrase, "contemplata aliis tradere": to hand over to others what we lovingly contemplate.[75]

But the source of our wanting to share the fruit of our contemplation with others is precisely the Spirit's gift of wisdom that makes us "taste" and "savor" God in contemplative prayer. Thomas discovered from experience that this contemplation is communion with God as our dearest friend, for, Thomas assures us, we cannot help wanting to speak and share our heart with our close friend. Contemplation is simply our being with the divine persons, our beloved friends.[76]

All of our reading, meditation, study and prayer are meant to draw us to this quiet contentment in the Trinity.[77] In contemplative prayer we commune with God intimately, not by thinking or reasoning but simply by an intuitive understanding, a peaceful serenity in the God we love: "Be still and know that I am God" (Ps 46:10; RSV).[78] We are meant to share generously with others the sweet fruit of this contemplation.[79] But from his own experience, Thomas knew that we discover this contemplative contentment in God especially when the gift of wisdom deepens in our life.[80] For since contemplation means not only knowing but also loving God,[81] the Spirit's wisdom fills us with a loving peace and union with the Trinity.[82] Our contemplation, therefore, is meant to deepen our love for God, just as love alone inspires us to "waste" time with God in contemplative prayer.

Thomas found that this love joining us to God abounds as both the source and the goal of our contemplation.[83] For since charity alone unites us to God, charity is greater than faith or hope, and greater even than the Spirit's gifts.[84] Thomas knew how we ourselves give our love in every gift we give, and how our own experience hints at the far deeper truth at the heart of the triune God. Every other gift of the Father and Son is given to us in and because of the Spirit of love, who is the very source of all other gifts they shower on us.[85] The Holy Spirit is the Father's and Son's first, great uncreated gift to us, their very love in person. And the Spirit's charity is their first and greatest created gift to us, through which we share in the very person of the Spirit, and by which the Spirit directs and guides us. Faith, hope, and charity are the very principle and root of the Spirit's gifts in us.[86]

Since the Spirit intimately dwells in us through charity (Rom 5:5), charity itself completes and unites all the virtues. It is when the Spirit's charity deepens in our heart that the Spirit's gifts also intensify within us.[87] Thomas himself experienced how intensely we live a "mystical" life when the Spirit's gifts are the source of all we say and do. Through these gifts our life and actions become a true sharing in God's own way of living, and charity itself shines as the very root and heart of the mystical life we live.[88]

The more deeply we love the triune God, therefore, the more our thoughts and actions begin to exceed what our own reason and power can do. This wonderful truth was radiant in Thomas' own life. The older he grew, the more his love for the Trinity deepened, and the more the gift of wisdom intensified in him. This gift of the Spirit was the source of his prodigious outpouring of writings as he neared the end of his life. Thomas learned by experience that our truly knowing God through the gifts of wisdom and understanding always gives us deeper love of God.[89] And the more we know of God's infinite good, the more we both love the God we know and feel impelled to share the riches of this God with others.

Thomas speaks of our beloved Father sending the Son and Spirit into our minds and hearts in missions that extend in time their unending coming forth from the Father in eternity. We were given the beloved Son in a visible way at the incarnation, just as the Spirit was sent to us at Pentecost. But the Father continues to send them to us invisibly to transform us through their imprints of wisdom and love.[90] They come to us inseparably, the Word through the gift of wisdom, and the Holy Spirit through charity.[91] The closer we grow to Jesus and the Holy Spirit, the more deeply we grow in wisdom and love.

The wisdom that filled Thomas is not simply any kind of knowledge of God, but, as he himself tells us, only that "sweet" knowing which is warmed with love and breaks into love's affection.[92] Indeed, the only source of true wisdom is the bond of charity intimately joining us to the Holy Spirit.[93] Here on earth, as well as in heaven, we truly know God only through charity's love. And the more we are united to God through love, the more wonderfully the gifts, especially of wisdom and understanding, flower in our lives, since they are filled with the Spirit's love.[94] Moreover, the Son and Spirit leave an intimate "seal" of wisdom and love within us, enabling us to enjoy the persons themselves.[95] In the experience of love, therefore, Thomas found the whole meaning of his pursuit of wisdom. He drank in the Spirit's wisdom through his contemplative study and prayer, and lovingly shared its fruit through his preaching, teaching, and writing.

When Thomas describes the effects of the Spirit's wisdom in our lives, he shows the depth of his own personal knowledge of mystical union as familiar friendship with God. As he so often does, he reflects on our experience of love: we may know many things about our beloved, but the deepest things we learn only through love. Paul wrote to the Philippian community, "I hold

you in my heart" (Phil 1:7). Thomas finds in these tender words
a description of all who love. We seem to have only one heart,
soul, and even life with our beloved. This is why a merely superficial knowledge of our dear one can never content us. The Spirit
of love "searches the very depths of God," Paul tells us (1 Cor
2:10). Yes, Thomas adds, just as the Spirit, the very person of
love between the Father and Son, alone knows their depths, we
ourselves cannot help wanting to know our beloved's inmost
depths.[96]

Thomas knew, therefore, how we truly know our dear one only
through love, and because of love. Love makes us see our beloved
precisely as lovable, and therefore in a different light than if we
did not love him or her. Through love, we become our dear friend
in some way; we want our beloved's true good, and long for the
deepening of our love and union with him or her.[97] But in wanting to be with our loved one, we are not simply choosing the delight of our friend's presence in a self-centered way. We simply
want to be with, to be *one* with, our beloved.

From his own close friendships with Albert and Reginald,
Thomas discovered that love unites us to our beloved friends; they
are part of us and we are part of them. Indeed, we seem to be
"another self" to each other.[98] Yet this is far more true of our
intimate closeness with the Lord; as Paul tells us, "Those who
cling to the Lord are one spirit with him" (1 Cor 6:17). In this
most tender of our human experiences Thomas finds a small hint
of what our "contemplating" God means. We want and need just
to spend time with the triune God, peacefully enjoying the divine
Persons as our beloved friends.[99] In contemplation, therefore, we
know God the way we know a dear friend, through love.[100]

Tasting God's Sweetness

Thomas knew that in our deepest friendships we reveal our
heart's secrets to our friend (John 15:15). He had discovered this
truth in his own close friendship with Reginald, to whom he confided all the secrets of his soul. This experience helped him to understand how the Spirit's wisdom entrusts the secrets of *God's*
heart to us.[101]

The gift of wisdom leads us to depths where our own study and
reasoning cannot take us, for God's love in our heart is both *what*

we know and *how* we intimately know God. Through the Spirit's charity, we experience the divine persons as our beloved friends, present within us, loving us intimately, unconditionally. This gift of becoming God's own friends and "equals" Thomas calls "experientia divini consortii," the experience of God's own intimate companionship.[102] Thomas found that this is the very goal of our mystical life: tasting by experience how sweet the Lord is.[103] As he tells us, "We can testify about something only in the measure that we have *shared* in it."[104] Thomas found that our understanding is made perfect by our "seeing" what we contemplate, and our wisdom is completed by our intimately "tasting" what we experience.[105] He learned from Dionysius that we know God and the things of God not by just by studying them, but even more by experiencing them through love.[106] When we know God by experience, Thomas adds, we "taste" God's sweetness through a knowledge only the Spirit's love can give us.[107]

Thomas reflects on how physical goods are outside us, giving us a "sweetness" unable to satisfy our deepest hunger. We experience their presence through our senses of seeing, hearing, smelling, touching, tasting. But God is not like these physical realities; God is not outside us, but rather within the very depths of our being.[108] And although all that delights us is sweet to us, physical sweetness delights only our bodily hunger, while spiritual sweetness delights our soul's hunger.[109] Present in our midst, in our inmost heart, the triune God gives us a sweetness enabling us to resist evil and to enjoy what is good.[110]

This is why the psalmist encourages us to "taste and see how sweet the Lord is" (Ps 34:8). In reflecting on this beautiful psalm verse, Thomas thinks of how, in feasting on earthly food, we first see and then are drawn to taste the food we see. But when we feast on spiritual food, we first taste the banquet of God by experience, and only then do we truly see and know the food we eat. We truly know God only in tasting God by experience.[111]

All that delights us in the world—truth, honors, possessions, pleasures—exists in God in unbounded fullness. All that is sweet to us on earth delights us only because it flows from the infinite sweetness of God, the fount of all goodness. As he reflects on this beautiful truth, Thomas cries out with unrestrained praise, God is *"superexceedingly* great, incomprehensibly sweet," infinitely delightful! Whatever pleasure we can find on earth, its unbounded fullness is found in God's sweetness.[112] Indeed, the God whose mercy is incomparably sweet is sweetness itself.[113]

Yet we may not always experience God as sweet. Sometimes this may happen because sin itself is blunting our taste for good. Thomas thinks of the experience of being sick. When we are ill, we lose our sense of taste, and delicious food begins to disgust us. Sin is like this sickness, ruining our taste for good food. We begin to be pleased by what is distasteful and to be disgusted by what is wonderful. But as we become healed of the sin that makes us "sick," we begin to savor truly good food, to take delight in what is good beyond all imagining, God's own sweetness.[114] For the "sweetness" of God is God's *infinite goodness*.[115]

Whether we realize it or not, we are always seeking this goodness of God in everything that we desire. Origen tells us that in all that we want, we are really thirsting for what our heart desires. If our eyes could ask for what they want, they would ask for beautiful colors. Our ears would ask for exquisite sounds, and our heart would ask for beauty and truth, for honor and love and peace. But at the very *root* of all our desires is our heart's ache for God's loveliness. This is why the psalmist urges us, "Take delight in the Lord and he will give you your heart's desire" (Ps 37:4). And we delight in the Lord, Thomas tells us, precisely when we love God with all of our heart and above everything else.[116]

We live this love by offering our every action to God as a sacrifice of praise. Paul himself urges us, "Do everything for the glory of God" (1 Cor 10:31). In commenting on this text, Thomas recalls how the Hebrew people offered to God both sacrifices and holocausts, but holocausts were sacrifices *completely* consumed for God's glory. We ourselves can dedicate a part of ourselves or our possessions to God, and so offer God a "sacrifice" of praise. But just as Jesus did on the altar of the cross, we can give the triune God *everything,* keeping back nothing for ourselves, and so offer our whole life to God not simply as a sacrifice but as a *holocaust* of praise![117]

Thomas writes that the psalm verse, "I will go around your altar" (Ps 26:6), reminds us that we are the temple holding the altar of our heart, and that the Spirit's charity burns on our heart's altar. The "temple" is also the Church, whose altar is Christ, and we need to "go around" this altar by surrounding Christ with *all* of our heart's affection. The "temple," too, is God who contains the "altar" of the divine mercy poured out on us. Thomas urges us to make our very life speak the psalmist's cry of praise and love: "The Lord is good to all; God's compassion is over all that God has made" (Ps 145:9).[118] Thomas loved to think of David as a wonderful model of this wholehearted love for God. David saw that his life and every good were from God; this is why, even in his weakness, he responded to God's love with all of his love.[119] Let us do as David did, Thomas urges us; let us content ourselves not simply with ordinary, bland, and even tasteless food—with just what we need to be saved—but with God's magnificent banquet, with the exquisite delicacies that are God's own sweetness.[120]

We taste God's sweetness more and more as our actions are increasingly the "fruit" of the Holy Spirit[121] who gives us the delicious harvest of charity, joy, and peace.[122] In the measure that we give ourselves to the Holy Spirit's sweet power, we begin to live the Beatitudes, experiencing heaven even now. The Lord himself promises us the joy of the Beatitudes, for we live this perfect life not by our own strength but by the Spirit's sweet power within us. "How happy are the poor in spirit, the kingdom of heaven is theirs. . . . Happy are the merciful, for they shall obtain mercy. How happy are the pure in heart; they shall see God. Happy, too, are the peacemakers, for they shall be called children of God!" (Matt 5:3, 7-9). Here is the great paradox: in these Beatitudes that turn the world's values upside down, we discover the true joy of a life filled with the Spirit's own sweetness.[123]

"Drinking" the Torrent of God's Delight

Thomas invites us not only to "taste" God's sweetness but also to "drink" its delights. The psalmist tells us, "You give them to drink of the *torrent* of your delight!" (Ps 36:8). Thomas discovered this "torrent of delight" in the very person of the Holy Spirit, the font of contentment within us. From his own experience Thomas found that we drink of the Spirit's torrent especially through imbibing the Spirit's wisdom in study and prayer: "The fountain of wisdom is an overflowing stream" (Prov 18:4). When we thirst with all of our heart for God's sweetness, savoring it in our prayer and study, the Spirit's delights grow more and more irresistible to us.[124] Thomas reminds us how easily we would get drunk if we held our mouth to a huge cask of wine and simply drank with abandon! If we would fasten our heart's ache for love to the font of God's own sweetness and drink with abandon there, our heart and soul would become drunk with the Spirit's delight.[125]

Thomas knew that we cannot help feeling distant from God at times. We may experience our prayer as empty and distracted, and it may seem that God is far away rather than intimately near to us. But God is simply "hiding," not from *us,* Thomas assures us, but only from our feelings. God does this only so that in our *feeling* God to be absent, we will long for God all the more. In "hiding" from our feelings while all the while staying intimately within us, the triune God stores up wonderful blessings of love for us, for God's sweetness is contained not simply in the gifts of good feelings, but in the deeper blessings of true peace, joy, and love. By "hiding" from our feelings now, Thomas tells us, the Trinity often teaches us to "taste" the very sweetness that is deeper than anything our physical senses can experience. We are living heaven's life even now through grace, therefore, but we do not always *feel* the sweetness of God's goodness. In heaven's joy, however, God's sweetness will no longer be hidden even from our senses but will be unveiled and lavished on us as our unending joy and fulfillment.[126] Forever we will enjoy God to the full![127]

The psalmist's words, "My soul *thirsts* for God, the *living* God" (Ps 42:2) were especially touching to Thomas. He knew that in everything we ask for or seek, we are trying to get what we need or want; our desires prompt all of our asking. But in all of our desires, whether we realize it or not, we are really thirsting for *God.* Our every desire is an ache to enjoy and to be contented with God's infinite sweetness. Thomas thinks of how catechumens thirsting for the Spirit in baptism know the meaning of this ache with special force. This is why, Thomas tells us, we sing this psalm on Holy Saturday and on Pentecost when the solemn baptism of catechumens takes place.[128]

Yet it is not only catechumens who thirst for God. Those who long for God with growing intensity sing this psalm with special vehemence. They have learned that the world holds nothing they desire, Thomas writes, and so they increasingly long to come home to the font of life. This is why we so fittingly sing this psalm not only at baptisms, but also at funerals, for it voices our thirst to come home to the font of unending life. Thomas thinks of how a "living" font or wellspring continuously surges not with stagnant but with living water. For Thomas, the beloved Father *is* this living font of love and grace. Our tender Father, he tells us, is the font from whom we long to drink: the more the Spirit's gifts take hold of us, the more our whole being begins to thirst for the living font of the Father.[129]

It was this thirst for heaven which the Holy Spirit inspired with increasing intensity in Thomas' own heart as he reached the very prime of his life. His entire life had been an astonishing thirst to proclaim God's glory, but he had learned that he could share with others only what he himself tasted of the Spirit's sweetness in his own life.[130] Thus he learned to yield himself completely to the Spirit, drawing his every breath from the Spirit of love.[131] This love made him so taste God's sweetness that he could not keep it locked within himself. He *had* to "preach the Gospel, in season and out" (2 Tim 4:2); he *had* to share the good news of Jesus with others. In the end, Thomas' thirst for God's glory became not only a sacrfice but a holocaust of praise. "Aglow with the Spirit," Thomas lived his life of preaching not from his own empty resources but from the wellspring of the Holy Spirit, "Giver of Life" within him.

Notes

[1] Can 84; Foster, *Life,* 114.
[2] In Gal 5, lect. 7.
[3] In 1 Th 5.
[4] In Jn 1, lect. 4.
[5] In 1 Cor 2, lect. 3.
[6] In Jn 3, lect. 1, 5.
[7] In Jn 6, lect. 8.
[8] In Gal 5, lect. 7.
[9] Ibid.
[10] In Jn 3, lect. 2.
[11] In 1 Cor 3, lect. 3.
[12] In 1 Cor 6, lect. 3.
[13] In 1 Cor 3, lect. 3.
[14] In Jn 14, lect. 4.
[15] In Gal 5, lect. 3.
[16] In Rom 8, lect. 1.
[17] In Rom 8, lect. 3.

[18]Ibid.

[19]Cf. ST I-II, 68, 1-8.

[20]In Ps 30:12.

[21]In Gal 4, lect. 3.

[22]In Gal 2, lect. 1.

[23]ST III, 25, 3, ad 4.

[24]In 1 Cor 2, lect. 3.

[25]In Gal 4, lect. 3.

[26]In Rom 8, lect. 3.

[27]In Gal 5, lect. 7.

[28]ST I, 43, 3.

[29]ST I-II, 68, 4; I-II, 68, 6.

[30]Cf. ST I-II, 68, 4.

[31]ST I-II, 68, aa. 1-8.

[32]ST III, 7, 5; III, 7, 1.

[33]ST III, 7, 5, ad 2.

[34]ST I-II, 68, 1; I-II, 68, 2, ad 1. For most of the insights that follow in this section on the Spirit's gifts, I am indebted to William J. Hill, O.P., who graciously let me use his notes from a graduate class on Thomas' theology of the gifts taught by Paul Philippe, O.P., at the Angelicum in Rome.

[35]It was from Aristotle that Thomas drew his initial insight on the spirit's gifts as an "instinct" within us. Thomas was famliar with the *Librum de Bona Fortuna,* a translation of Aristotle's *Ethicorum Eudemiae.* In Ethics 7.4 Aristotle writes that if we are moved by divine instinct, we do not follow the dictates of human reasoning but are moved by a higher principle which we experience as so natural and easy to us that it seems like "instinct." Thomas refers to the *De Bona Fortuna* and describes the gifts of the Holy Spirit as a certain "instinct" which perfects us for acts which are higher than those of the theological virtues (ST I-II, 68, 1).

Even before Thomas, Albert was the first to view the Spirit's gifts as habits whose action in us is higher than that of the theological virtues of faith, hope, and love, since through the gifts God moves us directly (Sent III 34, a 1). Thomas himself writes (Sent III d. 34, q. 1, a 1) that among the many opinions of the time about the nature of the gifts, he follows the opinion—which is Albert's— that the gifts are principles of acts higher than the virtues.

While Thomas draws from Albert's insights, he goes even further in his own explanation of the gifts. In his commentary on Lombard's *Sentences,* written in 1255, Thomas writes that the gifts are distinguished from virtues by their manner of operating; the virtues operate according to our human manner of thinking, but the gifts operate in a higher than human and therefore heroic manner (Sent III d. 34, q. 1, a 1). At this early stage of his life, Thomas also stresses that the gifts are given to us to perfect the virtues of faith, hope, and love. For all the virtues, except charity, have a radical imperfection because of their natural way of working within us, according to our own human measure and dictates of reason (*In Isaiam* 9).

But in his *Summa Theologiae,* written between 1270-72, we find deeper insight on the gifts. Thomas distinguished the gifts from the theological virtues in still another way, according to the power which moves us to our final goal of heaven, our own reason, or God the Holy Spirit. Through the gifts, the Spirit influences us to know and act in a way above our natural powers of reason (ST I-II, 70, 4).

[36]ST III, 7, 5, ad 1.

[37]CG IV, 21, 8.

[38]ST I-II, 67, 6, ad 3.

[39]ST I-II, 68, 4.

[40]ST I-II, 68, 2.

[41]ST I-II, 68, 2, ad 1.

[42]Truth q. 12, a 4; In Eph 5, lect. 7.

[43]ST I-II, 93, 6, ad 1.

[44]ST I-II, 68, 3, ad 2.

[45]ST II-II, 23, 2.

[46]Cf. ST I, 105, 5.

[47]ST II-II, 52, 2, ad 3.

[48]Cf. ST II-II, 8, 4, ad 1.

[49]ST II-II, 45, 4.

[50]Cf. ST I-II, 9, 1.

[51]Cf. Truth q. 13, a 3; ST I-II, 33, 3; I-II, 33, 3, ad 2; Truth q. 37, a 1.

[52]ST II-II, 9, 2, ad 1.

[53]ST II-II, 45, 2.

[54]Ibid.; ST II-II, 45, 4.

[55]ST I, 1, 6, ad 3.

[56]ST II-II, 8, 1.

[57]Ibid.

[58]ST II-II, 8, 6, ad 1.

[59]ST II-II, 8, 1.

[60]ST II-II, 8, 1, ad 3.

[61]ST II-II, 8, 1.

[62]ST II-II, 8, 6, ad 2.

[63]ST II-II, 8, 1.

[64]ST II-II, 8, 1, ad 2.

[65]ST II-II, 8, 5, ad 3.

[66]ST II-II, 8, 6.

[67]ST I-II, 8, 4.

[68]ST II-II, 9, 1, ad 1.

[69]ST II-II, 9, 1.

[70]ST II-II, 52, 2.

[71]ST II-II, 52, 2, ad 3.

[72]ST II-II, 139, 1.

[73]ST I-II, 68, 4.

[74]ST II-II, 19, 9.

[75]ST II-II, 188, 6.

[76]CG IV, 22, 3.

[77]ST II-II, 180, 3.

[78]ST II-II, 180, 1.

[79]ST II-II, 180, 2.

[80]ST II-II, 45, 6, ad 3.

[81]ST II-II, 45, 2.

[82]ST II-II, 180, 7, ad 1.

[83]ST II-II, 180, 8, ad 1.

[84]ST I-II, 68, 8, ad 1; Char a 2, ad 17.

[85]ST I, 38, 2.

[86]ST I-II, 68, 4, ad 3; I-II, 68, 8.

[87]ST I-II, 68, 5.

[88]ST II-II, 184, 1, ad 2; I-II, 68, 4, ad 3.

[89]ST II-II, 180, 7.

[90]ST I, 43, 5, ad 2.

[91]ST I, 43, 5, ad 3.

[92]ST I, 43, 5, ad 2.

[93]ST II-II, 45, 6, ad 2; I, 43, 5, ad 2.

[94]ST I-II, 68, 8, ad 3.

[95]Sent I d. 14, q. 2, a 2, ad 2.

[96]ST I-II, 28, 2.

[97]Com Div Nom ch. 2, lect. 4.

[98]ST I-II, 28, 2.

[99]Cf. ST I-II, 28, 4.

[100]ST II-II, 180, 2.

[101]In Jn 15, lect. 3.

[102]In Ps 33:9.

[103]Ibid.

[104]In Jn 1, lect. 4.

[105]In Ps 33:9.

[106]ST II-II, 45, 4; II-II, 45, 2; II-II, 97, 2, ad 2.

[107]In Jn 17, lect. 6.

[108]In Ps 33:9.

[109]In Ps 24:7.

[110]In Ps 45:4, 8.

[111]In Ps 33:9.

[112]In Ps 30:16.

[113]In Ps 24:7.

[114]In Ps 30:16.

[115]In Ps 33:9.

[116]In Ps 36:3.

[117]In Ps 19:1.

[118]In Ps 25:4.

[119]In Ps 17:2.

[120]In Ps 36:3.

[121]ST I-II, 70, 2.

[122]ST I-II, 70, 3, ad 4.

[123]ST I-II, 69, aa 1-4.

[124]In Ps 35:4.

[125]Ibid.

[126]In Ps 30:16.

[127]In Ps 13:2.

[128]In Ps 41:1.

[129]Cf. ibid.

[130]In Jn 1, lect. 4.

[131]In Gal 5, lect. 7.

10

Bread of Angels

The townspeople of Naples knew the story of the time Thomas had celebrated Mass there on Passion Sunday. His face bathed in tears, he had become so lost in the Eucharistic mystery that he seemed to be sharing in Christ's own sufferings. After a long time, several of the brothers had come up to him and gently nudged him back to his senses. After Mass, in company with some knights who were friends of his, they had asked Thomas what had happened. But he would say nothing.[1]

We do not know if Thomas would not or could not speak at that moment. But we do know that what happened to him on that Passion Sunday was not unusual; it was only more public. Those who had been present at other times when Thomas celebrated the Eucharist knew that often he became so absorbed in its mystery that tears would run down his face.[2]

Tears can speak depths in our heart which no words can say. Thomas' tears tell us secrets of his soul which he did not speak in his writings, secrets of his tenderness toward this sacrament of love that feeds lowly creatures with God. Like his father, Dominic de Guzman, Thomas could not hold back his tears before the mystery of a God whose love would go to such lengths for us. "Nothing is more a source of wonder than that *God* should become one of *us,*" Thomas had written.[3] But that God should become smaller still, small enough to become our food—this is a mystery before whose depths he could only fall down and adore.

Thomas the nobleman had seen the wretched poor fall on their knees to thank a worldly lord for crumbs of bread. Now, in the

Eucharist, Thomas found another image, in stark contrast to the first. Of ourselves we are the poorest of the poor. And yet we feast, not on a banquet of crumbs thrown to us by an earthly nobleman, but on the very flesh of God served to us by God. "O res mirabilis! Manducat Dominum, pauper, servus et humilis," Thomas cries out in his hymn, "Panis Angelicus": "O marvelous wonder! A servant, poor and lowly, eats God the Lord!"[4]

Thomas' Corpus Christi Texts

The story of how Thomas came to write the Corpus Christi texts, from which the above stanza of the "Panis Angelicus" is taken, must be told in the context of the love for the Eucharist which the evangelical movements inspired in the people of the thirteenth century. The Albigenses of southern France had been teaching that the human body and material creation are evil. God who is pure spirit could not, would not, be given to us in what is so lowly, so evil: the material realities of bread and wine.

Not everyone was seduced by the Albigensian heresy. People influenced by the evangelical movements that spread through the northern European countries, especially Belgium, responded with a ground-swell of devotion to the Eucharist. The Beguines, devout women attached to various churches and monasteries of the region, helped promote Eucharistic customs such as keeping the sacred host in a tabernacle in church, displaying the host on the altar, ringing bells at the elevation, and celebrating benediction of the Blessed Sacrament.[5]

Popular devotion in the diocese of Liège made it the center from which this Eucharistic devotion spread. A saint and recluse attached to the Church of Saint-Martin's of Belgium, Julienne of Mont-Cornillon and Eva, urged Robert of Torote, bishop of Liège, to establish a feast in honor of the Eucharist. This he did in the summer of 1246. But since Holy Week prevented the exuberant celebration this sacrament deserves, Robert chose the first Thursday after Trinity Sunday as the diocesan feast of Corpus Christi.[6]

The feast quickly spread from Belgium to Germany. A Dominican cardinal and papal legate in Germany, Hugh of St. Cher, was deeply moved by the Corpus Christi festivities he witnessed in

Liège. In 1252 Hugh promoted the celebration of the feast in the German territories under his jurisdiction. Other factors added to the spread of this feast to the whole Church. Jacques Pantaléon, who would become Pope Urban IV, himself had participated in the celebration as archdeacon of Liège, and personally knew both Julienne and Bishop Robert.

As pope, Urban had received numerous petitions to extend this feast to the whole Church. But he took no action until an extraordinary event prompted Italian people from Bolsena, a village near Orvieto where he was staying, to beseech him to promulgate the feast. A German priest, a pilgrim at Bolsena, had been troubled by doubts about the Eucharist. One day as he celebrated Mass, he saw that the corporal was stained with blood. After residents of Bolsena brought the corporal in procession to Urban, he decided to extend the feast of Corpus Christi to the whole Church. He also enlisted Thomas to compose the texts for this feast.

Urban's choice of Thomas stemmed from his strong admiration for the Dominican, whom he had come to know at Orvieto. Before Thomas arrived at Orvieto, he had been teaching with great success at Paris as a master of theology from 1256–59. But in 1259 his Dominican superiors assigned him to the Dominican convent in his native Naples. In September of 1261, Thomas was again reassigned as theology lector at the Dominican convent in Orvieto. A year later, Pope Urban IV chose Orvieto as his residence. Urban was delighted to have the opportunity of getting to know Thomas. As his esteem for Thomas grew, he began asking him to write scriptural and theological works for him.

The pope's most important charge to Thomas was composing the liturgical texts, the Mass and Divine Office, for a feast which would honor the Eucharist. As we have seen, local churches had been celebrating this feast for some time. Texts for its liturgy, therefore, had already existed before Urban enlisted Thomas to write one for the entire Church's use. "Composing" a liturgy thus meant that Thomas was commissioned to re-write existing texts as well as to create new ones.[7]

Thomas completed his texts in 1264. On August 11, 1264, in his papal bull *Transiturus,* Urban extended the feast of Corpus Christi to the whole Church, granting a large indulgence to those who would celebrate this liturgy.[8] The liturgy Thomas composed, called the "Roman" one to distinguish it from other Corpus Christi texts used in Belgium, Germany, and Cistercian abbeys, was celebrated in Orvieto sometime between August 11 and September 8, 1264.[9] The Dominicans did not adopt the Roman Corpus Christi liturgy until over fifty years after Thomas' death. But as early as 1312–17, Tolomeo of Lucca, a contemporary of Thomas, wrote that it was indeed Thomas who had composed "the Office for Corpus Christi in full, including the lessons and all the parts to be recited by day or night; the Mass, too, and whatever has to be sung on that day."[10] It is true that our present texts for the Feast date from a fifteenth-century Roman liturgy attributed to Thomas.[11] Yet the same themes appear so clearly in Thomas' other writings that contemporary scholarship is beginning to recognize in our present texts certainly the heart and often the hand of Thomas himself.[12]

Sharing Together in the Lord's Death and Resurrection

Thomas' friends remembered a remarkable experience which had shown them how deeply he had expressed in his writings on the Eucharist his own love for the "sacred mysteries" of the Lord's Body and Blood. This incident, witnessed by several prominent Dominicans, occurred when Thomas was teaching at Paris. Other theologians at the university, debating about their varying interpretations of the Eucharist, reportedly asked Thomas for his insights. Before he would begin his response, Thomas gave himself to a long period of prayer, begging the Holy Spirit to inspire his thoughts and words. Several of his Dominican brothers, including Reginald and the prior of the convent at Paris, saw Thomas place the papers with his own insights and those of the other theologians on the altar in church. During his intense prayer, they heard a voice say to him, "You have written well of the sacrament of my body, as well as can be said in human language by one still living this mortal life." Thomas remained lost in prayer; as they watched, the brothers saw him raised "nearly two feet from the ground."[13]

These brothers were not overly surprised by what they had witnessed. They knew that Thomas celebrated Mass every morning and that he assisted daily at Reginald's Mass. They had seen Thomas' tears as he celebrated the Eucharist and had recognized the truth which his biographer, Bernard Gui, later described:

Thomas' profound writings on the Eucharist flowed from the
same grace which had inspired him to celebrate the Eucharist every
day—not in a distracted, halfhearted way, but with the most ardent love and devotion.[14]

Thomas' tears as he celebrated the Eucharist in some way physically expressed his own deep insight into its mystery. His tears
as he celebrated Mass recalled for him other tears, tears we cannot hold back in sharing a final meal with someone dear to us—
as when a loved one is dying, or going away for a very long time.
We know that, if we could, we would make this meal last forever. When our beloved eats the food we have so lovingly prepared, she or he is feeding on our love. When our loved one is
gone, we will remember every small detail of this meal. Most of
all, we will hold in our heart the words and gestures of closeness
in this last "banquet" together, since even more than dining on
the food before us, we have feasted on the banquet of each other's
love.

Thomas could not help recalling his own experience of poignant times like these. He lets his soul's remembrance speak the
depths of meaning that he experienced in the Mass as Jesus' Last
Supper with us, his intimate friends: "We remember most deeply
final words, especially those spoken by departing friends," he tells
us. "At such a time, our affection for our friends is most enkindled, and the things which affect us most are most deeply impressed in our soul."[15] The final intimate meal together of beloved
friends: this is the experience of closeness which most illumines
for Thomas the profound meaning of the Mass as Jesus' self-
giving to us in anticipation of his death. In *this* meal, however,
we do not dine merely on the love *symbolized* in the food. In the
Eucharist, the thanksgiving meal prepared for us by Jesus, our
beloved friend *is* the very food we eat.

Perhaps Thomas knew the story about the enormity of peli-
cans' love for their young. He had heard that they will pierce their
own breasts with their beaks and feed their little ones with their
own flesh and blood before they will let them starve. They will
give themselves as food to their starving young ones. The prayer
attributed to Thomas, "Adoro Te Devote,"[16] cries out in praise,
"O Jesus Lord, *you* are the loving pelican!"

At the paschal meal, the last meal he celebrated the very night
before he would die, Jesus gave himself to his beloved friends
in words and gestures of the most profound intimacy. On the mor-

row he would not be able to say what he longed to say to them. He would be unable to do anything in the agonies of his asphyxiation except gasp for the next breath. But because of this last meal with his beloved friends, they would understand the saving meaning of his death. They would see that Jesus did not have his life wrested from him. He freely gave himself for them, knowing that they would betray and forsake him, and forgiving them even before they did so. In this Eucharistic celebration, Jesus makes his healing death present to his beloved friends before it will happen. By his love, he satisfies our longing to have this meal never end; he answers beyond all we could dream our hunger never to say goodbye, our thirst to keep our beloved friend Jesus with us always.

For this longing becomes, in the Eucharistic meal, not just hopeless yearning but wondrous reality for us. In the most profound way Jesus makes this meal a banquet which will never end, a feast in which we and people of every time and age into eternity itself will feed on the exquisite food that is God. In this feast, time itself is transcended; at this table, past, present and future become one. "O sacred banquet," Thomas cries out! "Banquet in which we feed on Christ, and recall his passion; banquet in which we are filled with grace, and a pledge of future glory is given us."[17]

Yet today and in every age, we need to be *joined* in an intimate way to this sacrificial meal in which Jesus has made present his saving death for us. This is precisely what each sacrament, most especially the Eucharist, does: unite us now to Jesus' saving death and resurrection[18] and pour out on us today the healing power of his blood.[19]

Thomas thus understood the meaning of the Eucharist in the context of his own experience of the sacraments as human realities through which the unseen God truly comes to us. Thomas was filled with the sense of how precious our humanness is to God, so precious that the Word has become flesh in order to dwell with us. And just as Jesus, God the Word, has come to us through the humanness of his flesh, Jesus continues to come to us today precisely through the humanness of the sacraments.[20] Flowing from Christ's passion, these sacraments are human signs that make us whole,[21] saving signs through which Jesus fills us with his own love in dying for us.[22] Just as the physical body of Jesus has given us the invisible God, Thomas tells us, the physical signs that are the sacraments truly give us the healing love of the invisible God.[23] Through what we can perceive, the Lord showers on us the love deeper than what we can perceive; physical realities we can see become the means of our encountering the God we cannot see![24]

Through the physical reality of these sacraments Jesus himself fills us with the same Spirit of love he poured out upon the world at Pentecost. This is true of every sacrament but especially of baptism, the foundational sacrament whose entire purpose, Thomas tells us, is to lead us to the Eucharist.[25] He reflects on how the same Spirit visible at Jesus' baptism fills our own hearts at our baptism: "The Holy Spirit descended *visibly* in a physical form on Christ at his baptism so that we might believe that the Spirit descends *invisibly* on all of *us* who are baptized."[26] Indeed, baptism derives its healing, divinizing power not only from the passion of Christ but also and inseparably from the Holy Spirit.[27] Deeper than the external action of the one who baptizes, therefore, is the interior action of the Holy Spirit; in the person of the minister of baptism, it is truly the Holy Spirit who baptizes us.[28]

Because we were baptized into one Spirit, we are now meant to drink of the one Spirit (1 Cor 12:13) by slaking our soul's thirst with the precious blood, the "sacramental drink made holy through the Spirit."[29] In the Eucharist, therefore, we receive not only Jesus, but also the Holy Spirit who filled Jesus with the love to die for us. From his own experience of the Eucharist, Thomas became convinced of the intimate link between baptism, joining us to Jesus in his death and rising (Rom 6:1-11), and the Eucharist, "memorial of the Lord's passion."[30] He saw that the death of Jesus shines as the cause of salvation for the whole world, the one remedy for our wounds and sin.[31] By plunging us into Christ's death, baptism heals us as truly as if we ourselves suffered and died with the infinite love that filled Jesus' heart.[32]

In this way baptism is the sacrament of *faith* flowing from Christ's passion and rooting us in Christ. But the Eucharist is the sacrament of *love* streaming from his passion as the bond of our perfection in charity (Col 3:14).[33] We are baptized, therefore, precisely so that we can receive the Eucharist: "By baptism we are ordained to the Eucharist."[34] While baptism unites us to Jesus, the Eucharist, sacrament of love, reigns as the crowning point and culmination of our baptism, giving us Jesus as our very food.[35]

The Eucharist as the Culmination of All the Sacraments

For Thomas, not only baptism but *all* the sacraments are meant to lead us to the Eucharist as their purpose and culmination. Confirmation, for example, perfects us with the Spirit's love precisely so that we will be drawn more powerfully to the Eucharist. The sacraments of reconciliation and anointing of the sick prepare us to receive the Lord more worthily. The sacrament of marriage signifies the union of Jesus with us, his Church, and it is this very same union of which the Eucharist is the most poignant sign.[36] The sacrament of ordination, too, is ordered in a special way to the Eucharist as its culmination, filling those who receive it with the Spirit of love so that they can preside in love at the Eucharistic celebration, the saving memorial of Christ's passion. "All the orders bear a relation to the Eucharist, the sacrament of peace granted to us by the shedding of Christ's blood."[37] Thomas shows us in this way the profound spiritual and theological source of his own intense devotion to the Eucharist, "the greatest of all the sacraments."[38]

With Dionysius, Thomas was convinced not only that all the sacraments lead us to the Eucharist, but also that all the sacraments should be completed by our sharing in the Eucharist as their culmination and goal.[39] For in the Eucharist we receive not only the love powerful enough to convert us completely to God,[40] but also the very person of Jesus, who unites himself to us in this sacrament most intimately of all.[41] Indeed, the Eucharist alone gives us Jesus in an intimate union with us as members of his own body: "The common spiritual good of the whole church is contained substantially in the sacrament of the Eucharist."[42] The Eucharist thus is the "consummation of our spiritual life and the purpose of all the sacraments."[43]

At the Lord's own command, therefore, we, his community of beloved friends, continue to celebrate in the Eucharist his saving death for all time. In the Corpus Christi Mass sequence, the "Lauda Sion" sung before the Gospel reading, Thomas cries out, "On this solemn day we recall the institution of the Lord's table. What Christ did at this supper he bade *us* also to do in his memory. Taught by his sacred command, we consecrate bread and wine as a victim for our salvation." In his prayer for the Corpus Christi liturgy Thomas begs God that, as we celebrate the Eucharist, we may do so, not in a distracted, halfhearted way, but with all of our heart, experiencing for ourselves the healing power of the Mass, the "memorial of the Lord's passion."[44] For this sacrament makes present the saving sacrifice of Jesus' death,[45] and enables us to partake of the fruit of the Lord's own passion.[46]

Bread of Life

Thomas loved to ponder how the Eucharist, the Lord's Body and Blood, is the fruit of the Mass, our Eucharistic ("thanksgiving") celebration of the Lord's death and resurrection. This saving meal is Jesus' most intimate act of *friendship* with us: on the night before he died Jesus gathered his *friends*[47] and celebrated with them the paschal meal. But in place of the bread and wine given as a sharing in the Exodus experience of old, Jesus anticipated his healing death and offered his own body and blood as our saving victim.

In the Corpus Christi sequence, Thomas recalls the Old Testament figures who could only foreshadow the love Jesus poured out in his saving death and resurrection and which he now makes present to us in the Mass. The Father's love for us is prefigured in Abraham, whose devotion made him willing to sacrifice even his beloved, his only son, Isaac. Jesus' saving death is prefigured in the blood of the paschal lamb, smeared on the the Hebrews' doorposts to save them from the plague's destruction. As an act of intimate communion with God, the people immolated and consumed this paschal lamb—a foreshadowing of the true Lamb whose flesh and blood now feed us with God.

Finally, as the Hebrew people wandered through the desert on the way to the Promised Land, God poured down manna from heaven to feed them—a pale symbol of the Eucharist which feeds us with the Bread of Angels. For as wonderful as this loving deed was, it could only hint at the unspeakable love now showered on us: "At this table of the new King, a new pasch of the new law ends the old phase. The new wipes out the old, truth makes the shadows flee, light eliminates the night!"[48] Now, we feed not on creatures—on manna or even a paschal lamb—but on God.

John tells us, "the Word became *flesh* and dwelt among us" (John 1:14). On the cross Jesus poured out upon us the saving power of his blood, the physical symbol of love no eye could see, nor heart imagine. Here in the blood of Jesus is healing for the entire world. Thomas sings in his Corpus Christi Vespers hymn, "Pange Lingua": "Write, O my tongue, of the mystery of the glorious body and precious blood poured out as the redemption of our world!" And the prayer, "Adoro Te Devote," which, if not completely from Thomas' own hand, surely expresses the sentiments of Thomas' heart, gives unrestrained praise before the Eucharist as the "memorial of the Lord's death," lavishing on us the saving power of Jesus' blood: "O loving pelican, Jesus Lord, wash my uncleanness in your blood. For one drop of your blood is enough to make the entire *world* whole and cleansed from every guilt!"

Our experience of intimate friendship thus became for Thomas the key symbol of the Eucharist as the mystery of Jesus' love— love so ardent that he gives us himself to eat. Thomas knew how love makes us long for a union with our beloved that is so profound, so intense and intimate that no closeness seems close enough. Only having our loved one literally within the depths of our heart and soul could satisfy our longing. Parents lovingly, jokingly say to their little ones, "You are so sweet I could eat you!" We smile when we hear these words, for we recognize the deep longing they express, an ache within each of us. Every intimacy we have with one we love is simply our attempt to achieve the impossible: union so close that we become one heart, one mind, one soul, even one body with each other.

The force of Jesus' love for us makes him long to be present with us even now in his human flesh. And so in the Eucharist, Jesus does not deprive us of his intimate physical presence even now, but continues to give us *himself* in his flesh and blood. We ourselves cannot help wanting to "live together" with our friends, Thomas tells us, and our own experience can only hint at the desire of Jesus, our beloved friend, to "live with" us. This is why he promises us as our joy for all of eternity his own human, physical presence. But even now as we wait for heaven Jesus gives us his bodily presence in this sacrament as the most intimate sign of his love for us. Thus Christ's "familiar" union with us in the Eucharist cannot help filling us with hope and joy.[49]

In "Pange Lingua," Thomas sings of that wondrous night on which Jesus, anticipating his passion, gave himself to us in the most intimate way possible as our sacred drink and our very food: "Given to us, born for us from the inviolate virgin, Jesus made his home with us in the world . . . and closed his life in a wondrous way. On the night of the Last Supper . . . he gave *himself* as food to the band of the twelve."

Thomas sees in the Eucharist our true medicine, perfecting and fulfilling, nourishing, healing, and strengthening us.[50] But for Thomas, the Eucharist is most of all our true food,[51] the intimate bread of life who is content only with being united to us in the very depths of our being.[52] The Eucharist does for our inmost soul infinitely more than earthly food can do for our body, for in it Jesus feeds us with his own flesh and blood to sustain and restore us, to make us grow and fill us with the most profound delight.[53]

The people of Thomas' time used bread as their staple of life. Thomas himself knew the delight of freshly baked bread, of feeding on its hardy goodness so sweet to all our senses. Yet he knew, also, that we can eat even the most delicious bread only piece by piece, and that it can nourish us for only a short while. Regardless of how hungry we are, we cannot push a table laden with food into our mouth at one gulp. And even as we enjoy what we have eaten, we soon become full, and can eat no more; yet within a short time we are hungry again.[54]

For Thomas, everything less than God is like this food. Earthly food, like all earthly pleasure, passes away with time. After we have had it for a while, we become surfeited, and our pleasure gives way to satiety, and then to disgust. When our initial enjoyment passes, we have only the memory of the pleasure we once had. But spiritual blessings like the peace and joy that are given to us in the Eucharist are not like this, Thomas assures us. We do not have to enjoy them only piece by piece, and their plenty never runs out! The more we enjoy spiritual blessings, the more they increase in us; their richness and pleasure never satiate or disgust us but stay with us forever.[55]

Jesus thus feeds us with *real* food that nourishes not only our body but our heart and soul as well. To satisfy our every hunger, Jesus gives us nothing less than himself, the living bread whose plenty never runs out, and of whose delight we can never have too much.[56] And unlike earthly bread, this food changes us into itself,[57] for through the Eucharist we "eat *Christ.*"[58]

Thomas encourages us to receive the Eucharist daily, for we need the Lord's intimacy and power within us not only on some days but every day. Just as we would not think of letting a day go by without eating earthly food to nourish and sustain our body, we need to be fed daily with the Lord's intimate presence in the Eucharist. "It is a *good* thing to receive the Eucharist every day, as long as we are properly disposed," Thomas tells us.[59] If for some reason we cannot receive the Eucharist sacramentally, he urges us to receive it spiritually through our desire. Indeed, he says, all of us *must* in some way receive the Eucharist, either sacramentally or spiritually, for it is the Eucharist that incorporates us into and unites us with Christ, our saving Lord.[60]

Yet Thomas knew that our mere presence at the Eucharistic celebration is not enough to make us experience the delight and healing power of the Lord's Body and Blood. We know how thoughtless and distracted our presence at the Eucharist can be, how devoid of our own personal investment and participation in the mystery. This is why Thomas was convinced that we truly experience the power of the Lord's passion and resurrection in the measure that we consciously give ourselves to the Eucharistic celebration through faith and charity.[61] For although Jesus comes to us intimately in the Eucharist, we experience his closeness only by consciously cleaving to him in a personal communion through love and faith.[62]

The prayer "Adoro Te Devote" describes the personal nature of this faith that alone truly feeds us with God in the Eucharist: "Humbly I adore you, hidden God, concealed under these forms. My whole heart submits itself to you; contemplating you, it totally fails. Sight, touch, taste in you are deceived; hearing alone safely is believed. I believe all that the Son of God has spoken, for nothing is more true than the word of Truth. On the cross your divinity alone was concealed. But here your humanity, too, is hidden. Yet, believing and trusting both, I seek what the penitent thief sought."

It is by our own personal faith, therefore—faith that we express inseparably as a community—that we truly share in the Last Supper which feeds us with God. In "Pange Lingua," Thomas invites us, Jesus' own community of beloved friends, to celebrate the Eucharist together with this living faith: "Let the old give way to a new rite, and let *faith* supply for our senses' defects." In "Lauda Sion," Thomas also invites us to experience the depths of the Eucharistic gift precisely by our faith: "We believe that bread becomes his flesh, and wine, his blood. What you do not understand, what you do not see, faith full of spirit makes firm!"

Thomas knew by experience that the outward sign of the Eucharist, bread and wine eaten, signifies the intimate union of Jesus with us in the depths of our being. The Eucharist is real power for us, therefore, only when our inner faith truly expresses what the sacrament signifies. Only faith unites us to Jesus and enables us to experience for ourselves the healing power of the Eucharist in our life.[63] Note that, for Thomas, our faith is not a matter of mere feeling, since we can have deep faith without feeling that we do. Indeed, our very desire to believe *is* belief. Our "worthily receiving" the Eucharist thus means, not that we are worthy to feed on God, but rather that we *want* to believe more deeply, and that we are trying to be free of all that holds us back from closeness to Jesus.[64]

Just as our desire to believe is itself belief, our desire to receive the Eucharist is also a true way we can feed on the Eucharist. At those times when we are not able to share in this sacrament itself, Thomas urges us to receive it through our desire. God is not bound to the sacraments as the only way to fill us with the saving power of Jesus' passion.[65] Since Christ himself comes to us in the sacraments, he can give us the reality of a sacrament without the actual sacrament.[66]

Thomas thinks of how babies can be filled with grace while still in their mothers' wombs, as John the Baptist was.[67] He reflects, too, on how, in cases of need, non-ordained persons can hear our confession, since the act of repentantly confessing our sins is more essential than the person to whom we confess them.[68] While this kind of confession is not the fullness of the sacrament, it is quasi-sacramental and a true share in the sacrament of reconciliation, truly giving us God's forgiveness, reconciling us both to God and to the Church community.[69] We do need the sacrament of reconciliation to forgive and heal our serious sin, but if we cannot receive this sacrament actually, Thomas was convinced that we can receive it through our desire.[70]

In the same way, Thomas considers how powerful our heart's desire for the Eucharist can be in giving us the intimate union with Jesus that is the Eucharist's key effect: "Spiritual food changes us into itself." Yet we can be changed into Christ and become incorporated in him by our desire, even without receiving the Eucharist sacramentally;[71] we can eat Christ's flesh and drink his blood spiritually by union with him through our faith and love.[72] In a special way, we can receive the Eucharist through desire, and, indeed, we are *commanded* to receive it (John 6:53) at least through desire.[73] And when we are unable to feel that we desire it, our very wanting to desire it joins us to the Lord's presence through the *Church community's* desire. We ourselves feed on the Eucharist spiritually in love and faith through our union with the community's desire.[74]

Bond of Charity

This insight shows Thomas' profound sense of the communal nature of the sacraments, especially the Eucharist. Thomas could not imagine our cleaving to Jesus simply as isolated individuals. Salvation means that God's own love makes us whole in Jesus, but we gain this wholeness in communion with one another. It is the love binding us together that shows we belong to Jesus: "By *this* shall all know that you are my disciples, if you have love one for another" (John 13:35).

As the memorial of Christ's passion, the Eucharist itself is the source of our growing in this love and union. Thomas found that feeding on this "food of unity" is the very means of our becoming more deeply united not only with the Lord but also with one another.[75] "The sacrament of the Eucharist pertains principally to charity, since it is the sacrament of the Church's unity. The Eucharist is the origin and bond of charity, containing Christ himself, in whose person the whole Church is united and incorporated."[76]

As these beautiful words show us, Thomas' profound sense of our intimate union with Jesus through love forms the context for his reflections on the Eucharist as the "bond of charity." Through love, Christ has joined us to himself in a bond so intimate that we are now members of his own body. Indeed, as Paul assures us (1 Cor 12:27), we are the very body of Christ. But we are also Christ's "fullness" (John 1:16), and through love's intimate union, everything that belongs to him belongs also now to us. "All spiritual understanding, gifts, and whatever can be present in the Church"—all of these Christ possesses to overflowing, and he now lavishes them on us. The wonderful gifts of Christ are made explicit in some way in the members of his Church. For example, as the one "who fills all in all" (Eph 1:23), Christ makes some of us wise with his perfect wisdom and others just with his perfect justice. Since we are Christ's mystical body, all of the gifts we have share in Jesus' own treasures for the good of the Church.[77]

Because we are truly his body, we are members not only of Jesus, but also of one another: we belong not to ourselves but to one another (Rom 12:5). Thomas found from his own experience the depth of this truth we confess when we proclaim, "I believe in the communion of saints." We are bound irrevocably to one another in faith and love, and we are meant to experience in our own lives the power of this truth. The good of each belongs to all, and everything that we are and do is meant to be a means of helping and healing the entire body. "We all are *one.* Thus, if we live in charity, we share in all of the good done in the entire world," Thomas tells us. And because of our union with each other in charity, we especially benefit those for whom we consciously do good.[78]

Thomas loved to ponder how the Church's one great "common good" is contained in person in the Eucharist.[79] As the Eucharist increasingly unites us to each other through faith and charity, we are meant to help each other more and more, in this way growing strong as one body.[80] When he reflects on this closeness to each other as members of one body, Thomas finds our bond with the whole community expressed in a special way through the two apostolic leaders, Peter and Paul, on whose faith our own is founded. Thomas contemplates how Peter himself was fast-knit to the Eucharistic community. Many people had left Jesus at his words, "This is my body; this is my blood," but Peter was Jesus' *beloved friend,* Thomas tells us, and he loved Jesus with the devotion of friendship-love. In Jesus, Peter also loved his brothers and sisters in the community; he "guarded his friendships and had a special affection for Christ. When he responded to Jesus, therefore, 'Lord, to whom shall we go? You alone have the words of eternal life,' Peter answered not simply for himself but also for the whole community."[81]

Thomas thinks, too, of how, in his letters to his communities, Paul would send not only his own greetings, but also those of the brothers and sisters to whom he was joined. In Paul's sentiments, Thomas hears the entire community described "in terms of sweet familiarity." Paul is not alone: the whole community is "with" him to console and help him. Other scriptural passages also express this profound, joyous communion. In helping one another as brothers and sisters, we become "like a strong city" (Prov 18:19). And because an "inseparable charity" fastens us to each other, it is "good and pleasant for us to dwell together in unity" (Ps 133:1).[82] The Eucharist which both signifies and gives us Christ, therefore, also signifies all the members of his body;[83] because of our intimate union with Jesus as his members, we are also bound irrevocably to one another. For the Eucharist is the "sacrament of *love*"[84] and thus the sacrament of the Church's unity:[85] "We, though many, are one bread, one body, who partake of the one bread" (1 Cor 10:17). Thomas saw how Christ has given us this sacrament precisely to feed us by uniting himself to us, his own members, even more intimately than physical food is united to our body. And because intimate union is charity's effect,[86] when we receive the Eucharist in faith, we receive and deepen our union not only with the Lord but also with one another. We experience this beautiful truth, for example, when we share in the Eucharist with someone we love. Each time we receive this sacrament, then, we deepen our union both with Jesus and also with one another as members of his body, the Church.[87]

Thomas was struck also by one particularly precious sign of the union which the Eucharist causes among us. In every Eucharistic celebration in every part of the world, we pray for those not present—and this would serve no purpose, Thomas comments, if the Eucharist did not help also those to whom we are bound in love.[88] Regardless of how small the number of those present, every Eucharist is universal in its healing effects, helping not only those for whom we pray but also "the entire Church, living and dead." For "the Eucharist contains the universal cause of all the sacraments, Christ himself,"[89] and since Christ is present in every Eucharistic celebration, the whole Church is present at every Mass, even if only one or two people are physically present.

In a remarkable passage written near the end of his life, Thomas shows his tender love not only for the Lord but also for the Lord's little ones. Thomas, who so loved the Eucharist himself, was unwilling to see children deprived of this sacrament. At a time when it was not customary in the Western rites for children to receive the Eucharist, Thomas found a way to explain how God's mercy provides for these little ones. The Eucharist so intimately binds us to one another, he tells us, that even children share in the community's faith. Little ones can receive the Eucharist even before their age allows them, through their union with the mature believing members of Christ's body. "That children are baptized means that they are destined by the Church to the Eucharist. And just as children believe through the Church's faith, they desire the Eucharist through the Church's intention. Through the Church's desire, therefore, little children receive the Eucharist's reality."[90]

Paul's profound insight that "we, though many, are one body in Christ" (Rom 12:5) thus inspired Thomas to see the entire Church as one mystic person with Christ in the unbreakable bond of charity. This sense of our intimate union with Jesus is particularly evident in Thomas' commentary on the psalms. He continually hears the voice of Christ himself praying in the person of his suffering members. When the psalmist prays for mercy, for example, Thomas hears Christ himself crying out as if he were suffering sin and wounds in his own body. Indeed, Thomas tells us, Christ so joins himself to us that our suffering becomes his suffering. Christ himself was sinless, but because we his members suffer the wounds of sin, Christ prays as if suffering these sins in his own body. When the psalmist cries out in fear, Thomas hears the voice of Jesus before his passion, crying out in fear. In his own human flesh, Jesus himself feared the tortures of his death. This is why the words of Psalm 22 are truly Christ's own sentiments before his passion. But now, for our sake, Christ prays the psalmist's words deep within each of us, his beloved members. For Paul's words are Christ's own assurance to us: "I hold you in my heart" (Phil 1:7); and *we* are Christ's "heart whom he especially loves."[91]

Christ thus prays the psalms now in us, the members of his body still being abused and tortured today.[92] He cries out the psalmist's words, "Why have you forsaken me?" (Ps 22:1) in the voice of those who are suffering. He cries out in the weak and feeble, in those afraid before the agonies of their own passion. All that his members suffer, Thomas tells us, becomes in some profound way the suffering of Christ himself, since the Church is his mystical body. "Christ is transformed into the Church and the Church into Christ and so they speak as one person."[93]

This intimate union is most tenderly expressed and deepened in the Eucharist, the sacrament of love that by its very nature forgives and heals our sin.[94] The closeness of Jesus to us cannot help filling us, therefore, with the most profound love and trust. "Because of such familiar union of Christ with us, the Eucharist is the sign of supreme charity and the uplifter of our hope!"[95]

Bread of Angels

"O sacred banquet, in which Christ is received, the memory of his passion is recalled, our souls are filled with grace and a pledge of future glory is given to us!" As we have seen, in this Magnificat Antiphon for the Corpus Christi Vespers, we find Thomas' profound insight into how the past, present, and future become one in the Eucharist. We feed on Christ here on earth so that we can be led to the whole purpose of the Eucharist, the unending delight of heaven where we will enjoy Jesus as the angels do. Our eating of Christ in the Eucharist is our way of sharing even now in that "eating" by which the angels enjoy Christ. For "eating" Jesus means enjoying not simply Jesus' love for us, but *Jesus himself!*

The angels in heaven enjoy Jesus in an unhindered way, as he truly is in himself. But the paradox of God's love is that even now, we ourselves, weak, mortal human beings, can feed on the Bread of Angels in the Eucharist and enjoy Christ as the angels do.[96] We feed on this Bread of Angels precisely to be filled with the unquenchable life that the risen Lord is. For the Eucharist causes heaven to well up in us *now,* at the same time that it brings us to heaven's perfect joy by its gentle power, full of delight.[97]

In his Corpus Christi sequence, "Lauda Sion," Thomas says, "Behold the bread of *angels,* made the food of *pilgrims,* true bread of children which must not be given to dogs. Good shepherd, true bread, Jesus, pity us. Pasture us, protect us, make us see your good in the land of the living. You who know all things and can do all things, you who feed us mortals *here,* make us *there* the dinner companions, the coinheritors and intimate *friends* of the company of the saints. Amen! Alleluia!"

Thomas finds in the Eucharist, therefore, the spiritual bread which gives us this unquenchable joy and peace of the angels even now. In the banquet of the Eucharist we feast on the very cause of the angels' and saints' joy; with them, we feed on God! And

feasting on the infinite pleasure of God, our soul's deepest longings are satisfied even now as a precious foretaste of heaven.[98]
This is why Thomas' reflections on the Eucharist resound with
the joy he himself experienced so often in this sacrament, a profound contentment in God's delight and "sweetness" within us.
He recalls the words of the Song of Songs: "Eat, O friends, and
drink, and be *inebriated,* dearly beloved!" (Cant 5:1). The Eucharist, Thomas tells us, inebriates us with God's sweetness. Babies instinctively turn away from food that is bitter, and just as
instinctively delight in what tastes sweet. We learn quickly by experience that food not only nourishes us but also can delight us!
Indeed, we learn very early to eat the foods that most please us.
Yet delicious food can please only our tongues, and only for a
little while. But God has food for us so sweet that it delights our
whole being, and forever. The Eucharist is not only infinitely
nourishing, Thomas assures us; it is also infinitely delightful, because it "inebriates us with *God's* own sweetness."[99]

In the Eucharist, therefore, we receive God's intimate kindness
refreshing our heart and soul with God's sweetness, infinite
enough to satisfy our every desire.[100] Thus the Eucharist cannot
help causing jubilant praise to well up from within us, the praise
that impels us to seek nothing but God.[101] Thomas' "Lauda Sion"
rings out with this joy flowing from a heart overwhelmed with
such love. That Jesus would desire such closeness to us that he
becomes our very food: *this* is a love before whose depths we must
shout our praises! "Praise your Savior, O Sion, praise your leader
and shepherd in hymns and canticles! Praise as much as you can,
as much as you dare, because the God who is greater than all praise
can never be praised enough! On this solemn day we recall the
institution of this table. May our praise be full and resounding,
may our jubilation be delightful and beautiful! A theme of special praise is set before us today, the living Bread, the Bread of
Life!"

And in his Corpus Christi Matins hymn, "Sacris Solemniis,"
Thomas voices his jubilant praise:

> May our gladness be joined to this sacred solemn feast. From
> the depths of our hearts, with deep feeling, let there be public cries
> of praise. Let the old things pass away and let everything be new:
> our hearts, voices, and works!

We recall the eve of that Last Supper. With his own hands the Lord gave his body to the disciples; all of him was given to all, given to each.

He gave the weak a tray of his body, he gave to the sorrowing a drinking cup of his blood, saying, "Receive this cup I give you, and all of you drink from it."

Bread of angels made bread of humans: this heavenly bread gives an end to the types! O marvelous, extraordinary wonder! A servant, poor and humble, consumes God the Lord.

We ask you, one, triune God, to visit us as we worship you. Through your way lead us where we tend, to the light where you dwell. Amen.

Pledge of Eternal Life

Thomas experienced the Eucharist as an infinite feast, an overflowing banquet whose food never runs out. Its sweet-smelling bread is the Bread of Life, satisfying our every desire. He thinks of the incomparable difference between the Eucharist and earthly bread: the more we eat of created bread, the more satiated and even disgusted with it we become. But the more we eat of the Bread of Life, the more we *hunger* for it! Because it "contains the very person of Christ,"[102] the Eucharist gives us infinitely more life than bread gives to our bodies. Jesus gives himself to us as food, food that not only nourishes us and makes us grow, but also that heals and delights us.[103]

Because Jesus is the Bread of Angels, he comes to us in the Eucharist not as a disembodied spirit but as flesh of our flesh, to feed and heal us in our deepest identities as persons of flesh and blood. Jesus heals us in the Eucharist through his risen *flesh*. "Christ gives life to the world through the mysteries which he accomplished in his flesh. Because the humanity of Christ in the Eucharist is united to the Word of God, his very *flesh* is *life-giving*."[104] Thomas recalls Augustine's words: "I am the food of the robust. Grow and you will eat me. But you will not change me into yourself; *you* will be changed into *me*."[105] Jesus comes to us, too, as medicine and healing for our every wound, the balm for our every physical or spiritual sickness.[106] Since the Eucharist "inebriates us with *God*," as we feed on it, we are more and more transformed into Jesus and made living members of his body.[107]

This healing of our human flesh through the Eucharist is a precious foretaste of our resurrection, when Christ will permeate even our bodies with his own unquenchable life. Present in the Eucharist "not only in his divinity, but also in the reality of his flesh, Jesus is the cause of resurrection not only of our souls, but of our *bodies* as well."[108] As he reflects on this mystery of the Lord's Body and Blood, Thomas cannot help finding its meaning illumined precisely in our experience of intimate friendship. "It is the special characteristic of friendship to live together with friends," he writes. We are not content with mere thoughts of our beloved friend; we want his or her physical presence! This common experience helped Thomas to see how Jesus' *friendship* with us has impelled him to become flesh of our flesh. And this same love of friendship has made him impatient to give us the joy of his *"physical* presence as our final reward."[109]

Thomas fills his Corpus Christi texts with the marvelous paradox of profound worship invaded by tumultuous joy before this wondrous sacrament that "inebriates us with God!" "To venerate worthily such a great sacrament," Thomas sings in "Pange Lingua," "let us fall headlong with our faces to the ground in worship. Let us cry out our praise and jubilation, our well-being, honor, and benediction to the Trinity. Amen!"[110]

In the hymn for Matins, "Sacris Solemniis," sung in the early morning of the Feast, Thomas bids us to welcome the day with glad shouts of joy: "May our extreme delight be joined to this sacred, solemn feast! Let our public cries of praise ring out with deepest feeling from the depths of our hearts. Let the old pass away and let everything be new: our hearts, our voices, our deeds!"

"Lauda Sion" also rings out with shouts of joy: "Praise your Savior, O Sion, praise your leader and shepherd in hymns and canticles! Praise as much as you can, as much as you dare, because the God greater than all praise can never be praised enough! On this solemn day on which we recall the institution of this table, let our praise be full and resounding, let our souls be full of delight and beauty!"

The Corpus Christi hymn for Lauds, "Verbum Supernum," with its concluding verses used for Benediction, "O Salutaris," voices our praise of the infinitely loving Word who becomes in human flesh *everything* for us: our food, our intimate companion, our final reward:

The Word of heaven came forth from the Father's right hand without leaving him. Having undertaken his mission, he came at last to the eventide of his life.

About to be handed over by a disciple to those jealous of him, Jesus first handed *himself* over to his disciples on a tray of life. He gives his flesh and blood under the forms of both bread and wine, so that he might feed our whole person made of two substances.

Born for us, he has given himself to us as our companion. Feasting with us, he has given himself to us as our food. Reigning now in heaven, he gives himself to us as our reward!

O saving victim who opens the gate of heaven! Hostile wars press around us; give us strength and your help.

Unending glory to the triune Lord who gives us life without end in heaven, our true home! Amen!

Even now, we cling through hope to this life promised us, anticipating its lavish fulfillment in heaven; because of Jesus, this life that cannot be snuffed out wells up in us even now! For Christ is unquenchable life, and in the Eucharist we receive him as the very source of life. Even more, Thomas assures us, inexhaustible life will well up from within us not only in hope but also in its full reality in heaven. Feeding on the Bread of Life, we will be brought to the infinite abundance of life itself.[111]

At the end of his own life Thomas showed how truly he himself had feasted not only with his mind, but also with his heart and soul and body on the Word made flesh, given to us in the Eucharist as our food and ecstatic delight. For Thomas, preacher of the Word, had also become "Eucharistic Doctor": he "held it in his *hands,* that Truth"[112] he loved and proclaimed. He not only had contemplated but also had *eaten* the Word of life, and countless times had tasted its tenderness within himself. Having held in his own hands the Word made flesh, the Word he had cherished and preached, Thomas hungered for him with vehemence at the end.

Cistercian monks, who had witnessed Thomas' last days at Fossanova, fifty years afterwards were still so deeply moved by the memory of Thomas' last Eucharist that their accounts cannot help touching our own hearts with their poignancy. As the end drew near, Thomas asked with much devotion to receive the sacred Body of Christ. Until that moment, he had become so weak that he could not move from his bed. But when the abbot brought him the Eucharist, Gui tells us, Thomas worshipped the Lord by an action in which he eloquently spoke the meaning of his entire life. With extreme effort he raised himself out of bed and prostrated himself in adoration.[113] "Falling prostrate on the ground, let us venerate so great a sacrament," he had written.[114] With his whole being, with his mind and heart and dying body, Thomas worshipped his Lord who had deigned to come to him. "Prostrate on the ground, weak in body, but with his mind, as it were, running strongly to meet his Lord,"[115] Thomas surrendered himself to the God who had continually fed him with his own flesh. "O loving pelican, Jesus Lord. . . ."

According to custom Thomas was asked if he believed that this was the Body of the Son of God. With intense devotion and tears, and in a strong voice Thomas cried out that he did.[116] "O marvelous, extraordinary wonder! A servant, poor and lowly, feeds on God his Lord."[117] With his face bathed in tears, Thomas received the "life-giving sacrament." Those around him could hear him pray, "O price of my redemption and food for my pilgrimage, I receive You. For *your* sake I have studied and toiled and kept vigil. I have preached *You* and taught *You*."[118] "Jesus, whom I now behold veiled, I ask you to grant what I so thirst for: that I may see your face unveiled, and that the sight of your glory may be my bliss."[119]

Notes

1. Gui, c. 26.
2. Gui, c. 15.
3. In Jn 6, lect. 4.
4. Corpus Christi Matins hymn, "Sacris Solemniis."
5. Weisheipl, *Friar,* 178.
6. Ibid., 178–79.
7. Ibid.
8. HE 22:25.

9. Weisheipl, *Friar,* 180–81. Not everyone has agreed that Thomas wrote this "Roman" liturgy attributed to him since the early fourteenth century. Thomas' close friend and secretary, Reginald, had compiled a list of Thomas' works after his death, and he makes no mention of the Corpus Christi texts. Some argue that the Order surely would have celebrated this liturgy sooner if Thomas, one of their own, had indeed written it (Weisheipl, *Friar,* 177).

But Weisheipl shows how complex the events were which delayed the universal celebration of Corpus Christi and why its liturgical texts were not included at first in the "official catalogue" of Thomas' works. Urban had promulgated his papal bull *Transiturus* extending the Feast of Corpus Christi to the whole Church on September 11, 1264. But Urban died the very next month, and his decree was not implemented. It was not until almost forty years later that Pope Clement V decided to implement previous papal decrees from the reign of Gregory IX until his time. In 1310, at the Council of Vienne, Clement V approved Thomas' liturgy for the Church's universal use (HE 22:25).

Clement V soon died, however, and the celebration of the Corpus Christi feast was delayed until 1317, when Pope John XXII promulgated Clement's decrees. The Dominican chapter meeting at Lyons in 1318 decreed that the Corpus Christi feast be observed in the Order. The next chapter, held at Vienne in 1322, recognized Thomas as its composer: "Since our Order ought to conform in the divine office to the Holy Roman Church in so far as possible, and particularly in an office which is a product of our Order by apostolic command, we now wish that the office of Corpus Christi, composed, as it is said, by the venerable doctor Thomas d'Aquino, be observed throughout the entire Order on the Thursday after the feast of the Trinity and throughout its octave" (Weisheipl, *Friar,* 183–84).

It is probable that the Dominicans in this way were apologizing for neglecting Urban IV's original decree of 1264, just as most dioceses had done (Weisheipl, *Friar,* 184).

[10]HE 24; Foster, *Life,* 131. See also Weisheipl, *Friar,* 177.

[11]As Weisheipl points out (*Friar,* 177–78) Antonio Pizzamano in 1497 included the Corpus Christi texts in the collection of Thomas' writings. Pius V in the sixteenth century, and Pius X in the twentieth century, had the texts revised.

[12]Weisheipl, *Friar,* 180–81. For recent research on this question, see Pierre-Marie Gy, "L'Office du Corpus Christi et S. Thomas d'Aquin: état d'une recherche," *Revue de Sciences philosophiques et théologiques* 64 (1980) 491–507.

[13]Gui, c. 24.

[14]Gui, c. 15; cf. Tocco, c. 29; Calo, c. 16.

[15]ST III, 73, 5.

[16]With regard to the Eucharistic prayer, "Adoro Te Devote," Weisheipl notes that though the weight of tradition "strongly accepts Thomas' authorship," historical documentation is not yet available which would prove his authorship beyond doubt, and recent scholarship has tended not to attribute this prayer to Thomas. See Weisheipl, *Friar,* 401.

[17]Corpus Christi Magnificat Antiphon, "O Sacrum Convivium."

[18]CG IV, 56, 1; Ap Creed, 54; ST III, 61, 1, ad 3; III, 62, 5.

[19]In Ps 45:3.

[20]ST III, 62, 5.

[21]CG IV, 57, 1.

[22]ST III, 62, 5.

[23]ST III, 61, 3.

[24]CG IV, 56, 7; ST I-II, 108, 1.

[25]ST III, 73, 3.

[26]ST III, 39, 6, ad 3.

[27]ST II, 66, 112; III, 66, 12, ad 3.

[28]ST III, 38, 2, ad 1.

[29]In 1 Cor 12, lect. 3.

[30]Prayer from the Corpus Christi Mass.

[31]CG IV, 55, 29.

[32]ST III, 69, 2.

[33]ST III, 73, 3, ad 3.

[34]ST III, 73, 3.

[35]CG IV, 61, 3; ST III, 79, 5, ad 1.

[36]ST III, 65, 3.

[37]ST Supp, 39, 4.

[38]ST III, 65, 3.

[39]In Jn 6, lect. 7; ST III, 65, 3; In Jn 6, lect. 6.

[40]In Ps 21:23.

[41]In Jn 6, lect. 6; ST III, 65, 3; III, 65, 3, ad 3.

[42]ST III, 65, 3, ad 1.

[43]ST III, 73, 3.

[44]See also ST III, 73, 5, ad 3; III, 79, 7, ad 2.

[45]ST III, 79, 7; III, 82, 4.

[46]ST III, 83, 1.

[47]ST III, 73, 5.

[48]Corpus Christi Sequence, "Lauda Sion."

[49]ST III, 75, 1.

[50]ST III, 79, 6.

[51]ST III, 73, 1.

[52]CG IV, 61, 3.

[53]ST III, 79, 1.

[54]In Jn 6, lect. 4.

[55]Ibid.

[56]Cf. ST III, 79, 5, ad 1.

[57]ST III, 73, 3, ad 2.

[58]ST III, 73, 5, ad 1.

[59]ST III, 80, 10.

[60]ST III, 80, 11.

[61]ST III, 79, 7, ad 2.

[62]CG IV, 55, 30.

[63]Sacraments; cf. In Ps 47:6.

[64]In Jn 6, lect. 7.

[65]ST III, 64, 7.

[66]ST Supp, 6, 1, ad 2.

[67]ST III, 68, 11, ad 1.

[68]ST Supp, 9, 3, ad 3.

[69]ST Supp, 8, 2, ad 2; Supp, 8, 2, ad 3.

[70]ST Supp, 6, 1.

71ST III, 73, 3, ad 2.

72In Jn 6, lect. 7.

73ST III, 73, 3.

74In Jn 6, lect. 7.

75Ibid.

76ST Supp, 71, 9; III, 79, 4; III, 67, 2; cf. III, 65, 3, ad 1.

77In Eph 1, lect. 8.

78Ap Creed.

79ST III, 65, 3, ad 1.

80In Eph 4, lect. 5.

81In Jn 6, lect. 8.

82In Gal 1, lect. 1.

83ST III, 80, 4.

84ST III, 79, 4; III, 79, 4, ad 3.

85ST III, 67, 2; III, 80, 5, ad 2; III, 83, 4, ad 3.

86ST III, 79, 5.

87ST III, 80, 4.

88ST III, 79, 7.

89In Jn 6, lect. 6.

90ST III, 73, 3.

91In Ps 21:11.

92In Ps 21:16.

93In Ps 21:1.

94ST III, 79, 4.

95ST III, 75, 1.

96ST III, 80, 2, ad 1.

97ST III, 79, 2.

98Cf. In Jn 6, lect. 4.

99ST III, 79, 1, ad 2.

100ST III, 79, 8.

101In Ps 21:22.

102ST III, 65, 3.

103ST III, 79, 1.

104In Jn 6, lect. 4.

105In Jn 6, lect. 7; ST III, 73, 3, ad 2.

106ST III, 79, 6.

107In Jn 6, lect. 7.

108Ibid.

109ST III, 75, 1.

110These stanzas translate the "Tantum Ergo" hymn used for Benediction.

111In Jn 6, lect. 6.

[112]Maritain, *Aquinas,* 118.

[113]Gui, c. 39. See also 1 Can 8; 10; 49.

[114]Corpus Christi Vespers hymn, "Pange Lingua."

[115]Gui, c. 39; Foster, *Life,* 55.

[116]Gui, c. 39.

[117]"Panis Angelicus," from the Corpus Christi Matins Hymn, "Sacris Solemniis."

[118]Gui, c. 39; Foster, *Life,* 55.

[119]Prayer, "Adoro Te Devote."

11

Eye Has not Seen

Thomas' Joy in Anticipating Death

The historian Tolomeo of Lucca recounts a touching story which Thomas had told about himself. It is a story a child would tell, and yet it reveals the paradox of Thomas' heart, at once absolutely profound and utterly simple. Brother Romanus, a Dominican of great learning, had succeeded Thomas as master in theology at Paris. But in the very next year after his appointment, Romanus died. One night Thomas dreamed that Romanus appeared to him. Thomas asked his friend how things were going for him. "Very well," Romanus replied. Thomas then got to the real question he wanted to ask him: "Is our vision of God in heaven anything like what people have written about it?" Romanus smiled. "Yes, but its manner is more noble." In fact, Romanus added, Thomas would know this for himself before long. As Thomas recounted his dream, Tolomeo recalled, "he seemed happy when he spoke of it." The following year, Thomas died.[1]

Thomas' smile as he remembered his dream stayed with him. When he heard that a loved one had died, he would peacefully join his own prayer to the Masses he would have celebrated for them.[2] The same contentment shone in Thomas as he approached his own death. One of the brothers at the monastery of Fossanova where Thomas died told of hearing that Thomas was "one of the wisest and best men in the world." And he did indeed seem to this brother to be a wonderful man. For during his final illness, the noble, learned Thomas had treated everyone in the most "humble, kindly and patient" way.[3]

When Paul speaks about the death of one who has fallen in love with Jesus, he pictures an athlete racing to the finish line with one tremendous final surge of energy. We experience this same surge of energy as we near home after being away for a long time. We find ourselves hurrying, rushing with new energy those last few miles. The closer we are to our loved ones, the faster we strain to get to them, to get "home."

Those who, like Thomas, have fallen in love with Jesus can begin to feel this same urgency as they approach their death. Thomas knew that by nature we certainly do not seek death; on the contrary, we run from it. And yet, as we grow closer to the Lord, our desire to be perfectly with the God whom we love can grow stronger even than our desire to live. An immense yearning for heaven can fill our heart, pulling us irresistibly home. Thomas was preaching these very thoughts to the people of Naples when he suddenly cried out the desire welling up in his heart, "And may God bring *us* there also!"[4]

Thomas was longing to go home. For Thomas, heaven *was* home. Perhaps only those who have lived as strangers in a foreign land thousands of miles away from their loved ones and all that they hold dear can know what Thomas means when he calls heaven *patria*. (Instead of referring to heaven with the usual Latin word, *caelum* ["sky"], Thomas almost always speaks of heaven as *patria*, our "homeland.") And he realized that the nearer we are to our loved ones, the more our love intensifies; the closer we are to our heart's desire, the more irresistibly we are drawn to it.[5]

Aristotle had written that a truly long life is one that is full, not necessarily of time, but of goodness. Thomas wholeheartedly agrees. When we have lived a *good* life, even if we die young, we have lived a *long* life! He recalls the words of Wisdom 4:13: "Being made perfect in a short time, they fulfilled a *long* time, for their souls pleased God."[6] Thomas knew that we naturally want to live, to be healthy and well. Our natural inclination is not to hate and abuse our body but rather to care for it. If we do discipline our body so that it will be more docile to our spirit, we are not hating our body but rather desiring its true good. Further, it can happen that the closer we come to the Lord, the more we begin to long for death, not because we hate our physical life, but because we desire the infinite loveliness of heaven more.[7] As Thomas grew older, he seemed to focus his every energy with increasing intensity on the God he loved. At Naples, where he spent his last years, he would celebrate the Eucharist very early every morning in the chapel of St. Nicholas. After attending another Mass he would begin his teaching, and then would write or dictate to his secretaries—sometimes to three secretaries simultaneously!—until the noon meal. After eating, he would return to his cell, rest during the siesta time, and then resume his writing. Like a sharp arrow, one of his contemporaries comments, all of Thomas' energies were increasingly focused directly on God.[8]

Toward the end of his time at Paris, Thomas had written, "Wisdom's ultimate effect is to fill us with peace."[9] Yet when he was writing this section of the *Summa,* he was already beginning to require of himself what his body and psyche could not long endure. He would write late into the night, sleep a short while, and pray into the early morning hours. In the years approaching his death, Thomas poured out his energies with growing intensity. In approximately thirty-six months, he produced over thirty-three major works. In the three short years of his second stay as master of theology at Paris, he composed the entire second part of the *Summa,* as well as commentaries on Paul's epistles and the Gospel of John. In addition, he wrote commentaries on the philosophical works of Aristotle, and prepared the material for key theological debates at the university.

Anyone looking on would see his fevered activity during this time as intense labor without rest or respite. And yet, paradoxically, as he gave himself to the increasing demands made upon him day by day, he began to be more and more lost in contemplation during his work. From his own experience Thomas learned that wisdom's labor fills us with a peace and joy so deep[10] that it no longer feels like toilsome labor: "Far from entailing bitterness or toil for us, wisdom makes the bitter sweet, and labor a rest!"[11]

What was the source of his remarkable productivity during these last years of his life? Thomas himself gives us the answer when he reflects on the words of Psalm 45: "My heart overflows with a goodly theme; my tongue is like the pen of a ready scribe" (Ps 45:1). Our own study, he tells us, parcels out wisdom to us only in small portions and over a long period of time. But when the

Holy Spirit possesses us and begins to direct our work, wisdom fills us like the rush of a mighty wind! Thomas recalls how the apostles experienced the Holy Spirit filling them like a sudden mighty flood. We, too, can be filled suddenly with a wisdom that God alone can give us. At times like these, the Holy Spirit makes our tongue "like the pen of a prolific writer." When the Holy Spirit inspires us, therefore, we are sometimes able to produce in a short time what others would take a lifetime to do, since the Holy Spirit writes "quickly" in our hearts![12]

During his last years—when he was only in his mid-forties and in his prime—the Holy Spirit *had* written quickly in his heart. Then everything changed. Several months before his death, Thomas was celebrating Mass one morning in the chapel of St. Nicholas at Naples. As we have seen, during that Mass, something happened which radically changed him. He had been feverishly composing the third part of his *Summa Theologiae* and was in the process of writing about the sacrament of reconciliation. But after Mass on that morning of December 6, 1273, he stopped writing. He refused to dictate to his secretaries as usual, and he completely "put away his writing materials." Reginald grew alarmed at this inactivity and asked him if he were giving up all of his great work. Thomas answered quietly, "I *cannot* go on." Fearing that Thomas' rigorous schedule had affected his brain, Reginald kept insisting that he continue his writing. But Thomas could only say, "Reginald, I *cannot*—because all that I have written seems to me so much straw."[13] "Such things have been revealed to me that all I have taught and written seems quite trivial to me now. The only thing I want now is that as God has put an end to my writing, he may quickly end my life also."[14]

Thomas had feasted on the Spirit's joy not only in his contemplation, but also and especially in sharing the fruit of his contemplation with others through his writing: "As with the riches of a banquet shall my soul be satisfied, and my mouth shall praise you with joy!" (Ps 63:5). But it was the triune God who had given him his writing vocation, and it was this same God who was now ending it. If Thomas could no longer write, if his mouth could no longer "praise God with joy" through his writing, he knew that his life's work and joy had come to an end. Now he wanted only to feast on God in the unhindered joy of heaven. After that Mass, Thomas never taught or wrote again; within three months he was dead.

Perhaps Thomas had suffered a stroke or a physical and emotional breakdown during Mass that day in the chapel of St. Nicholas. In the years preceding his death, he had been writing profound philosophical, theological, and scriptural works with incredible energy and speed. He had slept less and less. Perhaps the fevered work that had filled his days and nights had finally taken its toll. We do not know. But we do know that, whatever the emotional and physical impacts of this experience on Thomas were, they were inseparable from a profound mystical experience. The intellectual giant who had written and spoken volumes about God during his life now was reduced to silence. He could no longer speak about God. Compared to what he had glimpsed of God during those few moments in the chapel of St. Nicholas, his most profound insights and most eloquent words became for him worthless straw.

Yet, as Josef Pieper comments, this act of "falling silent" did not contradict Thomas' life as a preacher of the good news. In his very silence at the end, Thomas embodied the deepest insight he himself had articulated about God.[15] Since our finite minds can never contain in themselves the inexhaustible beauty of God, he had written, "this is the ultimate of our human knowledge of God: to know that we do not know God."[16] In his profound experience during that Mass in the chapel of St. Nicholas, Thomas showed us the true purpose of our words as we share the fruit of our contemplation with others: finally to *adore* together the God whose beauty we have contemplated and proclaimed.

The Glory of the Resurrection

Thomas himself experienced this increasing ache for the beauty of God, a yearning especially apparent when he speaks about the joy of our resurrection. In the year before he died, Thomas preached to the townspeople of Naples a series of Lenten sermons on the Apostles' Creed. In charge of the Dominican studium at Naples, he had been responsible for engaging someone to preach the daily sermons during Lent. He gladly undertook the charge himself, and his preaching was so moving that most of the townspeople came to hear him every day. In one of these sermons, Thomas reflected on our belief in the resurrection of the dead. He begins by assuring us that it is natural for us to grieve when our loved ones die. But even in our greatest pain, our faith in the resurrection can comfort us immeasurably. We suffer our loved ones' loss in death, but we also believe and trust that in a little while we shall see them again, and then nothing will ever part us! If we keep the joy of our resurrection before our eyes, therefore, we find ourselves consoled even in our loneliness.[17]

When Thomas reflects on the wonderful joy of heaven, he stresses that we will be together with our loved ones, never again to be parted, joined in a love that will be closer and deeper than ever before. Here on earth, we can be close only to those who are physically near us, and our mind is not always where our body is; we suffer from distractions that often take our thoughts a thousand miles away from where we are physically present. But in heaven our risen body will transcend the boundaries of time and space, and will take us wherever our mind wants to go. We will be always near our loved ones, even those still on earth. Gregory the Great tells us that "wherever the angels are sent, their course lies in God" (Homily 34 in Ev). The same will be true for us. Wherever we go, we will never be lonely or afraid, for we will see fully what we only glimpse now: that we are never outside the arms of God and those we love.[18]

Thomas turns his gaze to the risen body of Jesus, the cause of *our* risen glory. Paul had pictured the first ancestor of the human race as simply a living being. "Adam's" created soul could give him only a small portion of life, not unbounded life itself. And his sin made him the cause of our death, not the source of our life. But Christ, the new Adam, completely reverses the course of human history which the first "Adam" began: "The first Adam became a living being; the last Adam became a life-giving spirit!" (1 Cor 15:45).[19]

A created soul gave life to the first Adam, but the uncreated Spirit of God wells up as the source of life in the risen Lord Jesus. The first Adam merely lived and by sinning became the cause of death for us. But Jesus, risen Lord, not only lives; he *gives* us life, life that no power in the universe can wrest from us.[20] Jesus' glorious risen body thus shines as the magnificent pattern and cause of our risen glory.[21] Yes, Thomas says, "Christ himself will transform our lowly body" (Phil 3:21)—"a blessing we should greatly desire!"[22]

We should desire this magnificent culmination of our life precisely because Jesus, our risen Lord, has robbed death of its power, and has made everything utterly new! Jesus is God the Word, the very fountain of life, and even in his risen humanity he is the pattern and cause of our own resurrection.[23] Intimately present to all of us, and, indeed, to the whole universe and to all of history, the risen Lord causes unquenchable life to well up in us also.[24]

Thomas could not hold back the wonder he felt before the mystery of a God who would give us heaven's joy as our own inheritance. It is true that our creation itself is the gift of the infinitely good God's lavish love. But God's love has also transformed us from mere creatures into true daughters and sons of God. And *this* grace far surpasses even the gift of our being created.[25] Jesus alone is the true heir of heaven, the only Son of the Father by nature; but now all that belongs to him is given to us as our inheritance:[26] "If sons and daughters, then *heirs* also" (Rom 8:17)![27] Joined to Jesus through our baptism, we receive in a created way all that belongs to him.[28] Thus the Church Fathers did not tire of stressing, "God has become human that we might become divine!" Thomas agrees: "Our true bliss and goal is fully sharing God's own life, a gift which Christ's humanity lavishes on us."[29]

At the heart of Jesus' risen power flows the Holy Spirit, the "fount of water springing up into life everlasting" within us (John 4:14). The Spirit is luring us even now to the unquenchable life that awaits us as our own inheritance.[30] For we will be radiant with God's immense grandeur: "Once you were darkness, but now you are light in the Lord!" (Eph 5:8). Thomas pictures each of us in heaven as ablaze with dazzling light,[31] radiant with the Spirit's love shining from within us. Our great joy will be feasting on the splendor of love that will illumine our whole being: "The path of the righteous is like the light of dawn, which shines brighter and brighter until the fullness of day arrives in all its splendor" (Prov 4:18). Through grace, God's own glory will blaze in us as resplendent light, and God's love in us will shine as our most beautiful adornment.[32]

Thomas thinks of how often even now what we feel in our spirit overflows into our body. When we feel sad or lonely, our discouragement takes its toll on our body and shows on our face. But when we feel happy, our body seems to become more healthy and invigorated, and our face glows! Our experience now gives us a taste of heaven, where our spirit's joy will flood our body, and fill it with radiant beauty.[33] The Lord's own radiance will shine in our spirit and permeate every fiber of our body. And not only our body will share in our spirit's joy; the glory of our risen life will pervade the entire universe! Our bodies will glow with the Spirit's charm (1 Cor 15:44),[34] and all of creation, too, will glisten with the Spirit's radiance: "I saw a new heaven and a new earth" (Rev 21:1).

We know how we try to make our environment beautiful even now. We want to decorate our home with lovely furniture, with pictures, flowers, appealing colors. This very urge to live and work in a beautiful setting, Thomas tells us, inspires us to want the whole universe to glow with the beauty of our resurrection: since the whole universe is our home, we cannot help wanting it to shine with the glory of our resurrection![35] And God will fulfill our desire beyond all we could dream, for God, who is loveliness itself, fills heaven with every kind of beauty on which our soul and senses can feast.[36]

We all have experienced how everything around us darkens with gloom when the skies are gray. But when, after the rain, the sun bursts forth, everything around us seems to awaken with new splendor, to glisten with gorgeous sunlight. This experience of ours gives Thomas an intimation of heaven's splendor. At the end of time, all of creation will be magnificently transformed and glow with the most delightful color.[37] The heavenly bodies with their brilliant light will shine as the most glorious part of creation: "The beauty of heaven is the stars' glory, for the Lord enlightens the world on high" (Sir 43:9). The heavens themselves will radiate with splendor, and our senses will feast on God's beauty shining in their brilliance.[38] Creation's beauty will lure us to the loveliness of its creator: "By the creature's greatness and beauty, their *creator* can be seen and known" (Wis 13:5).

Yet Thomas finds a reciprocity even in our heavenly radiance. *Our* risen glory will permeate the whole universe, but the glory of the universe, in turn, will shine in *us!* Even the smallest creatures will share in the brilliance of the most immense heavenly bodies. And our bodies, composed of the universe's elements, will glow with the intense radiance of the stars, while the grandeur of the whole cosmos will gleam in us.[39]

Enjoying God

Yet even though the magnificence of the universe will dazzle us, heaven's joy far exceeds even this created glory. As Paul tells us, the very heart of heaven's joy is that "we shall always be with the Lord" (1 Thess 4:17). Thomas reflects on our own experience here on earth: we delight in our loved ones even when they are away from us, but we are most happy of all when they are with us![40] The more intimately we love our dear ones, the happier we are when they are near us.[41] Yet our happiness in our loved ones can never be complete here on earth; we always face the agony of saying goodbye to those we love, if not before death, then at the moment of death itself. Neither can we "see" the God we love "face to face" here on earth. This is why Paul himself wanted to know the gladness of being perfectly with his beloved Lord: "I want to depart and be with Christ," he tells his dear Philippian community (Phil 1:23). Thus the Lord assures us: "I will come again and will take you to myself, that where *I* am *you* also may be" (John 14:3). Then, in heaven, our desire to be always with our dear ones and with the God who loves us will be satisfied far beyond all that our heart could dream.[42] The psalmist's description of our ecstasy when we "see" God's "face" hints at our intense intimacy with God in heaven. The triune God will fill our heart with such glory[43] that even Moses' "speaking to God face to face" will pale in comparison.[44]

Thomas could not help thinking of the immense contrast between the delight that the triune God will be for us and *is* for us even now, and the limited pleasure that material goods can give us.[45] From his own experience he knew that nothing external, not even others' approval, can make us truly happy. The applause that others give us now can turn into disdain overnight, and the possessions we have today can be destroyed tomorrow. The more we have, the less satisfied we become, and the more we want. The older we grow, therefore, the more we learn that only contentment within us, not material goods outside us, can make us truly happy.[46] For joy is not inactivity, a matter of our passively receiving pleasure, money, or honor, but rather the summit of our own activity and inner actualization. True joy is an inner completion and fullness which we experience in the depth of our souls: "The kingdom of God is within you" (Luke 17:21)![47]

Because God has made us precisely for enjoyment,[48] we cannot help loving what is delightful. Every created pleasure, however, can give us only a miniscule hint of the sheer delight that God is for us in heaven. For God is infinite beauty, the good of every good, the font of all pleasure and delight! In beholding God, we will see every delight; in having God, we will experience every true pleasure; in knowing God, we will possess love's most intense joy.[49]

Thomas pictures heaven's delight as our increasing intensity in love. The deeper our love, the more intimately we will contemplate God and the more intensely we will delight in God. Our delight will increase our love and desire, and our desire, in turn, will widen our heart to receive more of God's riches.[50] The very heart of heaven, therefore, is *delight,* delight that is full and overflowing! Everything good we seek in this world, we will have beyond all we could imagine in heaven: "You shall see, and your heart shall rejoice" (Is 66:14)! In God we will find the most intense of all pleasures, the riches of all wealth.[51] Every delight, every possible pleasure will fill our heart to overflowing in God's infinite goodness.[52]

The divine persons have made us precisely for the infinite enjoyment of feasting our heart, mind, soul and senses on their goodness.[53] Our gladness for all of eternity will be not only enjoying God's gifts, therefore, but also "fully enjoying *God*"![54] As Thomas loves to say, since only God's infinite delight is enough to satisfy our insatiable desire for joy,[55] "nothing less than *God* is our bliss and inheritance."[56] "*God* is the reward and the joy of all our labors"![57] "We shall see, we shall love, and we shall praise!" Augustine had said. Yes, Thomas adds, God will satisfy our every desire beyond all our imaginings;[58] our inheritance as God's own children will be forever knowing, loving and enjoying *God!*[59]

Yet it is not only that *we* enjoy God in heaven, but also that the triune God enjoys *us,* and delights in making us happy. We know how much joy it gives us to make our dear ones happy; Thomas sees this as a small hint of how much the divine persons enjoy filling us with their own gladness. Yet we human beings can give our loved ones only external possessions as an inheritance. We cannot literally transfer to them the spiritual gifts within our own hearts; we cannot make our children inherit our inner peace, love, or joy.

We might think of someone who loves music suddenly receiving the gift of enjoying music with the very joy that a great artist
experiences. But this gift would be only a small hint of how God's
own pleasure is ours in heaven. The goodness of God is infinitely
"beyond our desire, our understanding, and our capacity." As
Paul tells us, "Eye has not seen, O God, what you have prepared
for those who love you" (cf. Isa 64:4; 1 Cor 2:9),[60] for we will
enjoy God with God's own joy! The divine persons, therefore,
give us not only the riches they are; they give us also the very enjoyment they have of their own goodness.[61]

This is why, as our charity grows deeper, we cannot help longing more and more for heaven,[62] since it is charity that enables
us to "enjoy God."[63] And because all that we do in love we do
with a free heart, heaven's perfect charity will make us utterly
free![64] Here on earth we so often withhold ourselves, giving God
and one another only small parts of who we are. In heaven we
will be freed finally of all our selfishness; the very heart of our
joy will be unreserved mutuality, intimate friendship-love. Finally
and forever, we will love God not simply with little pieces of ourselves, but completely and perfectly and with all that we are: "This
is our perfection and wholeness: to love God *fully* in return!"[65]

Thomas loved to think of what it will be like truly to love God
with *all* of our mind and heart, with *all* of our soul, and strength
(Luke 10:27). Our thoughts will always be fixed on God, beholding God in everything. We will love God with all of our affection, and for God's sake we will love absolutely every one and
everything in God. All of our thoughts, deeds, and affections will
be wholly turned to God.[66]

Enter into the Joy of Your Lord

Earlier in his life, when Thomas had been lecturing on Matthew 25:21-23, he had wondered why the evangelist writes, *"Enter
into* the joy of your Lord," and not, *"Receive* the joy of your
Lord." As he reflected on this passage, Thomas found his answer in our own experience. We are always seeking enjoyment
in whatever we do. But we know, too, the difference between the
intense delight we feel in spiritual blessings like God's own peace
and joy, and the passing delight we feel in merely physical pleasures or material goods. We know the joy that floods our soul when

we have been freed from a destructive habit or attachment, or when God's own selfless love seems to bind together our family and loved ones. Compared to this delight, the infinitely lesser "delight" that merely external goods or passing pleasures give us can never satisfy our soul's capacity for inexhaustible joy.[67]

We know, too, that we never have perfect joy or peace or security here on earth. Regardless of how content we may feel at a particular moment, we still are not free from some external trial or inner anxiety.[68] For while everything good gives us joy, not even the best goods can completely satisfy our soul's thirst for enjoyment here on earth. This is why the limited pleasures we gain from things less than our heart always enter into us, so that we "contain" *them*.[69]

Yet the Lord prays, "May *my* joy be in you, and may your joy be *full!*" (John 16:24). Thomas knew that joy fills us when our desires are satisfied, but our joy is perfect and full only when our desires are completely satisfied, and absolutely nothing is left for us to want.[70] *This* is the joy of heaven: joy to the *full!*[71] We have no anxieties, troubles, or fear, and the most perfect security and contentment fill us.[72] Because we have in God infinitely more than anything we could imagine or desire (1 Cor 2:9), infinite peace floods our soul, and absolutely every desire of our heart is satisfied to overflowing.[73]

Thomas recalls Augustine's beautiful insight that material goods like money, power, and success are blessings that are external to us, but spiritual goods like joy and peace fill the very depths of our soul. This is why heaven's joy is the most profound, the most intense interior joy of all, joy that cannot be wrested from us in the way that external goods can be taken from us, for the kingdom of heaven is *within* us (Luke 17:21).[74] God's immense joy does not enter us, therefore, since God's joys are greater than anything our heart could hold. Rather, *we* enter into the immensity of *God's* joy, and this joy contains and enfolds *us*. The gospel cry, therefore, is not, "Let the joy of your Lord enter you," but rather, "Enter into the joy of your Lord!" (Matt 25:21).[75]

Enjoying One Another in God

The psalmist's tender words, "The Lord is my shepherd, there is nothing I shall want" (Ps 23:1), struck Thomas with special force. The psalmist pictures the richness of God's heart as an overflowing feast, a feast at which we feed on God.[76] But we will also have one another in God. Even now, in the Spirit's charity, we love our dear ones with the very same love we have for God, and our union with them makes us want heaven for them as much as we desire it for ourselves.[77]

Since we can never be completely happy alone, our joy in heaven will be one another's love and companionship as well. The paradox is that in giving us themselves, the divine persons give us all of our loved ones, too, and more tenderly and closely than ever.[78] Love's perfect contentment[79] is our deepest joy in heaven. Even now we feel as if we have only one heart and soul with those we love; we consider them part of ourselves and love to have them near us. But the joy we have in their presence now gives us only a small taste of how much we will enjoy them in heaven. In perfectly enjoying God, we will all the more enjoy one another in God! We will never be lonely again; with friends and loved ones to share our blessings, our joy will be full to the brim. Our joy will be theirs, and their joy will be ours.[80]

Thus, all of the wonderful natural inclinations God has placed in us here on earth will not be destroyed but made perfect in heaven. By charity's inclination, we will love even more deeply those who are dearest to us, since the reasons we have loved them on earth will not disappear in heaven but rather will deepen immeasurably. Yet every one of these reasons will be incomparably surpassed by our loved ones' nearness to God. Of all of the qualities that now enchant us about those we love—their kindness, gentleness, strength, humor—in heaven, their closeness to God will be dearest of all to us.[81]

In heaven, therefore, we will be closest not only to those dearest to us, but also to those who are nearest to God.[82] Our delight will be in the company and friendship of all the saints and angels! And since we will love one another as ourselves and rejoice in each other's good as our own, the wonderful gifts of each of us will belong to all. As the pleasure and enjoyment of one increases, the delight of all will grow.[83] Indeed, in heaven our union with God and one another is so perfect that we all have only one will. We all want only what God wants, and God wants only what we want. In God's will, our own will is done, and the Lord is our crown of joy![84] Not only our desire for God, therefore, but also our every conceivable desire for good will be completely satisfied.[85]

Longing for Heaven

From his own experience Thomas knew that we desire and reach out only to a goal that in some way has already begun in us. A child with a beautiful voice learns to love singing, and the mature singer that the child one day will become already exists in the heart and soul and voice of this little one. In a similar way, we, too, long for heaven only because in some way heaven *already* exists in us.[86] For heaven's joy is intimately knowing God (John 17:3), and we begin this life of heaven even now through faith.[87] Jesus is the light shining in our heart, enabling us through faith to "see" God as a beginning of heaven's joy here on earth.[88] And heaven's delight deepens in us now precisely in the measure that we live the joy of the Beatitudes—blessed are the poor in spirit, the merciful, the pure of heart, the peacemakers.[89]

The key reason that heaven begins for us even now is that the Holy Spirit has been poured into our heart;[90] the Spirit of joy within us makes us taste eternity's joys even now! For eternity is not time that never ends, but rather life to the full that is always now. Time is life given to us in little portions, life that is gone from us, and life that we haven't yet lived. But heaven means unending, perfect joy, with no past to rob us of joys that have faded, and no future to tease us with joys we do not yet possess. There is only overflowing life, all of it lived in complete joy, and always *now!*[91] Thomas thinks of the psalmist's lovely words, "God your God has anointed you with the *oil of gladness"* (Ps 45:7). The Spirit is this "oil of gladness," anointing our hearts with joy (Rom 14:17), charity, and peace (Gal 5:22), and filling us with glad and expectant hope for heaven,[92] the one hope we should nurture above all other hopes![93]

As Thomas matured, this hope for heaven increasingly took hold of him. A lovely story is told of a time when, with some of his students, he was returning to Paris after a pilgrimage to St. Denis. As they approached Paris, they could see the splendor of its buildings. The students playfully asked Thomas if he would like to be lord of such a magnificent city, known everywhere for its beauty, grandeur, and learning. No, Thomas answered with a smile. "I would rather have Chrysostom's Commentary on Matthew!" Besides, he added, "If I had to concern myself with Paris, I would have no time for contemplation or studying Scripture, which gives me such joy. And the more we want worldly power, the less we long for heaven."[94]

Thomas knew the force of this longing for heaven from his own experience. The story of his last days fills us with the sense of how irresistibly he was being drawn to heaven's joy. We have seen how, on the morning of December 6, 1273, as he was celebrating Mass in the chapel of St. Nicholas at the Dominican priory in Naples, Thomas suffered a stroke or breakdown. More importantly, he underwent an intense mystical experience. After this day, all of his labors abruptly ended.

In an effort to cheer him, he was taken to see his sister whom he dearly loved, the Countess Theodora of San Severino, wife of the Count of Marisco. When he arrived, however, and Theodora rushed out to greet him, Thomas remained silent and withdrawn. Alarmed, the countess asked Reginald what was wrong with her brother: "He seems quite dazed and hardly spoke to me!" Reginald told her that Thomas had been like this since the Feast of St. Nicholas, and that since then he had written nothing at all.[95]

After this disappointing visit, Thomas was taken back to Naples. But soon he had to begin another, more arduous journey, even though he was already very ill. Pope Gregory X had summoned Thomas as an expert theologian to the Second Council of Lyons, scheduled to open in May, 1274. Sometime in the early spring of 1274 Reginald and a lay servant set out with Thomas for the council. Thomas had to travel by horse—an indication of how sick he was, for the Dominicans were required by their rule to travel on foot, like the beggars they really were. As he rode, Thomas sustained a blow to the head when he hit a tree, seriously injuring himself. This last assault was too much for his weak body. The little company took him to the castle of Maenza where his niece, Lady Frances, Countess of Ceccano, lived. Thomas had been a frequent visitor there, and it was there that he fell into his last illness.[96]

A charming story is told of Thomas' days at Maenza, a story that cannot help touching us with how human Thomas was, and how tenderly his beloved Lord cared for his every need, regardless of how small. Thomas had been unable to eat, but Reginald begged him to try to take some food. Thomas replied that he thought he could manage some fresh herrings if they could be obtained. Reginald answered that they *were* available—"across the Alps, in France or England!" But at that very moment a fishmonger arrived at the castle with a supply of sardines he regularly brought. When Reginald asked the man if he had any herrings, he replied that he had only sardines; yet when he opened one of his baskets he found fresh herrings. Everyone was amazed and overjoyed, because fresh herrings were "unknown in Italy!" Reginald rushed to tell Thomas that the good God had given him exactly what he wanted. When Thomas asked where he had obtained the herrings, Reginald said, "God has brought them!"[97]

Thomas stayed for a while at Maenza. But when he realized how sick he had become, he asked to be taken to the nearby Abbey of Our Lady at Fossanova, for he wanted to die in a religious convent. The Cistercians—perhaps to justify their keeping Thomas' body for over fifty years after his death!—reported that when Thomas entered their monastery ill and weak, he clung to the doorpost and uttered the psalmist's words: *"This* is my rest in this world, *here* I shall dwell, for I have chosen her."[98]

The abbot gave Thomas a room in his own apartments and had the monks care for him. Since it was winter, they gladly undertook the burden of keeping a fire burning in his room, carrying the wood for the fire on their own shoulders. In their desire to have some remembrance of their honored guest, the monks asked Thomas to write something for them. Although we do not have the text, we are told that Thomas did manage with great effort to dictate a brief commentary on the "Song of Songs" in gratitude for the monks' kindness to him.[99]

Thomas: Handing Himself over to God

In this loving gesture of giving to others, even in his last days, the wisdom he treasured in his heart, Thomas expressed at the end the content of his entire life. He had studied and written, preached and taught not in self-centered isolation but in self-giving love of God and his brothers and sisters in God. Indeed, in his very phrase defending the Dominican life of preaching, "contemplata aliis tradere," he had chosen the word *tradere*—not *praedicare* or *docere* or *dare* or a host of other words he could have used to signify what we are to do when we preach the Word we contemplate and love. The Corpus Christi liturgy attributed to Thomas uses the same verb, *tradere,* "to hand over," for Jesus' total surrender of himself to his disciples in the Eucharist. The

Corpus Christi hymn "Verbum Supernum" sings out, "About to be *handed over* by a disciple to those jealous of him, Jesus first *handed himself over* to his disciples on a tray of life." The Matins hymn "Sacris Solemniis," uses the same verb: "He gave to the weak a tray holding his body; he gave to the sorrowing a drinking cup of his blood, saying, 'Take what I *hand over* ("trado") to you and drink from this cup.' "

As we have seen, it was precisely at the Eucharistic celebration on that December 6, 1273, that Thomas suffered his life-changing mystical experience—a grace which one commentator interprets as an "unusually overwhelming experience of the Mass."[100] And in his phrase "contemplata aliis *tradere*"—"to hand over the fruit of our contemplation to others"—Thomas uses the same word for Jesus' handing *himself* over to us and for us at the Last Supper. In using the verb *tradere*, therefore, Thomas urges us to "hand over," to "surrender" totally to others what we hold in our minds and hearts. We are to do this in the same way that Jesus "handed himself over" to his disciples at the Last Supper, in the same way that he surrenders himself to us today in the Eucharist. Thomas himself had spent his life in communion with Jesus, "handing over" his whole being not only to God, but also to the dear friends whom God had given him.

The words of Ladislas Boros come to mind as we picture in our mind's eye these last hours of Thomas as he "handed over" to God one final time all that he was:

> [For theologians], theology is a mental effort to make life more beautiful and more luminous, to help their friends to overcome the sin of existential weakness. Thinking is for them a humble service to being, a welcoming and protecting of everything worthy of welcome and protection. They have experienced in themselves the suffering and poverty of human existence and therefore they try to think from those experiences. This they seek and this is important to them, not their own success or their own prestige. . . . With their thoughts [they] must try to do their friends some good. They must clearly think that "their salvation hangs on what they think and on what they say to others."[101]

Thomas would aggree that true preachers of the Word do not seek "their own success or prestige." His own last days showed how truly he had lived in communion with Jesus, who came to serve and to save. At the end, Thomas the nobleman humbly watched his brothers, Cistercian monks, carry in on their own shoulders the firewood needed to keep him protected from the winter cold. And Thomas the nobleman, now Thomas the beggar, could not help crying out, "Who am I that the servants of God should wait on me like this?"[102]

The Sweet Fragrance of Thomas' Life

Thomas died on the morning of March 7, 1274. Lord Francis, the Franciscan bishop of Terracina, came to Thomas' funeral, as did many lay people, especially noblewomen, since Thomas had many relatives in that area. Thomas' niece, Lady Frances, also came from Maenza. Yet, as we have seen, women were forbidden entrance into the cloister chapel where the funeral was to be held; Frances was told she had to wait at the gate. She cried so uncontrollably, however, that the monks had to carry out Thomas' body to her so that she could see it one last time.[103] Thomas' body was then placed before the high altar. For the funeral of this great, humble man, no official of the Dominican Order found it necessary to attend, nor was there even an official representative of the Dominicans present for the Mass. Reginald preached at the funeral, telling of how he had been a confidant as well as confessor for Thomas for many years. "Before God I declare that I have always found him like a little child in his purity; and I am certain that he never willingly committed a mortal sin."[104]

For two years, Thomas' body was quietly kept at the Cistercian monastery where he had died, and the Dominicans made no attempt to reclaim his body. But in January, 1276, a Dominican, Peter of Tarentaise, became pope, and the monks at Fossanova began to fear that Peter would try to return Thomas' body to the Dominicans. But the Dominicans did not reclaim his body.[105]

As time passed, the townspeople began hearing rumors that the monks had exhumed Thomas' body and cut off his head, which they then "hid in a secret place" in a corner of a chapel behind the choir. If the monks had to give up Thomas' body, they would not be deprived of his head! The removal of Thomas' head, however, probably did not occur during *this* particular exhumation. But seven months after Thomas' death the monks did exhume Thomas' body, and a sweet fragrance filled the air.

Then in 1281 or 1282, Dom Peter of Montesangiovanni, the newly elected abbot, had Thomas' body exhumed yet again and put under a stone slab in a greater place of honor on the Gospel side of the high altar. Reginald had already taken Thomas' right thumb—probably before the funeral in 1274—and given it to Hugh de Billom, bishop of Ostia, later made a cardinal.[106] Seven years passed. Then Thomas' body was *again* disinterred so that the monks could bury it in a more honorable place on the other side of the high altar! The same sweet fragrance filled the air at this exhumation also.[107] Abbot Nicholas of Fossanova, who had been present at Thomas' death and had seen him receive the Eucharist with tears, testified that he himself had smelled the fragrance of Thomas' body both at this and at the first disinterment.[108]

Still *another* disinterment took place in 1288 at the request of Thomas' sister, Theodora of San Severino; she wanted one of Thomas' hands! The body seems to have been complete even at this time. Peter of Montesangiovanni, who had known Thomas for ten years and who cared for him at the end, said that Thomas' body was incorrupt, and there was still hair on his head! In a charming account, Peter tells us that all that was missing was one hand "which the countess of San Severino had. There was also a dent near the tip of the nose as if a mouse had bitten it. The body had a good smell!" Peter testified at the canonization process that he himself, as well as many other monks, smelled the "sweet fragrance" of Thomas' body when it was exhumed.[109]

In order to keep the best part of Thomas' remains, the monks removed Thomas' head, possibly in another exhumation in 1303, when the Dominican, Benedict XI, was elected pope. But Benedict died in 1304, and *still* the Dominicans made no serious attempt to recover Thomas' body. It probably was at the disinterment of 1303, however, that the monks boiled Thomas' body to remove the flesh from his bones. In this way, they could keep his bones in a smaller casket, with less probability that the casket's location would be discovered! William Tocco later testified at the canonization inquiry that he had seen some of Thomas' bones in a chest at Fossanova in 1319.[110]

Finally, in 1368, Pope Urban V ordered that Thomas' body be taken to Toulouse, birthplace of the Dominican order. This solemn translation took place on January 28, 1369. Here Thomas' body remained with the Dominicans until the French Revolution, when it was transferred to the Church of St. Sernin. On October 21, 1974, as part of the celebration in Toulouse of the seventh centenary of Thomas' death, his body was transferred to the restored Church of the Jacobins, where it now lies. The cathedral of Naples claims to have a bone of Thomas' left arm, and the Church of the Minerva at Rome preserves Thomas' right arm.[111]

There is symbolic irony in these remarkable stories of Thomas' body giving off a "sweet fragrance" long after death, and of its being exhumed, hidden, and then cut apart so that people could have a piece of him even after death! The huge Thomas, so physically large in life, had so completely "handed himself over," had so totally given himself away his whole life long, that little even of his physical body remained after death. Thomas' corpse now lies in a very small casket, large enough to hold the body of a child. And indeed, in many ways, Thomas' simple casket *does* hold the body of a child. For this was the paradox of Thomas' great mind and soul: he treasured his profound insights in the heart of a child.

The small casket holding the little that remains of his bones speaks eloquently of his great heart. Like Jesus, Thomas had held on to nothing for himself: "contemplata aliis *tradere.*" Let us hand over the fruit of our contemplation to others, he had written. And as he had written, so had he lived. The "sweet fragrance" of his body after death spoke with eloquence of the fragrance of his life and insights which he had so generously shared with others. In all that he had said and written, Thomas had poured forth only the Spirit's sweet aroma. Now, in death, his very body, temple and home of the Holy Spirit from whom he had drawn everything he had preached and taught and written, continued to pour forth the Spirit's sweetness.

In the end, this "sweetness" of Thomas was victorious even over his enemies. During his life, he had suffered from the attacks of jealous, less gifted rivals; these same attacks continued with more vehemence after his death. Subsequently, at both Paris and Oxford, various teachings considered inimical to the Christian faith were condemned; some propositions attributed to Thomas were included in these condemnations.[112] Yet the attempts to discredit him met with no lasting success. On the contrary, his influence spread to other nations. It is true that Thomas had no real "pupils"; all his life he remained ultimately alone, with no one who could be a true companion to him in his intellectual labors and no one who could continue his work.[113] Yet, Bartholomew of Capua tells us, after Thomas' death, people everywhere were reading his works enthusiastically. Indeed, Bartholomew adds, Thomas' writings "can be read with ease and profit by everyone," for even common people and those of "modest intelligence," clamor for them![114]

It is touching to read of how the enthusiastic Arts faculty at the University of Paris poured out their affection on Thomas after he died. *They* clamored not only for his writings[115] but also for his very body! The theology faculty, among whom Thomas had twice served, give him no "corporate expression of esteem."[116] But the young Arts faculty expressed their admiration of Thomas in a letter they sent to the General Chapter of the Dominicans meeting at Lyons in 1274.

First of all, they begged the Order of Preachers to send them Thomas' body. "We beseech you, out of our gratitude and devout affection . . . to grant us the bones of him now dead whom we could not recover alive." In this way, their beloved Thomas, who continued to be with them through his writings would also "by the remembered presence of his tomb in our city, live on for ever in the hearts of our posterity." The professors then inquired about philosophical works which they had asked Thomas to write for them and which he had begun at Paris. They begged that these, as well as copies of several other works Thomas had promised to send them, be sent to them "without delay!"[117] Finally, they wrote that they would appreciate it greatly if any other new writings of Thomas on logic would be sent to them, writings which, when Thomas was leaving, they had taken the liberty of asking him to send them.[118]

This young faculty had recognized the truth in Thomas' works and by their response to him had anticipated the vindication that he would receive a half century after his death. When Pope John XXII canonized Thomas in 1323, he finally put to rest the attempts to discredit Thomas' writings with these words, "Thomas alone has illumined the Church more than all the other doctors together!" The censures against Thomas at the University of Paris were withdrawn the next year. The Oxford condemnations were never officially withdrawn, but in practice they had no force. In the fourteenth and fifteenth centuries, the works of Thomas were translated into Greek and Hebrew. And at the Council of Trent in the sixteenth century, after the Bible was enthroned on the altar as God's Word, Thomas' *Summa Theologiae* was placed upon the altar, as a sign of honor for this work so full of the Holy Spirit's wisdom.[119]

Early in his life Thomas had taken these words of Hilary as his own: "I owe this to God as the chief duty of my life, that my every word and sense may speak of *God!*"[120] In season and out, for his whole life long, with his every word and sense, Thomas had spoken of God. And precisely in doing so, he had lived his "spirituality," a life absolutely identical with himself, drawn at every moment from the Spirit of love. In his sermon on the gospel parable of the sower and the seed (Mark 4:3-20), "Exiit qui seminat," Thomas cries out with wonder over the grace of being called to the preaching mission, the privilege of sharing with others the fruits of our contemplation: "O human race, how many have sown the Word in you, and what a precious seed! The whole Trinity has sown this seed in you—the Father has sown peace; the Son, truth; the Spirit, charity. The angels, and apostles, the martyrs and confessors and virgins have all sown the Word in you!"

Thomas once wrote that what we say *now* wells up from the small portion of wisdom within us; but in *heaven* our words will pour forth the unbounded wisdom we contemplate without interruption.[121] From this abundance of wisdom which he now enjoys in heaven, Thomas would surely tell us, "Since we are surrounded by so great a cloud of witnesses, let *us* also lay aside every weight and run with perseverance the race that is set before us, looking to Jesus the pioneer and perfecter of our faith, so that we may not grow weary or fainthearted!" (Heb 12:1-3; RSV).

For, Thomas assures us, if such an abundance of the Spirit's love is poured out upon the world when even one person preaches, how much more will this be so when an entire Order of Preachers—and, indeed, the entire community of believers—fills the world with the Word of God![122] In company with these sowers of the seed and with Thomas himself, may we ourselves recognize and claim with joy our own call to "hand over," as an act of friendship, the fruit of our contemplation, generously sharing our faith with others, and proclaiming the good news of God's friendship to the world!

Notes

[1]HE 23:16; Foster, *Life,* 139.

[2]I Can 81.

[3]I Can 19; Foster, *Life,* 88.

[4]Our Father.

[5]CG I, 91, 5.

[6]Ten Com.

[7]In Eph 5, lect. 10.

[8]I Can 77.

[9]ST II–II, 45, 6, ad 3.

[10]ST II–II, 9, 4, ad 1.

[11]ST II–II, 45, 3, ad 3.

[12]In Ps 44:1.

[13]I Can 79; Foster, *Life,* 109

[14]Gui, c. 27; Foster, *Life,* 46.

[15]Pieper, *Guide,* 158.

[16]Pot 7, 5, ad 14.

[17]Ap Creed.

[18]ST Supp, 84, 2.

[19]In 1 Cor 15, lect. 7.

[20]Ibid.

[21]ST III, 54, 2.

[22]In Eph 1, lect. 1.

[23]ST III, 56, 1.

[24]Ibid.; III, 56, 1, ad 3.

[25]ST III, 23, 1, ad 2.

[26]Ibid.

[27]ST I–II, 114, 3.

[28]ST III, 58, 4, ad 1.

[29]ST III, 1, 2.

[30]ST I–II, 114, 3.

[31]In Phil, Prologue.

[32]In Ps 25:5.

[33]In Ps 50:5.

[34]ST III, 54, 1, ad 2.

[35]ST Supp, 91, 1; Supp, 91, 4.

[36]In Ps 25:5.

[37]ST Supp, 91, 4.

[38]ST Supp, 91, 3.

[39]ST Supp, 91, 4.

[40]Cf. ST II–II, 28, 1.
[41]Comp Theo II, 9.
[42]In 1 Th 4:2.
[43]ST II–II, 26, 13, ad 3; III, 1, 6.
[44]In Ps 41:1.
[45]ST I–II, 2, 1.
[46]ST I–II, 2, 4.
[47]ST I–II, 3, 2, ad 4.
[48]ST I–II, 25, 2.
[49]Comp Theo II, 9.
[50]ST I, 12, 6.
[51]Our Father.
[52]Ap Creed.
[53]ST II–II, 23, 7.
[54]ST III, 49, 5, ad 1; In Ps 22:3; ST II–II, 17, 2.
[55]ST I–II, 3, 2, ad 1; CG IV, 54, 3.
[56]In Rom 8, lect. 3.
[57]Ap Creed.
[58]Ibid.
[59]In Eph 5, lect. 3.
[60]In Eph 2, lect. 2.
[61]ST III, 23, 1.
[62]ST II–II, 23, 8, ad 3.
[63]ST I–II, 114, 4; II–II, 28, 1, ad 3.
[64]ST I–II, 114, 4.
[65]ST III, 46, 3.
[66]Rel St 4.
[67]In Mt 25, lect. 2.
[68]Ap Creed.
[69]In Mt 25, lect. 2.
[70]ST II–II, 28, 3.
[71]In Ps 5:8.
[72]Ap Creed.
[73]ST I–II, 1, 5.
[74]In Jn 6, lect. 4.
[75]In Mt 25, lect. 2; ST II–II, 28, 3.
[76]In Ps 22:1.
[77]ST II–II, 17, 3.
[78]Cf. Ibid.
[79]ST I–II, 26, 2, ad 3.
[80]In Ps 5:8.

[81]ST II–II, 26, 13.

[82]Ibid.

[83]Ap Creed.

[84]Our Father.

[85]ST II–II, 28, 3.

[86]ST I–II, 114, 3, ad 3.

[87]Truth q. 14, a 2.

[88]In Ps 35:5.

[89]ST I–II, 69, 2; I–II, 69, 3.

[90]ST I–II, 114, 3; I–II, 115, 3, ad 3.

[91]CG III, 61, 2.

[92]In Ps 44:5.

[93]In Ps 4:7.

[94]Gui, c. 34.

[95]I Can 79; Foster, *Life,* 109–10.

[96]Gui, c. 37.

[97]I Can 50; Foster, *Life,* 95.

[98]I Can 80; Foster, *Life,* 110. See Synan, "Aquinas and His Age," 13.

[99]Gui, c. 38.

[100]Tugwell, *Albert and Thomas,* 267.

[101]Ladislas Boros, *Faith: Conversations with Contemporary Theologians,* trans. Donald D. Walsh (Maryknoll, N.Y.: Orbis Books, 1989) 10.

[102]Gui, c. 38; Foster, *Life,* 55.

[103]Gui, c. 40.

[104]Gui, c. 41.

[105]Foster, *Life,* 80–81, n. 96.

[106]Ibid.

[107]I Can 49; Foster, *Life,* 97.

[108]I Can 8; Foster, *Life,* 85.

[109]I Can 80; Foster, *Life,* 111.

[110]Foster, *Life,* 80–81, no. 96.

[111]Ibid.

[112]On this controversy, see Weisheipl, *Friar,* 313–43, especially 335–38, on the specific propositions involved. After Thomas' death, Averroistic teachings took increasing hold of the Arts faculty at Paris. Augustinian theologians, inimical to the "worldly" philosophy of Aristotle and the rationalism of Averroes, were increasingly critical of the situation. Stephen Tempier, bishop of Paris, was pressured by Pope John XXI to investigate which errors were being taught at Paris and by whom. In 1277 Tempier published a list of 219 philosophical propositions—most of them Averroistic—which he considered inimical to the faith. Among those propositions were some that he attributed to Thomas, without naming him directly. Shortly afterward, the Dominican archbishop of Canterbury, Robert Kilwardby, issued a similar but shorter list.

[113]Pieper, *Guide,* 21.

[114]I Can 83; Foster, *Life,* 113.

[115]As we have seen, Thomas had written many of his commentaries on Aristotle in order to help the young Arts faculty at Paris to withstand the inroads of Latin Averroism.

[116]Foster, *Life,* 156, n. 1.

[117]These were the Commentary of Simplicius on the *De Caelo et Mundo,* an Exposition of Plato's *Timaeus,* and *De Aquarum Conductibus et Ingeniis Erigendis.*

[118]Foster, *Life,* 154.

[119]Vann, *Aquinas,* 66–67.

[120]CG I, 2, 2.

[121]In Ps 36:21.

[122]Rel St 14.

Select Biblioigraphy

Editions of Complete Works of Thomas Aquinas[1]

S. Thomae Aquinatis Opera omnia ut sunt in Indice Thomistico. Curante R. Busa. Stuttgart: 1980.

S. Thomae Aquinatis Opera omnia. Parmae: 1872.

Doctoris Angelici diui Thomae Aquinatis Opera Omnia. Studio ac cura S. E. Fretté. Paris: Vivès, 1876–79.

S. Thomae de Aquino Opera omnia. Ed. Leonina. Rome: 1882–.

Select Works of Thomas Aquinas

1. *An Apology for the Religious Orders.* Trans. J. Procter. Westminster, Md.: Newman, 1950.
2. "Beati qui habitant." In T. Kaeppeli, "Una raccolta di prediche attribuite a S. Thommaso d'Aquino." *Archivum Fratrum Praedicatorum* 13 (1943) 88–94.
3. *The Catechetical Instructions of St. Thomas Aquinas.* Commentaries on The Apostles' Creed, The Ten Commandments, The Sacraments, The Our Father, The Hail Mary. Trans. Joseph B. Collins. New York: Joseph F. Sagner, Inc., 1939.
4. *Charity.* In *Saint Thomas Aquinas on Charity.* Trans. Lottie H. Kendzierski. Milwaukee: Marquette University Press, 1960.
5. "Les Collationes in decem preceptis de saint Thomas d' Aquin. Edition critique avec introduction et notes." Ed. J.-P. Torrell. *Revue des Sciences philosophiques et théologiques* 69 (1985) 5–40, 227–63.

6. *Commentary on Aristotle's Ethics: Books 8-9 on Friendship.* In *St. Thomas Aquinas On Aristotle's Friendship: Ethics, Books 8-9.* Trans. Pierre Conway, O.P. Providence College Press, 1951.

7. *Commentary on the Epistle to the Ephesians.* Trans. M. L. Lamb, O.C.S.O. Aquinas Scripture Series, Vol. 2. Albany: Magi Books, 1981.

8. *Commentary on St. Paul's Epistle to the Galatians.* Trans. F. R. Larcher. Aquinas Scripture Series, Vol. 1. Albany: Magi Books, 1966.

9. *Commentary on Saint Paul's First Letter to the Thessalonians and the Letter to the Philippians.* Trans. F. R. Larcher and Michael Duffy. Aquinas Scripture Series, Vol. 3. Albany: Magi Books, 1969.

10. *Commentary on The Gospel of St. John.* Part I. Trans. James A. Weisheipl, O.P., and Fabian R. Larcher, O.P. Aquinas Scripture Series, Vol. 4. Albany, New York: Magi Books, 1980.

11. *Compendium of Theology.* Trans. Cyril Vollert, S.J. St. Louis: B. Herder Book Co., 1947.

12. *Disputed Questions: Truth.* Trans. Milligan, McGlynn, Schmidt. 3 vols. Chicago: Regnery, 1952-54.

13. "Ecce Rex tuus." In J. Leclercq, "Un sermon inédit de saint Thomas sur la Royauté du Christ." *Revue Thomiste* 46 (1946) 152-66.

14. "Exiit qui seminat." In T. Kaeppeli, "Una raccolta di prediche attribuite a S. Thommaso d'Aquino." *Archivum Fratrum Praedicatorum* 13 (1943) 75-88.

15. "Germinet terra herbam virentem." In P. A. Uccelli, "Sermone inedito di S. Thommaso d'Aquino sulla Natività della Santa Vergine." *I Giglia Maria* 12 (1874) 125-43.

16. "Homo quidam fecit cenam magnam." In L. J. Bataillon, "Le sermon inédit de saint Thomas." *Revue des Sciences philosophiques et théologiques* 67 (1983) 360-65.

17. *Officium de festo Corporis Christi.* In *Opuscula Theologica.* Vol. II. Rome: Marietti, 1954.

18. *On the Power of God.* Trans. English Dominican Fathers (L. Shapcote). Westminster, Md.: Newman Press, 1952.

19. *On the Truth of the Catholic Faith.* Trans. Pegis, Anderson, Bourke, O'Neil. 5 vols. New York: Doubleday, 1955-57. Reprinted: Notre Dame University Press, 1975.

20. "Osanna Filio David." In T. Kaeppeli, "Una raccolta di prediche attribuite a S. Thommaso d'Aquino," *Archivum Fratrum Praedicatorum* 13 (1943) 75–88.
21. *Quaestiones quod libetales.* Ed. Raymond Spiazzi, O.P. 8th rev. ed. Rome: Marietti, 1949.
22. *Quodlibetal questions 1 and 2.* Trans. Sandra Edwards. Toronto: Pontifical Institute of Mediaeval Studies, 1983.
23. *The Religious State, The Episcopate and the Priestly Office.* Trans. of *The Perfection of the Spiritual Life.* Ed. and trans. F. Procter. Westminster, Md.: Newman Press, 1950.
24. *S. Thomae Aquinatis Expositio Salutationis Angelicae. Introductio et Textus.* Ed. I. F. Rossi. Piacenza: 1931.
25. *The Sermon-Conferences of St. Thomas Aquinas on the Apostles' Creed.* Ed. and trans. Nicholas Ayo, C.S.C. Notre Dame: University of Notre Dame Press, 1989.
26. *Sermones.* In *Sermones et opuscula concionatoria.* Ed. J. B. Raulx. Paris: 1881.
27. *Sermones.* In J. B. Schneyer, *Repertorium der lateinischen Sermones des Mittelalters für die Zeit von 1150–1350.* Beiträge XLIII 1–9. Münster, 1969–80.
28. *Summa Theologiae.* Latin text and English translation. 61 vols. London: Blackfriars in conjunction with Eyre & Spottiswoode; New York: McGraw-Hill, 1963–81.
29. *The Summa Theologica of St. Thomas Aquinas.* Translated by the Fathers of the English Dominican Province. 5 vols. Westminster, Md.: Christian Classics, 1981.
30. *Super Dionysium De divinis nominibus.* Rome: Marietti, 1950.
31. *Super Epistolas S. Pauli Lectura.* Ed. Raphael Cai, O.P. Vol. I. 8th rev. ed. Rome: Marietti, 1953.
32. *Super Evangelium S. Ioannis Lectura.* Ed. Raphael Cai, O.P. 5th rev. ed. Rome: Marietti, 1952.
33. *Super Evangelium S. Matthaei Lectura.* Ed. Raphael Cai, O.P. 5th rev. ed. Rome: Marietti, 1951.
34. *S. Thomae Aquinatis et S. Bonaventurae Balneoregiensis sermones anecdoti.* Modéne: 1869.
35. *The Three Greatest Prayers.* Trans. L. Shapcote. London: Burns, Oates and Washbourne, 1937. Reprinted: Manchester, N.H.: Sophia Institute Press, 1990.

Select Biographical Sources

The following key primary sources were edited by D. Prüm-
mer, O.P., and J. H. Laurent, O.P., and published in volumes
attached to the *Revue Thomiste* between 1912 and 1934 under the
title *Fontes Vitae Sancti Thomae Aquinatis* (FVST):

36. Calo, Peter, O.P. *Vita S. Thomae Aquinatis.* In D. Prüm-
    mer, ed., FVST, 2-55.
37. Gui, Bernard, O.P. *Vita S. Thomae Aquinatis.* In D. Prüm-
    mer, ed., FVST, 161-263.
38. Tocco, William, O.P. *Vita S. Thomae Aquinatis.* In D. Prüm-
    mer, ed., FVST, 57-160.
39. The First and Second Canonization Enquiries. In M. H. Laur-
    ent, ed., FVST, 265-510.
40. Accounts of the canonization. In M. H. Laurent, ed., FVST,
    511-32.

A reprint of much of the above material is given in Ferrua:

41. Ferrua, Angelico. *S. Thomae Aquinatis Vitae Fontes Praeci-
    puae.* Alba: 1968.

There is also information about Thomas in:

42. Tolomeo of Lucca, O.P. *Historia Ecclesiastica* 22.17-23.16.
    In L. A. Muratori, ed. *Rerum Italicarum Scriptores* 11.
    Milan: 1724.

An English translation of most of Gui's account, as well as the
First Canonization Enquiry and the relevant chapters on Thomas
from Tolomeo of Lucca's *Historia Ecclesiastica* can be found in:

43. *The Life of Saint Thomas Aquinas: Biographical Documents.*
    Trans. and ed. Kenelm Foster, O.P. Baltimore: Helicon
    Press, 1959.

Selected Studies

Bataillon, L.-J. "Approaches to the Study of Medieval Sermons."
    In *Leeds Study in English,* NS 11, 1980, 19-35.
_____. "Le sermon inédit de saint Thomas *Homo quidam fecit
    cenam magnam.* Introduction et édition." *Revue des
    Sciences philosophiques et théologiques* 67 (1983) 353-68.

_____. "Les sermons de saint Thomas et la *Catena aurea.*" *St. Thomas Aquinas 1274-1974: Commemorative Studies* 1. Toronto: Pontifical Institute of Mediaeval Studies, 1974, 67-75.

_____. "Les sermons attribués a Saint Thomas: questions d'authenticité." Albert Zimmerman, ed. *Thomas von Aquin: Werk und Wirkung im Licht neuerer Forschungen.* Miscellanea Mediaevalia, 19. Berlin, New York: Walter de Gruyter, 1988, 325-41.

_____. "Un sermon de S. Thomas d'Aquin sur la parabole du festin." *Revue des Sciences philosophiques et théologiques* 67 (1983) 360-65.

Boros, Ladislas. *Faith: Conversations with Contemporary Theologians.* Trans. Donald D. Walsh. Maryknoll, N.Y.: Orbis Books, 1989.

Boyle, Leonard E. *The Setting of the Summa theologiae of Saint Thomas.* Gilson Lecture 5. Toronto: Pontifical Institute of Medieval Studies, 1982.

Chesterton, G. K. *St. Thomas Aquinas.* Garden City, N.Y.: Doubleday Image, 1957.

Colledge, Edmund, O.S.A. "The Legend of St. Thomas Aquinas." *St. Thomas Aquinas 1274-1974: Commemorative Studies.* Toronto: Pontifical Institute of Mediaeval Studies, 1974, 13-28.

Douie, Decima L. *The Conflict between the Seculars and the Mendicants at the University of Paris in the Thirteenth Century.* Aquinas Society Papers 23. London: 1954.

Gilson, Etienne. *The Christian Philosophy of St. Thomas Aquinas.* With a Catalogue of St. Thomas' Works by I. T. Eschmann, O.P. Trans. L. K. Shook, C.S.B. New York: Random House, 1956.

_____. *Reason and Revelation in the Middle Ages.* New York: Charles Scribner's Sons, 1954.

Goodich, Michel. *Vita Perfecta: The Ideal of Sainthood in the Thirteenth Century.* Monographien zur Geschichte des Mittelalters, Vol. 25. Stuttgart: Anton Hiersemann, 1982.

Grabmann, Martin. *The Interior Life of St. Thomas Aquinas: Presented from His Works and the Acts of His Canonization Process.* Milwaukee: Bruce Publishing Company, 1951.

Gy, Pierre-Marie. "L'Office du Corpus Christi et S. Thomas d'A-
     quin: état d'une recherche." *Revue de Sciences philosop-
     hiques et théologiques* 64 (1980) 491–507.

————. "Le texte original de la tertia pars de la *Somme Thé-
     ologique* de S. Thomas d'Aquin dans l'apparat critique
     de l'édition Léonine: Le cas de l'eucharistie." *Revue de
     Sciences philosophiques et théologiques* 65 (1981) 608–16.

Kaeppeli, T. "Una raccolta di prediche attribuite a S. Thommaso
     d'Aquino." *Archivum Fratrum Praedicatorum* 13 (1943)
     75–88.

Leclercq, J. "Un sermon inédit de saint Thomas sur la Royauté
     du Christ." *Revue Thomiste* 46 (1946) 152–66.

Le Goff, Jacques. *Medieval Civilization 400–1500.* Trans. Julia
     Barrow. London: Basil Blackwell, 1988.

Maritain, Jacques. *St. Thomas Aquinas.* London: Sheed and
     Ward, 1931.

McInerny, Ralph. *A First Glance at St. Thomas Aquinas: A
     Handbook for Peeping Thomists.* Notre Dame: Univer-
     sity of Notre Dame Press, 1990.

Mollat, Michel. *The Poor in the Middle Ages: An Essay in So-
     cial History.* Trans. Arthur Goldnammer. New Haven
     and London: Yale University Press, 1986.

Murray, Alexander. *Reason and Society in the Middle Ages.* Ox-
     ford: Clarendon, 1978.

Pieper, Joseph. *Guide to Thomas Aquinas.* Trans. Richard and
     Clara Winston. Scranton, Penn.: Pantheon Books, 1962.

Principe, Walter, C.S.B. *Thomas Aquinas' Spirituality.* The
     Etienne Gilson Series 7. Toronto: Pontifical Institute of
     Mediaeval Studies, 1984.

Schneyer, J. B. *Repertorium der lateinischen Sermones des Mit-
     telalters für die Zeit von 1150–1350.* Beiträge XLIII 1–9.
     Münster, 1969–80.

Synan, Edward A. "Aquinas and His Age." *Calgary Aquinas
     Studies.* Ed. Anthony Parel. Toronto: Pontifical Insti-
     tute of Medieval Studies, 1978, 1–25.

————. "Saint Thomas Aquinas: His Good Life and Hard
     Times." *Thomistic Papers* 3. Ed. Leonard A. Kennedy,
     C.S.B. Houston: Center for Thomistic Studies, 1987,
     35–53.

Torrell, J. P. "La practique pastorale d'un théologien du XIIIe siècle: Thomas d'Aquin prédicateur." *Revue Thomiste* 82 (1982) 213–45.

Tugwell, Simon, O.P., Trans, ed., and intro. *Albert and Thomas: Selected Writings.* New York: Paulist Press, 1988.

Uccelli, P. A. "Sermone inedito di S. Thommaso d'Aquino sulla Natività della Santa Vergine." *I Gigli a Maria* 12 (1874) 126–43.

Vann, Gerald, O.P. *Saint Thomas Aquinas.* New York: Benzinger Brothers, 1940.

Verbeke, G., and D. Verhelst, ed. *Aquinas and the Problems of His Time.* Nifhoff, The Hague: 1976.

Walz, Angelus, O.P. *Saint Thomas Aquinas: A Biographical Study.* Trans. Sebastian Bullough, O.P. Westminster, Md.: Newman Press, 1951.

Weisheipl, James A., O.P. *Friar Thomas d'Aquino.* Rev. ed. Washington: The Catholic University of America Press, 1983.

_____. *Thomas d'Aquino and Albert His Teacher.* The Etienne Gilson Series 2. Toronto: Pontifical Institute of Mediaeval Studies, 1980.

Zimmerman, Albert, ed. *Thomas von Aquin: Werk und Wirkung im Licht neuerer Forschungen.* Miscellanea Mediaevalia, 19. Berlin, New York: Walter de Gruyter, 1988.

¹There is at this date no critical edition of all of Thomas' works. In 1880 Pope Leo XIII established the Leonine Commission to produce such an edition but the project still has not been completed.

Index